Pop Music in School

Eight contributions making the case for using pop music in schools. The book both provides the background many teachers will want and gives accounts of several projects which have been successfully tested in the classroom. The new edition contains a postscript, which describes the many important developments in pop music since 1975, including an assessment of the new wave. The extensive bibliography and discography have also been thoroughly revised and brought up to date.

An accompanying cassette includes classroom performances of some of the pieces referred to and provides an impressive demonstration of what can be achieved.

Pop Music in School
New edition

Edited by

GRAHAM VULLIAMY
Department of Education, University of York

and **ED LEE**
Senior Lecturer, Garnett College, London

CAMBRIDGE UNIVERSITY PRESS
Cambridge
London   New York   New Rochelle
Melbourne   Sydney

RESOURCES OF MUSIC

General Editor: John Paynter

Contents

Published by the Press Syndicate of the University of Cambridge
The Pitt Building, Trumpington Street, Cambridge CB2 1RP
32 East 57th Street, New York, NY 10022, USA
296 Beaconsfield Parade, Middle Park, Melbourne 3206, Australia

First published 1976
New edition 1980

Printed in Great Britain
at the University Press, Cambridge

Library of Congress Cataloguing in Publication Data
Main entry under title:
Pop music in school.
   (The Resources of music)
   Bibliography: p.
   Discography: p.
   Includes index.
   1. School music — Instruction and study — Addresses,
essays, lectures. 2. Music, Popular (Songs, etc.) —
Addresses, essays, lectures. I. Vulliamy, Graham.
II. Lee, Edward. III. Series: Resources of music series.
MT1.P64   1980   784   79-7708
ISBN 0 521 22930 8 hard covers
ISBN 0 521 29727 3 paperback
(First edition ISBN 0 521 20836 X hard covers
          ISBN 0 521 09968 4 paperback)

Notes on contributors

Ed Lee lectures in English at Garnett College, London. His previous teaching experience includes teaching both English and music in technical colleges, colleges of education and adult education. He has had wide musical experience in dance bands, jazz groups and rhythm and blues groups, but his most important musical venture was as full-time professional with CMU, a progressive rock and theatre group, which recorded an LP, *Open Spaces*, for Transatlantic Records. His other books include *Music of the People* (Barrie and Jenkins, 1970), *Jazz: An Introduction* (Stanmore Press, 1972) and *Folk Song and Music Hall* (Routledge and Kegan Paul, 1980).

Malcolm Nicholls has directed music at Countesthorpe College since it opened in 1970. His first teaching appointments were in Birmingham, first at Dame Elizabeth Cadbury Bilateral School (eleven to eighteen years) and then at Portland Secondary School (a secondary modern). He has also organised musical activities for young people at the Midlands Art Centre, Edgbaston.

Tony Robins was a late entrant into teaching, having been in the Bank of England for eleven years previously. His first teaching post was as head of music at Millom School, Cumberland (eleven to eighteen, comprehensive). He moved from there to be head of music at Sir Leo Schultz Senior High School, Hull (thirteen to eighteen, comprehensive).

Dave Rogers lectured part-time in liberal studies at Cambridgeshire College of Arts and Technology, where he made considerable use of pop music in his teaching. He has also run his own record shop. He is the author of *Rock 'n 'Roll* (Routledge and Kegan Paul, 1980) and is currently writing a book on Rock Music.

Piers Spencer is head of music at Woodberry Down School, North London (eleven to eighteen, comprehensive). He has previously taught music at the Sweyne School, Rayleigh, Essex (eleven to eighteen, comprehensive) and at Westcliff High School for Boys, Southend (a grammar school). He spent from 1973 to 1975 as a research student at the University of York music department investigating music composed and improvised by secondary school children.

Graham Vulliamy lectures in sociology in the Department of Education at the

University of York. He has previously taught liberal studies and sociology at Cambridgeshire College of Arts and Technology. His practical musical experience consists of having played the drums in various semi-professional rock groups, one of which he also managed. From 1971 to 1972 he was a research student at the London Institute of Education studying from a sociological perspective the various ways in which music teaching is defined in different educational institutions. He is the author of *Jazz and Blues* (Routledge and Kegan Paul, 1980) and a co-author of *Whose Music? A Sociology of Musical Languages* (Latimer, 1977).

Acknowledgements

Thanks are due to the following for permission to use copyright material:
Cover photograph: Times Newspapers Ltd, photographer Peter Boyce.
Cartoon (p. 5): *Giles* and Beaverbrook Newspapers Ltd.
Extract from 'Jazz Fantasia' from the *Complete Poems of Carl Sandburg* (p. 108): Harcourt Brace Jovanovich, Inc.

Preface

Curriculum development advances on a number of fronts but it is especially significant whenever it seeks to free a subject from the restricting bounds of cultural assumptions. We have reached this stage with music in education. A lot is happening. As a curriculum subject the scope of music is broadening all the time. It is offering far more than it has ever done before, and large numbers of young people are actively involved. From beginnings in a restricted curriculum whose appeal was, in the main, to a limited number of classically trained choral singers and orchestral musicians, music flourishes now as a many-headed plant. There are numerous opportunities for musical experiences in different forms to meet differing needs.

Yet in all this advance the absence of pop and rock music is particularly noticeable. The acceptance of pop music in schools has been slow; in general because of misunderstandings and assumptions about the nature and purpose of the music. These assumptions are commonly accepted but rarely questioned. The authors of this book aim, from the start, to dispel the myths. And having brought this complex and varied musical scene into perspective they demonstrate, from first-hand experience, the importance of this music in the general education of young people. Their practical advice is extremely valuable, and it comes at a time when, as teachers, we are more than ever open to ideas about curriculum change. The structure of school organisation is opening up. There is movement away from the restriction of short lesson periods. With a greater degree of flexibility in the timetable comes an increased need to review the content of a subject, its rationale in the whole educational scheme, and its relevance to those who are taught. Where music is concerned this must mean taking into account the musical interests of those we teach and considering these interests, as far as we can, from a position of involvement and first-hand knowledge. Only thus can we hope to widen the perspective of school-based activities, relating them to the reality of experience beyond the school.

Department of Music,
University of York

JOHN PAYNTER

Introduction

GRAHAM VULLIAMY and ED LEE

The aim of this book is to provoke discussion about pop music and its possible use in education, and to stimulate practical work based upon this. This is done in the belief that pop music is valuable both as a teaching aid and in itself. We believe it to be of particular importance to the teacher who is concerned, not so much with specialist music education but with music as a part of the general education of the pupil.

We are aware that many people have been highly critical of the values which they feel to be associated with pop music. Such a stance is often the real basis for opposition to or lack of interest in pop music and this is why reasoned arguments, including detailed considerations of the music itself, often fail to produce any significant changes in their attitudes. Certainly questions of moral and cultural value are of the greatest importance; it is impossible to act in a morally responsible way without having answered them satisfactorily. However, the editors have found that the many years they have spent listening to, playing and talking about pop music have been of such significance in the development of their own responses to and thought about music that they have in fact provided satisfactory answers to these questions of value; the editors must therefore agree to differ from such critics. Thus, since a consideration of the moral and wider social values underpinning varieties of pop music would clearly need a book in itself, we have decided to confine our efforts largely to the exploration of the practicalities of using pop music in schools. The reader who wishes to investigate the moral issues further is referred to the Bibliography. Here it is sufficient perhaps to suggest that there is a tendency to condemn the whole of pop culture on the basis of viewing only part of it. In addition we feel that such critics are prone to misinterpret even that part of it which they do investigate.

Pop music can be seen as especially valuable in the light of current educational thinking. It is clearly relevant to the real experience of the pupils and is a strong source of motivation to them in a variety of ways. At the same time the way in which pop is normally created accords with the adolescent's natural desire for independence and might fruitfully lead towards pupil-centred, self-directed work. In addition playing in a pop group involves pupils working together closely, an experience from which much can be learned about human relationships.

[1]

A general problem with pupil-centred learning is that teachers tend to fear a loss of control – a theme that is considered by a number of contributors to this book. However, the teacher might also argue that in this case the situation could be made even more difficult by his own ignorance, often exaggerated by rapid changes of fashion in pop. Such considerations need not apply, since we feel that pop should not be taught in the traditional manner, in which the teacher is the master of a body of facts which are then studied in a set order and in prescribed ways, the whole operation being directed by him. Instead the teacher should start by seeing his pupils as already possessing a considerable knowledge of pop music, which they are strongly motivated to expand. What he brings to the situation, which they do not have, is a body of ideas and concepts about music (e.g. rhythmic precision, harmonic progression), together with the skill to turn these into audible realities. If the teacher is prepared to apply his musical knowledge and understanding to the pupils' facts, the possibility of a real dialogue emerges, particularly if the teacher is willing to recognise the limitations of his own knowledge in this area and so temporarily revert to being a pupil. At the same time the pupils, in having to communicate with the teacher, could take a more active part in the educational process. This is surely a situation to be welcomed, because in so many subjects it is inevitable that the process will tend to be one-sided: the teacher is the authority and the pupil the uninformed recipient.

A further benefit is that the work itself can become more exciting for the teacher, as well as for the pupil. To come to grips with new facts and ideas must inevitably reshape, modify and deepen the teacher's existing conceptions of the nature of music. We are convinced that in facing this challenge, the teacher is likely to find an excitement and freshness in his work, which is all too easily lost in the current educational scheme of things.

Since this book is a collection of articles by contributors who combine teaching experience with considerable practical involvement with pop, a few words on the structure of the book may be of help.

The book begins with an account of the history of pop music by Dave Rogers, which it is hoped will provide teachers with a frame of reference for the later chapters. It could also act as a valuable source of material for musical appreciation. We have decided to leave this chapter as it was written in 1975, since Dave Rogers has brought it up to date in his new contribution 'Pop into the eighties', which appears as the Postscript to this new edition. The two remaining chapters of Part One then offer a defence of pop music purely as a musical experience and also as an educational study.

In chapter 2 Graham Vulliamy shows how his sociological training forces him to question many of the accepted ways in which music is talked about. People often express an opinion, believing it to be absolute and unquestionable, when in fact its validity depends very much upon their position in both history and society. In particular this chapter questions many of the assumptions often made by both right and left wing critics of pop music – assumptions such as the argument that pop music is primarily a commercial product and therefore necessarily of poor quality. Rather, it is argued that from a musical point of view pop has been undervalued, either because of lack of knowledge or because of a misunderstanding of its aims.

Part One closes on a more practical note with a second chapter by Graham Vulliamy (chapter 3), in which he examines the external and organisational pressures upon a teacher who wishes to introduce new methods. He argues strongly from case studies that a revolution in the musical life of a school can be brought about when the structure of the music department changes to a more 'open' one. Many teachers will recognise the analogy with the integrated approach in some primary schools. A point about the suggested 'open' approach to school music teaching worth stressing is that whilst we see the use of pop music as a valuable (and previously neglected) part of the musical education of pupils we do not see it as in any way *replacing* other approaches to music teaching. In fact one of the benefits of an 'open' music department, where a variety of approaches is encouraged, is that much of the prejudice of both pupils and teachers concerning different styles of music is likely to be broken down.

After a note by Ed Lee on conventions for notating Afro-American music, Part Two begins with a description by Piers Spencer of a project, designed to fit into a traditional music teaching framework. The course uses the blues as an approach to musical creativity — the blues being chosen here because it has stylistic features common to nearly every genre of Afro-American music. Examples of this work and similar illustrations from other chapters are given both in notation and on the recording of pupils' work. In his second chapter, chapter 5, Piers Spencer explores the concept of creativity as related to Afro-American music and illustrates the classroom possibilities with a number of examples of pupils' work. He is particularly concerned to suggest how a teacher may comment constructively upon creative work, especially that of the academically less able. Chapter 6 is an account by Malcolm Nicholls of the 'open' music department in action in a school. He describes in detail the work of particular pupils and his examples on the recording illustrate clearly the range and high quality to which school pop music can aspire.

Tony Robins in chapter 7 shows that pop can also be very suited to work which is more teacher-directed. He suggests ways in which one can deal with larger numbers of pupils since it is not always possible, for practical reasons, to work with smaller groupings. An important section of this chapter deals with the practicalities of buying equipment and, in particular, that which is used by the rhythm section. The importance of the latter in pop music cannot be overstressed.

Chapter 8 is by Ed Lee and makes further practical suggestions for the music teacher, including some observations on classroom instruction in playing the acoustic guitar. It also gives some indication of the value of and potential for integrating music with other areas of the school curriculum.

At the end of the book there is a Bibliography and Discography, together with a Postscript for the new edition covering the main developments in pop music since the first edition of the book.

One final word of explanation is needed. So much discussion of pop necessitates reference to the main areas of musical experience, but there seems to be no standard nomenclature. To avoid confusion we have therefore adopted the following definitions throughout the book:

Classical music is that part of the music of Western Europe from the Middle Ages to the present which forms the basis of conservatory training.

Avant garde music refers to that area of classical music which has seriously challenged the assumptions, aims and mode of creation of earlier classical music. We have in mind here the work of composers such as Berio, Stockhausen and Cage.

Afro-American is the term used for those styles of music which can be traced, in some of their aspects at least, to the merging of an African tradition of music with that tradition, European in origin, which thrived in the southern states of America in the nineteenth century. Examples of such styles might therefore include jazz, blues, soul, Tamla Motown and rock music. Since a range of terms is used to denote the main stylistic areas of Afro-American music, the reader must infer from the context the author's exact intention, as the contributors sometimes differ in their usage.

Rock covers a vast area of music ranging from the more technically adventurous groups (e.g. Pink Floyd, King Crimson), whose music is to be found predominantly or even exclusively on LP records, to the more commercially orientated post-1964 derivations of earlier rock'n'roll to be found on singles records (e.g. the earlier records of Slade).

Mass pop covers the wide range of styles (e.g. pop-rock, ballads, Motown) associated with the Top Ten singles.

Both rock and mass pop are influenced by Afro-American musical values to a greater or lesser extent; where the influence is strong and the music is actually played by black people the generic term 'black music' is often used. Many music commentators, together with a number of contributors to this book, refer loosely to both these areas simply as 'pop music' and the term 'pop music' is used rather than 'popular music' to delineate those areas of a popular music tradition which have been appropriated by young people in the post-1956 period.

It must be borne in mind, however, that these terms and their definitions are intended to provide no more than a basic frame of reference. In common with most classifications they are to some extent arbitrary.

PART ONE

1 Varieties of pop music: a guided tour

DAVE ROGERS

"We KNOW you ain't showing Rock 'n' Roll. That's why we're coming in to bust the joint."

Daily Express, Sept, 13th, 1956

1

In the summer of 1955 an American film, *The Blackboard Jungle*, opened in this country. It starred Glenn Ford and was an adaptation of Evan Hunter's novel — disturbing at that time — about a young teacher's struggle to get through to his students in a tough New York Trades School. The film portrayed a youth situation, was violent (for its period) and was competently acted. It had also had two predecessors with similar ingredients: Marlon Brando's *The Wild One* and James Dean's *Rebel Without a Cause*. But *The Blackboard Jungle* contained something more which causes it still to be remembered today: Bill Haley singing the song 'Rock Around The Clock' over the opening credits and in a featured spot within the film itself.

This was the lone messenger heralding the imminent arrival of rock'n'roll in Britain. Not just as a new form of popular music — indeed it was universally challenged by its detractors as possessing no musical value whatever — but as a focal

[5]

point for a newly-recognised and increasingly volatile social force: youth, or to be more accurate to the terminology of the time, the teenager.

There were a few disturbances that summer at cinemas where the film was shown. As far as the press were concerned, it was Teddy Boys who caused them, inflamed by the music, jiving in the aisles, singing along and stamping their feet in time to the 'jungle rhythm'. But it was not until the following year that rock'n'roll, violence, the Teddy Boy and by extension teenagers in general all became locked in one enormous equation. It was Bill Haley again who did it, starring this time in the all-rock'n'roll film *Rock Around The Clock*, which brought in its wake not just disturbances but sometimes riots in cities throughout the United States and Europe.

Looking back now, it is perhaps easy to ridicule those guardians of the public order who felt impelled to make utterance on the twin subjects of youth and rock'n'roll. Just as with jazz in the twenties, to some Americans it all seemed part of some unbelievably pernicious Communist plot, and there could be no denying to them that it was unmusical and obviously inspired by the devil:

Rock'n'roll is a means of pulling down the white man to the level of the Negro. It is part of a plot to undermine the morals of the youth of our nation. (Asa Carter, Secretary of the North Alabama White Citizens' Council)

Nor was that all, for the results would be even worse:

The effect will be to turn young people into devil-worshippers, to stimulate self-expression through sex, to provoke lawlessness, impair nervous stability, and destroy the sanctity of marriage. (Rev. Albert Carter, Nottingham Pentecostal Church, 1957)

Bearing those words in mind, it is instructive to listen again to Bill Haley's recording of 'Rock Around The Clock'. It sounds a little innocuous, hardly in the rabble-rousing class of, say, a new 'Marseillaise'. And yet, even now, it retains a punch and an immediacy which is instantly recognisable and which, at the same time, caused it to shout aloud above the bland, stale 'safeness' of those eternally middle-aged, early fifties crooners with whom there could be no identification for the new teenager.

This is perhaps the main reason underlying the force of its impact: youth's feeling of identification with the music and its performers. Rock'n'roll was music *for* young people *by* young people. Everything about it suggested a power and style in keeping with movement and change. Rock'n'roll threw out links with Dean's *Rebel Without a Cause* and Brando's motor-cycle gang, not so much sneering at social convention and traditional mores as the Rolling Stones were to do later, but rather ignoring them; providing for a generation — 'the self-defined, astride the created will' — the final boundary fence of a new world that lay between childhood and the responsibilities of becoming an adult. It is this world which Thom Gunn views from the periphery:

Seeking their instinct, or their poise, or both,

One moves with an uncertain violence
Under the dust thrown by a baffled sense
Or the dull thunder of approximate words.
('On The Move', 1969, p. 15)

while Chuck Berry, standing on the inside, merely provides what is necessary — celebration:

I've got no kick against modern jazz,
Unless they try to play it too darn fast,
And change the beauty of the melody
Until they sound just like a symphony.
That's why I go for that rock'n'roll music
Any old way you choose it,
It's got a back beat, you can't lose it,
Any old time you use it,
It's gotta be rock'n'roll music
If you wanna dance with me.
(Berry from 'Rock'n'Roll Music', Jewel Music)

2

See, that's one thing that made rhythm and blues different from the old-fashioned blues . . . The singer is singing and, instead of just guitars twanging, the horns played whole notes, rolling those riffs near the ends of the choruses — you know, whole notes with little melodies attached to them. (The blues musician Johnny Otis)

Musically, rock'n'roll was a fusion of black blues and country and western music into a more immediate and urgent sound and style. The final impetus to the emergence of rock'n'roll was given by the development of a faster, more confident blues form, urban rhythm and blues, on the West Coast of America and in Chicago and New York. From Kansas City came other important ingredients — an emphasised bounce to the music, and the use of the saxophone as a harsh bridging instrument between vocals — both derived from the jump bands of the forties.

But the country element is also of fundamental importance. Thus several of Elvis Presley's early recordings made in Memphis in the mid-fifties were of country songs. The important point about these, though, is that Presley sings them in a blues voice. To him, the styles were not dissimilar — he had grown up listening to both and both came naturally to him. As producer Sam Phillips exclaims at the end of one of the takes of 'Blue Moon of Kentucky': 'Hell, that's different. That's a pop song now, everybody!' (*Good Rockin' Tonight*: Bopcat Records 100.) Most of the early rock'n'roll artists possessed this country leaning except the Negroes for whom country and western was not part of their cultural tradition. Their background was the blues. Hence Chuck Berry stays with rhythm and blues and Jimi Hendrix with blues and blues-based progressions, while Little Richard has at times turned merely to another branch of the black musical heritage — gospel music.

The very rapid progress of pop music over the past twenty years has been characterised by two things over and above all others. The first is a process of cross-fertilisation and the second is an increased eclecticism of style. The extensive growth of pop has always of course been helped considerably by the commercial interests involved, anxious to see the music as yet another money-spinning manifestation of what in this country was perhaps misnamed the 'Affluent Society', and in the States was part of the Eisenhower administration. But commercial forces do not by any means wholly account for the new musical situation which now exists. Whereas at one time broadside ballads and folk songs from Britain crossed the Atlantic and found a fertile home in the Appalachian Mountains, jazz (in the twenties) and rock'n'roll (some three decades later) have reversed this process. In the last seventy years music originating in America has found a creative home in this country.

Musical cross-fertilisation between the two countries has continued at an accelerated rate through the sixties and seventies to the point where we now find musicians from different cultures and backgrounds — British and American, black and white, folk, blues and jazz — meeting, playing together and, in the best examples, creating not a bastardised, hybrid form, but a vibrantly alive type of new music, which tends in many cases to go far beyond mere eclecticism.

The true artist makes a virtue of his borrowings from other cultures or other areas of his chosen art form, and uses these to create a more valid and personal artistic statement. This is no less true of music than of the other arts. For example, in 1962 Bob Dylan was as derivative of his Woody Guthrie/urban folk antecedents as any other young singer. But as he developed both as a person and as an artist he borrowed from the blues form and rock'n'roll in his work of the mid-sixties; while more recently he has been influenced by Nashville and country and western music. In all this he has shown himself to be no mere copyist. He has created from his borrowings a musical style which, though it owes debts to its origins, transcends them by being resolved into a personal statement which is Dylan's own. At the same time he both transforms and innovates within his musical heritage.

However in the Britain of the fifties, rock'n'roll was not immediately embraced by all sections of youth. From my own experience I would suggest that in many a grammar and public school pop music was regarded with disdain by some in favour of a more respectable preference for jazz of all descriptions, from the Modern Jazz Quartet through Benny Goodman back to Bix Beiderbecke, and even, despite their commercial success, for Chris Barber and Ken Colyer.

In the main, it was working-class youth which acted as midwife to the birth of rock'n'roll in Britain. Perhaps it was they who felt more keenly the opportunities and freedom brought by affluence and rock'n'roll, and who had more need to assert their own definition of their role in society. The middle classes, urged on in their beliefs by the media, tended to equate rock'n'roll with violence, with a lower class of person, felt vaguely to be a criminal in some undefined way, and above all of course with the Teddy Boy. It was middle-class youth who were, later in the fifties, to swell the ranks of the CND movement, crowd out the trad jazz clubs, and affect a uniform of sloppy sweaters, jeans and duffel coats.

The backgrounds of some of the British pop singers of the time reinforced the linking of rock'n'roll with working-class youth. Terry Dene had been a messenger boy from Blackfriars, Billy Fury worked on a tugboat on the Mersey, while Tommy Steele, this country's 'answer' to Elvis, had been a merchant seaman from the age of sixteen.

Ambivalent attitudes towards the pop singer abounded. He had to appeal to the teenagers, but his stage movements did not have to be too suggestive nor his music too wild. This was in order that he might win a wider audience and so increase his earning power. (Even the biggest rock'n'roll stars of the fifties — Presley, Billy Fury, Gene Vincent and Little Richard — submitted, albeit sometimes unwillingly, to this taming process.) He must be both rebel and boy-next-door: dangerous and mis-understood, yet somehow safe and acceptable. He had also to be inaccessible but not the unreachable star: not too far away to be untouchable, yet not too close to his fans lest the magic should die. In short, his life was managed and guided so that, however brief his career as a pop singer, his profits would be maximised, even if, as sometimes certainly happened, outrageous contract terms meant that the singer worked, literally, only for the benefit of his promoters. Finally, if at all possible, he had eventually to be capable of metamorphosis into an all-round show-biz enter-tainer, capable of appealing to the whole family. Such was the ideal of the managers of the fifties, for rock'n'roll was seen at the outset as just another fad, to be super-seded in a few months by something new (the hula-hoop or the calypso?) which could be even more lucrative if the entertainment industry could discover soon enough what it was to be.

And so perhaps it might have been, were it not for a form of do-it-yourself music which sprang up only in Britain: skiffle. Lonnie Donegan, one-time banjoist with Chris Barber, was its foremost and most successful exponent. George Melly describes the beginnings of skiffle thus:

Ken Colyer, the traditional band-leader, was the first to institute the 'Skiffle Session' . . . Apprehensive that even his loyal public might find a whole evening of ensemble jazz a little hard to take, he broke it up by allowing his banjo-player Lonnie Donegan to change over to guitar and sing a few folk-blues drawn mostly from the repertoire of the American Negro folk-hero Huddie 'Leadbelly' Ledbetter.
These sessions were so popular that when Chris Barber left Colyer to set up on his own, taking Donegan with him, he kept them in as part of the act.
'Rock Island Line' was originally issued as one of the tracks on a Barber LP but was requested so often on radio programmes that it was eventually reissued as a single and, by May 1956, was Number 1 in the charts. (Melly, 1970, p. 28)

Thus was a movement born — a movement which had no parallel in the States until the college campus folk boom of the early sixties. It was a craze initiated by a music which, rhythmically and in its vigour, could be happily confused and associ-ated with rock'n'roll. Throughout the country would-be musicians formed them-selves into skiffle groups. For after all — and herein lies its importance — the instru-ments necessary to form a skiffle group were easily come by. All you needed was a washboard and a thimble to scrape against it, and to complete the rhythm section a 'double-bass' which was an old tea-chest, with a broom-handle fixed to one corner and a piece of string stretched from the top of the handle to the opposite corner of the chest — the player plucked the string and an adequate noise came out. The biggest part of the outlay was a guitar, but this was not so expensive as to put it out of reach of a collection of saved-up pocket money.

When the skiffle boom died, many of the groups carried on. Some of these, such as the Shadows and the Beatles in their 'Quarrymen' days, eventually formed the nucleus of the 'beat' and rhythm and blues bands of the early sixties, and laid the foundations of the many and varied forms of pop music of the seventies. However, though such groups continued playing, they were largely unknown to the general public, for by the turn of the fifties the entertainment industry was again dominant. At first surprised by the success of this raucous, uncivilised music, it had very quickly learned the rules of the new game, and by 1959 was again safely in control of its mass production.

The rise of rock'n'roll nevertheless had begun a revolution. From that point onwards, it is possible to contradict the assertion that record companies can dictate tastes. In fact, they generally find it very difficult indeed to predict with any accuracy what the record-buying public is going to want next. This does not mean of course that large-scale promotional campaigns and TV and radio exposure have *no* effect on sales. In the summer of 1974, for example, a technicians' strike blacked out the BBC TV programme 'Top of the Pops' over a period of several weeks. Records released in that period by Gary Glitter, the Rubettes and Sweet, acts which depend largely on visual appeal, lost their accustomed outlet, and their nationwide audience, and consequently sold very badly indeed.

Nevertheless the industry tends to do well by riding on the back of an already-established trend, not by initiating one. Most of the larger record companies, for example, turned down the Beatles in 1962; and even when EMI had finally signed them up, they were very doubtful as to the group's potential. The industry would thus appear to be concerned with maximising profits and minimising risks. This suggests that the record industry is really only concerned with the *number* of records sold, and not with the *content* of its products; if so it would obviously be desirable to predict or control what the public might wish to buy. However, a consideration of the facts is illuminating. Simon Frith in an excellent article in *Rock File 2* in 1974 investigates the sales of single records during the period 1 September 1972 − 31 August 1973. A total of about 2000 singles aimed specifically at Top Twenty success was released in that time. Of these, only 180 became hits — that is to say, a success rate of something like one in eleven. This seems to me to indicate a rather haphazard way of doing things, and certainly does not suggest that the industry is even confident in its predictions, let alone that it can confidently dictate consumer preference.

3

Instead of yakety saxes and greasebox bass, the big black sounds of classic rock, we all got stuck with Disneyland. (Nik Cohn, in 'A WopBopaLooBopaLopBamBoom')

By 1959 the rather shaky foundations of modern pop music had received a number of shattering blows. It was to be some years yet before the power of audience taste, as I have suggested above, combined with the demand for artistic control by the musicians, which I shall trace in detail later, were able to transform the nature of a substantial area of the music industry.

In America, besides the disappearance of Presley into army service, a string of catastrophes had taken place to help put paid to 'that rock'n'roll music'. Chuck Berry was sent to prison for two years for alleged offences under the Mann Act, Little Richard left rock to join the church, Chuck Willis died having recorded the ironically-titled 'Hang Up My Rock'n'Roll Shoes', and Buddy Holly, the Big Bopper, Ritchie Valens and Eddie Cochran all died in crashes while travelling between shows. The Sun record company in Memphis where Presley and Jerry Lee Lewis began their careers was failing badly; and then, as if to knock the final nail in the coffin, came the Payola scandals of 1959.

'Payola' is the term used to describe money or goods with which record companies bribe disc jockeys to plug their records. The various court cases resulting from the exposure of this practice served to make the companies so cautious that they made sure they released only safe, emasculated Tin Pan Alley songs. It was back to 1951 and Johnny Ray, Patti Page and Frankie Laine, except that this time they used teenage singers. At the same time they kept their stranglehold on pop music by literally picking up off the street any likely-looking young face and, regardless of whether he could sing or not, fashioning him into a 'star'. Fabian is the perfect example, and the whole idea is caught beautifully in the humorous exactitude of Stan Freberg's 'Payola Roll Blues', included on *The Many Sides of Rock'n'Roll*, Vol. 3 (United Artists Records). All of this eventually led to the discrediting and virtual disappearance of rock'n'roll in America.

Although what I have described above obviously had its effects in this country, the impact was far less; and aided by an influx of younger would-be musicians from the skiffle boom, rock'n'roll, and its parents, blues and rhythm and blues, safely flourished. In fact from the late fifties on, British rock music has had far more of a basis in black music (blues and rhythm and blues) than has music originating in America.

The British groups who were part of the mid-sixties rhythm and blues boom took their music from several sources: the guitar style of B.B. King, the Chicago city blues of Slim Harpo, Muddy Waters, Chuck Berry and Bo Diddley, as well as rhythm and blues found on Ahmet Ertegun's Atlantic label featuring Ray Charles, the Coasters, the Drifters and others. From the more immediate past, 'Twist and Shout' and 'Do You Love Me' came from Detroit and Berry Gordy's all-Negro Tamla Motown company.

All the above music has its roots in the blues: all of it was learned and played by British groups. Most white American musicians (whether influenced by Presley and the rock'n'rollers or not) had their musical beginnings in folk music, in which category I include both urban folk of the Woody Guthrie—Pete Seeger strand and country and western music.

Jeff Nuttall has drawn a similar parallel allied to his view of the two traditions of teenage culture, the English classic and the American romantic styles. The music of the classic mode, from Teddy Boys through the mods and the skinheads to the current preoccupation with soul music, has been Negroid in origin, emphasising sharpness, cool sophistication and a predominantly urban setting. However,

the romantic tradition follows an image which is fundamentally frontier-western. From the first prairie motor-cycle gangs to the current hippies the fascination has been for the nomadic figures of the Old West — for cowboys (motor cyclists) and Indians (hippies). Hell's Angels are seen by Hunter Thompson to be the immediate descendants of the Oakies, prairie farmers who were displaced by the big banking concerns in the thirties. Consequently the romantic tradition responds to the strong strain of country and western that crept into R'n'B with Elvis to become rock'n'roll, finally to culminate by way of Dylan and commercial folk, in the mountain music pastoral mood of The Band. (Nuttall, 1970, p. 118)

To see all this more clearly it is essential that we examine the backgrounds of some of the more important and representative musicians of the last fifteen years on both sides of the Atlantic.

One of the first manifestations in Britain of experimentation with the blues form occurred in 1961 when Alexis Korner, who nearly ten years before had been with Donegan as part of Chris Barber's skiffle line-up, formed his own band called Blues Incorporated. They played in London at the Marquee Club; included in the band's ranks were Jack Bruce, Graham Bond, Ginger Baker and Cyril Davies. Davies and Korner had known each other for some time and had often backed visiting American blues singers (Muddy Waters had high praise for Davies' harmonica playing on one of his early visits). Bruce, Bond and Baker had, like most other members of Korner's band, spent some time playing in jazz bands, both traditional and modern. What made them turn away at the end of the fifties was an increasing frustration with the lack of direction in jazz at the time, a growing interest in blues and, because of their background, jazz-tinged rhythm and blues. Bond, for example, while at no time losing interest and proficiency in his alto sax playing, turned to the electric Hammond organ; he alternated between both instruments for the rest of his life. (He died as a result of an accident in 1974.) Meanwhile the various line-ups of Blues Incorporated in the years 1961 to 1964 were prophetic of what was to come. Mick Jagger occasionally stood in as singer, Charlie Watts (drummer with the Rolling Stones) was a member, while pianist Nicky Hopkins, who turns up again and again through the sixties as session player on records by the Stones and Jefferson Airplane, and as a solo artist and member of the Jeff Beck Group and the American band Quicksilver Messenger Service, was in an offshoot of Korner's band, Cyril Davies' Allstars.

This then was the core of what I will call the first generation of modern blues musicians produced in this country. The effects are obvious. When Graham Bond, Jack Bruce and Ginger Baker left to form the Graham Bond Organisation, their playing, although not specifically aimed at the Top Twenty, influenced many of the younger artists then entering the music business. Jon Lord of Deep Purple has stressed how much his early keyboard-playing owed to Bond's style; John McLaughlin was a later member of the Bond Organisation before he joined Miles Davis. Subsequently he played in Tony Williams' Lifetime, before forming a musical partnership in the early seventies with the American Carlos Santana. Finally Rod Stewart worked first with Peter Green, the force behind the late sixties English blues revival band Fleetwood Mac, and then with Nicky Hopkins in the Jeff Beck Group. Stewart finally joined up with the mid-sixties 'mod' band Small Faces where his singing drew upon all his previous experience, as well as showing the influence both of more recent soul music and of the fifties rock singer, Sam Cooke.

In terms of wide acceptance, all the musicians I have referred to had to wait until after 1966 and the formation of Cream by Bruce, Baker and Eric Clapton. For it was here that what I have called the first generation began to fuse with the second in the person of Clapton, who began his career with the Yardbirds. While Blues Incorporated and the Bond Organisation were playing in clubs through the early and middle sixties they received recognition from only a fairly small following, composed in part of what came to be called 'mods'. Those who did receive commercial recognition and the financial profits were the younger groups passing through the gateway opened for them by the success of the Beatles, the Rolling Stones, the Yardbirds, the Kinks, the Animals, Manfred Mann and the Who.

This of course poses the question of why it was that younger groups, rather than Blues Incorporated or Graham Bond, gained the larger audience. I think the answer probably lies in the prevailing mood of the times and in the nature of pop music itself. It was still necessary to have an idol — someone who did not necessarily have to be a brilliant musician but who personified the fantasies, aspirations and rebelliousness of an adolescent audience. There has to be at some stage an identification by the audience between the group and the gang; for example, the Who were associated with the mods. At first the younger bands supplied this in the tradition of Presley and the early Cliff Richard. But these new people were closer and more solidly real: the days of gold lamé suits for pop singers had temporarily passed.

Additionally the songs echoed more than ever before the feelings, preoccupations and lives of the audience. The Rolling Stones ('I Can't Get No Satisfaction') and the Who ('My Generation') became — and ten years later remain — folk-heroes through their stance and style and their songs, ingredients which in the best of pop music are indistinguishable from each other. Even though it has been studied at length in many surveys of the sixties, Pete Townshend's 'My Generation' is still worth quoting in full, for although it is very much of its time, it exactly catches the uncertain forcefulness of adolescence and hence is perhaps timeless. Also, and very importantly, it speaks like Berry's 'Rock'n'Roll Music' with authority from the inside:

People try to put us down
Just because we get around.
Things they do look awful cold
Hope I die before I get old.

This is my generation, baby . . .

Why don't you all f-f-f-fade away
Don't try and dig what we all say
I'm not trying to cause a big sensation
I'm just talking 'bout my generation.
This is my generation, baby,
My generation.
(Fabulous Music, 1965)

Spurred on by the Beatles and the Stones, the younger groups carried all before them. But this time with a difference. There had never before been such an underpinning of musicianship nor such a wealth of talent centred on one movement. There was now a profusion of small clubs like the Marquee in cities throughout the country, not just in London, the traditional music capital. Thousands of groups were playing in clubs, village-halls, pubs and the newly-built chain of Mecca dance-halls up and down the length of Britain. Richard Mabey (1969) has estimated that there were more than ten thousand groups playing rhythm and blues by 1964. Obviously not all of them were professional or even earning a living wage from their efforts, but the main point is that they were playing. They took their repertoires from black music and in many cases, again an innovation, they were writing their own material, often paying tribute to their acknowledged masters in the process.

This then was the second generation, copying and creating, and being copied themselves: the Pretty Things, for example, modelled themselves initially on the Stones, but set out to be even more outrageous to adult standards. The clubs were the breeding ground of modern British pop. To exemplify this, we need look no further than one typical week in August 1964. The Bond Organisation and the Art Woods were playing at the 100 Club; Manfred Mann and the American blues singer and pianist Mose Allison were at the Marquee; Georgie Fame, John Mayall, Herbie Goins and Zoot Money were booked at the Flamingo; Van Morrison's Them at the Attic; and the T-Bones and the Yardbirds at the Crawdaddy; whilst at the Scene were the High Numbers, soon to change their name to the Who. This kind of intense musical atmosphere created a demand for groups which resulted in an excellent practical apprenticeship for band after band; and the constant night after night exposure to packed audiences proved a spur to mastery of technique previously unequalled in any mass musical movement in this country.

4

New York

Dear Beatles,
    . . . Perhaps you are not aware of this fact, but you are the first happy thing that has happened to us since the tragedy on November 22nd. You are the first spot of

joy to come to a nation that is still very much in mourning, although the grief is now personal and unpublicised. It is for this reason that I extend my thanks and, somewhat arbitrarily, those of my fellow Americans, to you.
(From an American fan letter, quoted in Braun, *Love Me Do*)

But what of the United States at this time? During this same period there was no corresponding upsurge of interest in rhythm and blues. Nonetheless there were young musicians forming themselves into bands scattered throughout the country. If they were not generally playing blues, what kind of music were they involved in?

There was no profusion of small clubs as there was in Britain; but there were large groups of young people, and hence would-be musicians, on college campuses. The music they had generally turned to was folk. There was nothing either new or vital being created in the field of rock'n'roll: Langdon Winner aptly sums it up by calling post-Payola American rock

. . . nothing more than an obscene requiem played by those who had assassinated an art which had once been so full of life. (1969, p. 44).

Some, but not many, turned to jazz. The majority took part in what rapidly became a folk revival almost on a par with Britain's skiffle excitement some four years earlier.

This was the period of the rise of Bob Dylan and Joan Baez, responding in song to the beginnings of the civil rights movement in the lunch-counter sit-ins of 1960, and moving to concern at and eventually direct condemnation of the actions of their country in rapidly accelerating the war in Vietnam. Not by any means all of the music thus created was as meaningful. Too often the ideas descended into the hootenanny style, when, in the disc jockey John Peel's words ' . . . they sang songs about prohibition, civil war, lynching, and other things about which they knew nothing'.

A similar criticism could have been and was levelled at Britain's skifflers, but the essential importance of both movements remains the same: out of this welter of hootenanny singers and folk groups, politically committed or not, emerged many of the outstanding rock musicians of the later sixties. Marty Balin (later of Jefferson Airplane) and John Sebastian along with many others played in or at least visited Gerde's Folk City in Greenwich Village and there met and were influenced by Dylan and Baez. The Mamas and Papas, Country Joe and the Fish, and the Grateful Dead were involved in folk, while Jorma Kaukonen of Jefferson Airplane was at one time singing in folk clubs in the San Francisco Bay area in company with Janis Joplin.

Thus a great many musicians came through a formative period of involvement with folk, either as active participants or merely as listeners. Perhaps this is not as surprising as it may seem. As I have tried to show, the blues heritage was not part of the conscious background of white America, whereas country and western and folk (urban and country) most definitely were. It can rightly be argued of course that blues music is even less part of a cultural heritage for British musicians, but here there was no barrier preventing the inculcation and influence of the music. Here it was free to grow and be extended as a matter of course: in the States, amongst the majority of the white population, racial considerations ensured that quite the reverse was true.

It would however be quite wrong to deduce that there was no black music achieving widespread popularity in America during the early sixties. The rhythm and blues tradition carried on without a significant break through into the sixties, growing stronger all the time. Since the late forties it had centred mainly on Atlantic Records and its subsidiaries. It is significant that many of the early rock'n'roll hits were white copies of songs first recorded by black artists on Atlantic: Joe Turner's 'Shake Rattle and Roll', for instance, was heavily bowdlerised by Bill Haley and his Comets. In the fifties the song sometimes mattered more than the performance. But although Atlantic continued to prosper into the sixties, there were by this time three other main outlets for black music. One was provided in Phil Spector's productions of black groups like the Crystals and the Ronettes; the second came from the Chess studios in Chicago and was much closer to the blues in that the artists concerned were Willie Dixon, Chuck Berry, Muddy Waters and Bo Diddley, all of whom were from the rhythm and blues tradition. The third major outlet became Detroit where in 1960 Berry Gordy's Tamla Motown records commenced production with Barrett Strong, Mary Wells and Smokey Robinson's Miracles, and eventually expanded to embrace the careers of the Temptations, Diana Ross and the Supremes and Stevie Wonder.

However, the most popular black recordings in the early sixties were rarely seen in terms of their roots and background: they were Top Twenty hits in a world of pure commercialism. This is not to say that they were not good or deserving of success — generally they were better then than at any time since — but they went unrecognised as such. They were not accorded the authority they possessed until the advent of the Beatles caused some of these antecedents of British rhythm and blues to be more widely appreciated both in Britain and in their country of origin.

It is at this point, with the arrival of the Beatles in America in January 1964, that the transatlantic musical cross-fertilisation mentioned earlier received its biggest and longest-lasting impetus. The Beatles' impact on American rock music cannot be overestimated. A typical comment is by Paul Kantner of Jefferson Airplane:

I, along with forty billion others, came along with John, Paul, George, and 'Help' . . . I can remember like when they first came out, Jim McGuinn was the first cat that I knew that really got onto them. He used to sit in the Troubadour playing 12-string guitar singing Beatle riffs. Just for hours on end . . . But they started it all, yeah. Kingston Trio, God! Who was before the Kingston Trio? Elvis Presley? The Beatles did a lot of it. Everybody I know used to sing Beatle riffs. God bless them, every one! (Gleason, 1969, p. 138)

The Beatles and the Rolling Stones succeeded in galvanising and reviving the ailing American rock music of the time in such a complete way that some people still believe pop music began with them. The Beatles' success can be put down to four factors. First, they reintroduced white America to the power and vitality of black music. Second, the brashness and confidence with which they interpreted it in live performance and on record harked back to the better rock'n'roll of the fifties. Third, their enthusiasm and unaffected personalities — 'the four, lovable mop-tops' — produced an audience-identification and a hysteria which, despite the similar success of the Osmonds in the early seventies, remains unequalled; it is perhaps impossible to bring it about intentionally. Lastly, they demonstrated the power inherent in mastery of the technique of using electric instruments:

Today, the least accomplished electric bands at high school gymnasium dances have at their command sounds and techniques which would have astounded even the most talented musicians of the Eisenhower years (Winner, 1969, p. 45).

For a long while, anything British was marketable in the States. Spurred on by the Beatles and the Stones and a steady succession of other British groups, former folk singers laid aside their acoustic guitars and turned to the business of making electric music. Jim McGuinn and David Crosby (later of Crosby, Stills, Nash and Young) formed first the Beefeaters (anything British would do . . . !) and then the Byrds. The early recordings the group made had a distinct Beatles sound and flavour. But when this imitative period was over, eclecticism linked with genuine creativity took its place. As the Byrds, they fused their electric style successfully with Dylan's folk songs and their own. The media called it 'folk-rock', but Dylan himself had already set the pattern by appearing at the Newport Folk Festival in 1965 backed by the rock group, then called the Hawks, now known simply as the Band.

On that occasion the audience was hostile, as it was the following year when Dylan and the Hawks gave a similar performance at the Royal Albert Hall. There exists a live bootleg recording of this concert (Trade Mark of Quality Records), and it contains some of the most exciting rock music ever played. The audience, wanting Dylan to conform to their image of the purist folk singer, has been barracking and catcalling throughout. Finally, a single voice shouts the word 'Judas!'. As Dylan retorts 'I don't believe you — you're a liar', he and the band move into the final number and the ultimate answer: a beautifully played, menacing and insulting version of 'Like A Rolling Stone' aimed directly at his audience. Like all great music, it cannot be adequately described, it must be heard.

5

The thing that happened, I think, historically is that in a certain sense the workers took over the means of production and the audience began to make records for itself. (Interview with Ralph Gleason)

A pattern had already emerged as a result of the events of 1963—4 which was leading to a greater degree of freedom on the performer's side. The situation now existed where an artist could create, innovate and advance musically without being tied irrevocably to the non-creativity inherent in the traditional commercial machine. By the beginning of 1965 the musician had embarked on the liberation of his music from these unnatural strictures.

It was a result of several factors. The new groups of the time had brought with them into the recording world an independence based on their having played together in clubs, not under the best of conditions, for some time before coming to the notice of the wider public or the record companies. They also came from different musical backgrounds; whether folk, rock'n'roll, blues or jazz mattered little. The conjunction of these influences sparked off new directions. Because of the unprecedented success of British music in the States, the doors of that country were opened wide (or, at least, as wide as the Musicians' Union would permit) to British bands, who took with them their own ideas to be passed on to American groups, and who brought back with them American methods and techniques to be disseminated here. Before 1964 the idea of a British rock group being allowed to use an American recording studio would have been unusual to say the least. Yet the Rolling Stones recorded 'Satisfaction' and most of their third LP in Chicago. Now the practice is commonplace and invites little comment, except occasionally a comparison of recording methods and studio 'feel'.

Once in the studio, these new groups took every opportunity to learn to use the machinery for themselves. Up to this time the men in charge of managing, promoting and recording pop music tended to be middle-aged and sometimes hostile towards rock'n'roll. There were exceptions. Phil Spector in New York and Joe Meek in Britain are the two who spring most readily to mind. What was to happen in the mid-sixties was that some of the groups themselves were to become their own producers. The important move by the artist towards control of all areas of the production of his music had at last begun.

This was inevitable if only because of the independence of the new groups. Record companies were no longer presented with a malleable singer ignorant of the ways of commercialism, but rather, in John Peel's words, 'tight, mutinous little gangs' who knew their own minds and, furthermore, knew their own music. It was not easy to manipulate these new people. Many of them came from the provinces, and the majority tended to be better educated and more assertive than their counterparts of the fifties. Mick Jagger, for example, had been a student at the London School of Economics, Spencer Davis was a modern languages graduate of Birmingham University, while a sizeable proportion of the remainder had been art students. As such of course they fitted very easily into that strange Swinging London of the sixties, as Christopher Booker describes it in *The Neophiliacs*:

with its suddenly risen legions of pop singers and pop artists, its fashionable young dress designers and interior decorators and fashion photographers, its discotheques nightly crowded with Beatles and Rolling Stones, its hundreds of casinos, its new National Theatre and its daring young playwrights and daring young film-makers and daring strip-tease clubs, with its skyline dominated by the gaunt outlines of soaring new glass-and-concrete towers — all set against a seemingly timeless background of Rolls-Royces and Changing the Guard at Buckingham Palace and the swans on the lake of St. James's Park. (1969, p. 16)

'Classlessness', according to Booker, was the keynote, and the emphasis, illusory and oversimplistic as we may see it now, was on youth, style, originality and success, rapidly achieved and as rapidly rewarded.

This host of other groups, then, launched themselves headlong onto the downhill race-track of the trail blazed by the Beatles and the Stones. Each fitted somewhere into the space left between the extremes of the wider-based pop appeal of the former to all ages and classes and the harsher, wilder music of the latter rooted in the rhythm and blues tradition. Those who ultimately stayed the pace were those who displayed originality, possessed a personal, recognisable identity, and who were capable of maintaining valid statements. These few were Manfred Mann, the Yardbirds, the Kinks, the Who, the Animals and the Spencer Davis Group. Each contributed in its own way, and ultimately developed into something more than merely the sum of its parts.

To some extent the prevailing publicity machine helped enormously in these groups' rise to prominence (whereas their rise to maturity originated from themselves). People talked of the 'Liverpool Sound' and record executives eagerly grabbed at any new band that came from that city, only slowly realising that this boom was not confined to Liverpool alone, but was manifesting itself in London (Yardbirds and Stones), Birmingham (Spencer Davis), Newcastle (Animals), and Manchester (Hollies, Freddie and the Dreamers) as well. Each company felt compelled to secure its own Beatles-success story. Decca had turned down the Beatles in 1962, but came up with the Stones and the Who; EMI may have turned down the Who in 1964, but at least found Manfred Mann and the Yardbirds to add to the profits made for them by the Beatles and the other Liverpool groups they had under contract from Brian Epstein; Pye gained the Kinks, giving the company a new lease of life after the demise of Lonnie Donegan and the Twist. In addition the ITV show 'Ready Steady Go' with its irresistible slogan 'The weekend starts here' provided a mass arena for the music through its admirable policy of encouraging new groups, as well as new and untried sounds on record.

Of the groups mentioned above who stayed the pace of the mid-sixties, those who were committed to blues and rhythm and blues — Yardbirds, Spencer Davis, Manfred Mann, Animals — are those who subsequently broke up and produced many of the musicians who have come into their own since. From the Yardbirds came Jimmy Page of Led Zeppelin and, pre-eminently, Eric Clapton, who left the group when it achieved national success with its first hit to join John Mayall's then little-known Bluesbreakers; he later went on to become part of Cream. He is perhaps primarily a musician and patently uninterested in the commercial star-system. He sees as unnecessary and beside the point the adulation poured upon him since the days of Cream:

People get hung up saying Blind Faith was one half of Traffic and one half of Cream. They couldn't accept it was a new band with something different to say. (Interview in *Melody Maker*, 1970)

The Spencer Davis Group produced Stevie Winwood, who left to form Traffic in 1966, a band which still retains its excellence and flair for experimentation. And while Manfred Mann, at the time the most commercially pop-orientated of the six, has recently broken new ground musically with his Earth Band, the Animals produced not only Alan Price, writer of the Oscar-winning score for 'O Lucky Man', but also Chas Chandler who moved onto the managerial side with first Jimi Hendrix and more recently Slade.

The Yardbirds, Spencer Davis, Manfred Mann and the Animals were the more overtly musically-orientated bands: from them have come many of the most influential musicians of the last ten years. The Kinks and the Who followed a different path. The former, via the developing talent of Ray Davies, left behind the gut-pounding bass sound of 'You Really Got Me' in favour of gentler and more lyrical social statements and cameos, while still retaining the hard, bitter edge to their music. Davies is as much a performer as a writer, and thus it is necessary to see him sing, say, 'Celluloid Heroes' in order to grasp the dignified pathos and self-allusion of the chorus:

I wish my life was a non-stop Hollywood movie-show,
A fantasy world of celluloid villains and heroes;
Because celluloid heroes never feel any pain,
And celluloid heroes never really die.
(Davray Music, 1972)

The sharpness of sound in Davies' work is allied to an incisive English social comment and a music-hall awareness that has become more evident over the last few years. In fact, although his background was in rock'n'roll, Davies sometimes seems to stand fairly and squarely in the tradition of English music-hall and to have affinities with past performers like George Formby. Listening to perhaps his finest work 'Muswell Hillbillies' however proves that even in the seventies this is by no means an anachronism.

The music of the Who makes no concessions at all. It always was, and still is, hard-driving rock'n'roll, but, as in 'My Generation' and latterly the song-cycles 'Tommy' and 'Quadrophenia', rock with a lyric relevance to its time. 'My Generation' has long been regarded as the anthem and epitome of inarticulate, pep-pilled youth, with the added impressionism contained in Townshend's stuttering guitar-phrasing echoing the jerkily-enunciated vocal. Along with the Stones' 'Satisfaction' this is surely the rock'n'roll statement of the sixties, just as any of Chuck Berry's songs sum up the fifties. They give articulate form to the prevailing mood of the youth of the time, while achieving longevity in their continuing relevance. The Who still perform Eddie Cochran's fifties song 'Summertime Blues' and it provides a platform from which they can take off into 'My Generation'. Townshend once attempted to sum up the 'powerful force' of rock'n'roll, its stimulus, its brashness, its overall embrace and effect:

It's like saying, 'Get all the pop music, put it into a cartridge, put the cap on it and fire the gun.' Whether those ten or fifteen numbers sound roughly the same. You don't care what periods they were written in, what they mean, what they're all about. It's the bloody explosion that they create when you let the gun off. It's the event. That's what rock'n'roll is. That is why rock'n'roll is powerful. It is a single force. It is a single impetus and it's a single force . . . (*Rolling Stone Interviews*, Vol. 1, p. 108)

6

And if it's true all so true that you can't live up to everyone's expectations, and if it's true you cannot be all things to all people, and if it's true you cannot be other than what you are . . . then you must be strong of heart if you wish to work the problem out in public, on stage, through work before 'them' who fully expect and predict in print their idol's fall. (Lou Reed of the Velvet Underground)

Alone among the groups of the mid-sixties, the Kinks, the Who and the Stones have managed to stay together without breaking up or undergoing undue major personnel changes. This may well be partly due to the dominant creative forces of their respective leaders, each contributing the majority of the group's music and direction, seeing their compositions in terms of the group as a unit. But if these three have continued in more or less their original form, what caused the others to split up?

The answer is that no group of people will advance in ideas or technique at the same pace. Given an interest and ability in creative musical expression, an artist will move freely, often from band to band and musician to musician, in order to further this progression. Hence constant shifting of personnel has become a characteristic feature of rock groups over the last ten years, bringing in its train, as we have already seen, a meeting between the different musical generations in blues, jazz and rock.

The pressures attendant on becoming a 'star' cannot be discounted either. The rapid elevation to such a status by the media and an often uncaring publicity machine has frequently brought emptiness and confusion to the pop musician. John Lennon in an interview with *Rolling Stone* magazine dealt at length with this topic:

Those were the most humiliating experiences, like sitting with the Governor of the Bahamas when we were making 'Help!' and being insulted by these junked-up middle-class bitches and bastards who would be commenting on our working-classness and our manners. I couldn't take it, it would hurt me, I would go insane, swearing at them, whatever, I'd always do something. One has to completely humiliate oneself to be what the Beatles were, and that's what I resent. I mean I did it, I didn't know, I didn't foresee; it just happened bit by bit, gradually, until this complete craziness is surrounding you and you're doing exactly what you don't want to do with people you can't stand, the people you hated when you were ten. (Wenner, 1973, p. 18)

And with all this would go a tremendous increase in pace: months-long tours of different countries, a feeling of being constantly under a microscope, and often the only impression left by a country or a city would be arclights on stage and the insides of hotel rooms and jet aircraft. This pressure, coupled almost inevitably in such a situation with the taking of drugs of all kinds for energy, release and comfort, has taken its toll of a number of the finest musicians of the last decade: Brian Jones, Janis Joplin, and Jimi Hendrix amongst them. This has become so much a part of the rock image that an American magazine recently ran a readers' poll to discover 'The Rock Star Most Likely To Die Next'.

But the break-up of the mid-sixties groups was also helped by a growing awareness of new ideas and philosophies, musical and otherwise, emanating from the burgeoning music scene centred on San Francisco — 'The West Coast Sound'. The way had been paved for this breakthrough in the records of first Dylan and the Byrds, and then, in 1966, Frank Zappa's Mothers of Invention and the Jefferson Airplane. By the end of the year more and more was being heard of the term 'psychedelia' and the concept of 'acid-rock' — first coined as a handy title for the music of the Grateful Dead and evolved when they were providing a backcloth of sound to Ken Kesey's Acid Tests — huge, meandering days-long parties where guests were freely invited to sample LSD (at that time the drug was still legal in California, or perhaps more accurately, not yet illegal). Tom Wolfe in *The Electric Kool-Aid Acid Test* says of their music that

disappearing down so many microphones and hooked through so many mixers and variable lags and blew up in so many amplifiers and rolled around in so many speakers and fed back down so many microphones, it came on like a chemical refinery. There was something wholly new and deliriously weird in the Dead's sound. (1969, p. 223)

There were new lyrics too, prepared for by Dylan's rambling image-filled marathons, and finding one outlet on the West Coast in songs dealing in fantasy — some, though not all, drug-inspired:

One pill makes you larger
And one pill makes you small;
But the ones that mother gives you
Don't do anything at all —
Go ask Alice
When she's ten feet tall.
(from 'White Rabbit' by Jefferson Airplane, Copper Penny Music, 1966)

The impact of all this on Britain was to increase the direction-seeking of British bands: new ideas for a new time in a new age. Not the least of the influence was due to the West Coast groups' development inside a closely-knit community which itself had been affected by the community of groups they had witnessed in Liverpool. But that particular community had almost disappeared even by 1964, for the centre of the British recording industry was, and still is, London. Pop in this country tends to be far more nationally-inclined than the regionalism of the States will permit. The San Franciscan bands had the managements and the studios in their own city, so they did not have to move; rather, people like Janis Joplin and Steve Miller moved to San Francisco. Implicit in all this was the intangible factor that California had always been regarded as somewhere special — witness the Beach Boys' 'California Girls' and Berry's 'Promised Land'. In addition it had historical and romantic connotations as the region to which the nineteenth-century settlers had made their great trek west. And aside from California in the early sixties having constructed its own myth with the surfing craze and the freer, sunnier life-style that went with it, San Francisco had already become a haven for the 'beats' of the forties and fifties:

Visualise the Haight in 1960, before its present population arrived. In that year, rising rents, police harrassment, and the throngs of tourists and thrill-seekers squeezed many beatniks out of the North Beach district, three miles away. They started looking for space in the Haight-Ashbury, and landlords here saw they could make more money renting their property to young people willing to put up with poor conditions than to black families. For this reason, a small, beat subculture took root in the Flatlands and spread slowly up the slope of Mount Sutro. By 1962 the Haight was the centre of a significant but fairly unpublicised bohemian colony.
   Although fed by beats and students from San Francisco State University, this colony remained unnoticed for several years. One reason was its members' preference for sedating themselves with alcohol and marijuana instead of using drugs that attract more attention. Another was their preoccupation with art and their habit of living as couples or alone. This living pattern was drastically altered in 1964, however, with the popular acceptance of mescalin, LSD and other hallucinogens, and the advent of the Ginsberg—Leary—Kesey, nomadic, passive communal electric-and-acid-oriented life-style. (Smith *et al.*, 1970, p. 100)

But, musically, the wheel had turned full circle. Whereas the influx of British groups in 1964—5 had been eagerly seized on by the Americans, the time had now come for a reappraisal of American music and its new departures set in motion by the British impact. Group after group 'went psychedelic', in that they played with new sounds and instruments and were seen to develop new philosophies, both political and apolitical. Some of the music became gentler in imitation of the more relaxed and folk-influenced music of the West Coast; some of the lyrics became harder in their attitudes towards social and political injustice. And as 1967 drew on, the aimless 'flower power' summer was inflicted on the nation.
   When the furore finally died down, it became evident that much of it had proved a blind alley as far as creativity and originality were concerned. The more dedicated musicians like Clapton and Winwood carried on largely undistracted; but although the Pied Piper of the Beatles' *Sergeant Pepper* album may have pointed towards the gates of dawn, for many the following day was to be overcast and rather dismal: in fact, very English. Some came away wiser and with a host of new ideas, a few of which were to be brought to fruition, while the rest fell on stony ground. But the most important effect was the inception of an international musical fellowship: henceforth the meeting ground and the influences were to become worldwide.

7
I'll be your mirror
Paint what you are
In case you don't know.
(From 'I'll Be Your Mirror' written and performed by Nico and the Velvet Underground)

As for social or political comment as a part of the stance of the modern pop lyric, as happens with all innovations in popular culture, it has had its bandwagon hour and has now been properly assimilated. Its power should not be overestimated, though it can be considerable. Its very success is a measure of how international concern (echoed in song) has become over issues far wider-ranging than those contained in the American Union songs of the thirties. Concern is no longer rural but universal: Lennon and others merely echo this as Guthrie in his dustbowl ballads and Pete Seeger with his 'Little Boxes' did for earlier generations. It is only when pop is filtered through the commercial machine that lyrics become stale, bland and meaningless. Otherwise there is much to choose from; whether one agrees or not with the standpoint should not be at issue. Thus Lennon's total commitment to the removal of British troops from Northern Ireland in his 1972 album *Sometime in New York City* and his insistence on seeing the soldiers as murderers may be termed naïve but we should try and balance against that the excellence of the product as a piece of rock music. There are now few barriers to the choice of subject-matter for pop songs, and this is surely all to the good. In the recent past, issues as various as ecology, pollution, the war in South East Asia and racial discrimination have all been dealt with, and some of the bands, themselves, albeit mostly American like the MC5 and Country Joe and the Fish, have been active in the political sphere. It is this kind of activity which Carl Belz (1969) points to in vindication of his thesis that certain styles of pop music come into the category of genuine folk art — springing from the people rather than manufactured for them.

One important change which has occurred in the last ten years is the increase in specific social comment in black music. In 1966 LeRoi Jones wrote prophetically:

. . . it is my thought that soon, with the same cycle of the general 'integrated' music bizness, the R'n'B songs will be more socially oriented. (1968, p. 208)

As it turned out, he was right. Although there were such songs emanating from Motown and Atlantic in the early sixties ('Uptown', 'On Broadway', 'Spanish Harlem'), they seemed more commercial offerings than totally committed to what they implied. And even what they implied was often a watered-down version of what actually existed. Jones saw this increasing criticism as a good thing, just as Eldridge Cleaver viewed the mixed results of the Twist at the opening of the sixties:

The Twisters, sporting their blue suede shoes, moved beyond the ghost in white shoes who ate a Hot Dog and sipped Malted Milk as he danced the mechanical jig of Satan on top of Medger Evers' tomb. (Cleaver, 1969, p. 181)

8

Sometimes it seems to be a profane liturgy of the doomed and the despairing, but more frequently it is a hymn of hope or an unbridled affirmation of dark defiance. (Phyl Garland in *The Sound of Soul*)

The black rhythm and blues of the fifties has by now largely merged into what is called soul music through a marriage with the gospel style. Throughout the history of black music, right up to the fifties, the blues and gospel had an uneasy relationship. Gospel musicians and singers, rooted in the church, looked upon the blues, with its subject matter of poverty, social movement, and often inescapably explicit sexual innuendo, as music inspired by the devil. There exists a fascinating recording of Jerry Lee Lewis (a white Southern rock'n'roller) being persuaded by his producer during a studio discussion that to sing rock'n'roll will still be in keeping with his Christian faith because he will be making people happy and therefore carrying on God's work (*There's Good Rockin' Tonight*, Bopcat Records). Soul music then generally includes the more heart-felt, emotionally-committed aspect of gospel, denser sound-patterns and a larger range of instrumentation (a tendency which emerged in the sixties).

Bill Millar, in his indispensable book *The Drifters*, mentions the Falcons' 1959 recording of 'You're So Fine' as possibly the first modern soul record. The Falcons were from Detroit, which is also of course the home of Tamla Motown Records. Tamla Motown and Stax Records from Memphis did most in the sixties to define popularly what constituted soul music, Motown in the process lending their name to one of the music's subdivisions. But in retrospect it is plain that Motown, an all-black company, had managed by the mid-sixties merely to define a middle ground. Their aim was to corner both the black and white markets, to cross over from the rhythm and blues pure soul area to the pop field, watering down what to whites might be the more emotional excesses of the music so as to make it slide more easily over the palate of a non-black audience. As Millar puts it, referring to the mid-sixties:

Various performers began to use the same backing track for different songs and Tamla Motown became synonymous with the word 'factory'. Paradoxically, the public consider technical perfection to be more important than bringing out the soul of the performer. (1971, p. 83)

In the late fifties the Drifters had pioneered the use in rhythm and blues and soul of different instrumentation and arrangements: string sections, large orchestrations, and Latin American rhythms. By the mid-sixties, Tamla Motown had largely followed suit. The whole process has given birth in the seventies to extraordinary success for something best called 'sweet soul'. Stemming mainly from Philadelphia ('The Philly Sound') and the writing and production work of Thom Bell, Kenny Gamble and Leon Huff, it tends to give a muted bass-led, 'sweet' string sound almost complete predominance. The singing, whether from an individual or a vocal group, 'the soul of the performer', often becomes one of several layers of sound: the voice has become one more musical instrument. Like a number of other branches of soul, this is music produced primarily for the discotheque where the demand is for dance music with few, if any, changes in mood or pace in the course of a single record.

Not all of it is like this however. Undoubted excellences tend to occur if the personality and interpretation of the performers is allowed full rein. This is certainly so in the cases of Stevie Wonder and Al Green, and pre-eminently with Smokey Robinson. Robinson was lead singer and song-writer with the Miracles through the sixties, has now turned to solo singing, producing and writing for other performers, and has been made a vice-president of the Tamla Motown Corporation. His songs and interpretations remain some of the finest to come from pop music in recent years. The songs themselves are highly literate, and even within the short three-minute time-span of a pop single manage effortlessly to convey a variety of intricate emotional moods. And like the best of pop music, they are equally viable on different levels — put bluntly, you can dance to them *and* listen.

Robinson and Wonder write their own songs; in this they are like Bob Dylan, the Beatles (taken both as a group and as individuals after the break-up of the group), and the late Jimi Hendrix. It is these artists who have had the greatest influence on pop music as it has developed over the last ten years. They have total control over all aspects of the production of their own music and this must provide a large part of the explanation of that influence.

Robinson and Wonder (along with Otis Redding, who died in a plane crash probably before his full potential had been reached) have provided much of the best and most consistent black music of the period. Dylan, almost single-handed, pushed a whole generation towards social and political awareness; and in so doing redefined the language of the popular song. It's a very long way from 'I Get A Kick Out Of You' to Dylan's depiction of society in 'Desolation Row':

Cinderella, she seems so easy;
'It takes one to know one', she smiles,
Then puts her hands in her back pocket
Bette-Davis-style.
Then in comes Romeo, he's moaning,
'You belong to me, I believe',
Till someone says, 'You're in the wrong place,
     my friend,
You'd better leave';
And the only sound that's left
After the ambulances go
Is Cinderella sweeping up
On Desolation Row.
(Blossom Music, 1965)

The Beatles reintroduced an appreciation of the roots of rock'n'roll, and still continue as individuals to add to what must in the final analysis be seen as one of the finest bodies of popular song of the century. Their work is increasingly being seen as an essential reference point for all mid-century youth culture and pop music.

Finally, Hendrix, who died in tragic circumstances in 1970, was, indisputably, the master of the electric guitar and its extensive amplified possibilities. His style and experimentation have affected almost every lead guitarist of the seventies; even several years after his death his music still sounds avant garde. Taking long, flowing blues lines as his base, he would mould and melt these into the most sustainedly intelligent use of electronic feedback, distortion and volume that had been heard at that time, especially in improvised form.

9

I know
It's only rock'n'roll
But I like it
Like it
Yes I do
I like it.
(The Rolling Stones from 'It's Only Rock'n'Roll')

But what of the present? What is being made of these influences? We have now a situation where a country style can be adopted in the melodic lines and personal lyricism of, say, Neil Young, in the guitar counterpoints of the once-acid Grateful Dead, and in the work of Elton John and Rod Stewart. There is a growing number of talented singer/songwriters, reflecting in their songs, not banal commercial clichés, but their own backgrounds, commitments and environments; out of many it will suffice to mention Van Morrison and David Bowie here. British bands, though not always fully understanding their chosen medium, have taken black music as their base, and in many cases, for example the Average White Band and Alex Harvey, have proved themselves not only highly competent but innovatory as well. Further, musicians have become more aware of their influences and sources and have learned to use them to best advantage. To listen to Roxy Music, one of the most original British bands of the seventies, is to realise that even thirties' style and traditional German song have a place in current pop, and that the terms rock'n'roll, country, rhythm and blues, and even the blues itself, no longer apply only to a particular locale or historical period, but have been creatively absorbed into the best of present-day music.

If there is an avant garde to the pop music of the seventies then it is the experimental area inhabited by such groups as Pink Floyd, Soft Machine, Hatfield and the North and Tangerine Dream. The last-named is a German band now recording in this country for Virgin Records, a small independent company which has characterised itself in a very short time by its policy of recording and releasing music which many a larger company would regard as too experimental and too much a minority taste to be commercially worthwhile. One of Virgin's first releases was Mike Oldfield's 'Tubular Bells', a long and intricate work utilising a large variety of instruments most of which were played on the recording by Oldfield himself. Paradoxically, in view of their policy, this record has deservedly been exceptionally successful in terms of sales.

Soft Machine and Pink Floyd both began in the mid-sixties, the latter outliving 'psychedelia' to produce a string of artistic as well as commercial successes, culminating perhaps with their album *Dark Side Of The Moon*. Whilst experiments with sound, taped effects (a kind of direct musical impressionism) and playing in extended form have been their direction, they manage perhaps to occupy a middle ground between mass popularity and outright experimentalism. Soft Machine on the other hand lean far more heavily towards improvised jazz. Their keyboards player Mike Ratledge has proved the mainstay of the band over the last ten years, and he has provided the basis of their work, developing music in extended form further than any other band, and eschewing even the strictures present in recorded music dictated by the length of time available on an LP record.

Hatfield and the North and Tangerine Dream probably have their best work still to come. Hatfield and the North combine in their work a variety of rock music influences together with more jazz-based improvisations often in complex time signatures, while Tangerine Dream, in common with a number of other German bands, are advancing into the area normally associated with avant garde classical music. They tend to use electronically synthesised sound rather than conventional acoustic or electric instruments, both in live performance and on record. In a recent interview with Michael Wale, Mike Leckebusch, a German TV producer heavily involved with rock music, has described German rock music thus:

There's no musical pop or rock tradition, there's only tradition in classical music, and a tradition in the sort of experimental classical music like Stockhausen, Schoenberg, and that's the region where German groups come in very strong, because this is what they've learned, what they know, and they don't have the feeling for American or English, or Anglo-American rock or blues, because we haven't had it here, there's no tradition of that, because we were cut off from 1933 until 1945, and everything had to develop then. So now I think there is a chance for new German rock music with the classical tradition or the electronic tradition. (Wale, 1972, p. 318)

Nor is this all, for yet another avenue has opened up in recent years. I have laid stress on black music stemming from the United States, but what must not be ignored is the impact of reggae, a music and style indigenous to the West Indies. Those who were first in Britain to claim this music as their own were the skinheads of the late sixties, following the lead of much of the West Indian immigrant population of this country. Not only the music but also the Jamaican clothes and dance-styles were seized upon. It is noticeable that, whereas the Teddy Boys of the fifties achieved notoriety in the Notting Hill race riots aimed primarily against the then growing West Indian population, by the time of the skinheads West Indian culture had been largely absorbed and any targets for gratuitous violence, though still racial in origin, had become the newer immigrants, the Pakistanis and Indians.

Musically, the reggae style had been filtering into Britain since the early sixties. Earlier forms, notably ska and bluebeat, had been successfully adapted into the repertoire of Georgie Fame, and the first reggae-style hit record was arguably Millie's 'My Boy Lollipop' in 1964. Heavily influenced by American rhythm and blues, the music had its origins in Jamaica in the fifties and, like skiffle in this country, could be played with relatively cheap or home-made instruments. Like the early blues, part of its subject matter and drive comes from suffering, and in its initial forms it was the preserve of working-class street musicians.

But it is also a music that is often closer to Africa than America. This is due partly to the vocal style and the rhythms employed, but it is also because of the influence of a mystical, political, and religious cult known as Ras Tafarianism. Space is too limited to delve into this at any length, but part of a Ras Tafarian's belief lies in seeing Ethiopia as a kind of spiritual homeland, and Hailie Selassie as King:

The Ras Tafarians gave a philosophical base to the musicians from which they could work: 'Peace and Love is the message' until Africa's children are freed from Babylon. Babylon is any place or any thought ultimately accountable to white social and political influences. (Courtney Tullock in *Rolling Stone Record Reviews*, Vol. 2, 1974, p. 208)

It would be invidious to single out any particular reggae artists for mention, suffice to say that Jimmy Cliff, Bob Marley and the Wailers, Prince Buster and Laurel Aitken have produced some of the best reggae to be heard in this country. Meanwhile as the seventies progress, more and more British musicians are following the lead of Lennon, McCartney, Paul Simon and even the Rolling Stones in using Jamaican recording studios and adopting reggae styles into their music.

Performers are also aware of the ambiguous nature of the commercial milieu in which they work. Rod Stewart adds a new perspective in 'Maggie May', when, having sung of the break-up of his relationship with the girl, he inserts into the song his real self as rock'n'roll singer:

I suppose I could collect my books
    and get on back to school,
Steal my daddy's cue and make a living
    out of playing pool,
Find myself a rock'n'roll band
That needs a helping hand ...
(Chappell & Co. Ltd, 1971)

David Bowie does a similar thing, when he creates a 'persona' in his songs, such as his character Ziggy Stardust, who mirrors his creator's own real-life success. Bowie has carried this much further than Stewart, by dramatising a 'persona' in his stage performances, sometimes using the techniques of mime which he learnt from Lindsay Kemp; he then finishes his act with a song called 'Rock'n'Roll Suicide', aping from start to finish the commercial myth of the rise and fall of a rock'n'roll superstar.

Thus we return once more to the commercial machine — the industry which in the first half of the seventies seemed to have its sights set firmly on a yet younger section of youth. One could argue that the first shots in the battle were fired with the deliberate creation of the Monkees in 1966 in the exact image of the Beatles, but this is by the way. The fact remains that the Osmonds, Gary Glitter, Sweet, etc. were designed to appeal primarily to an age-group which has its upper limit at fourteen. Youth, even extreme youth, is good copy. In commercial terms success was high, whilst the musical content was polished and well-performed, even though there seemed to be little 'soul', merely an excess of show. As such, however, it was perhaps reflecting the need in the early seventies for simpler forms of pop music as a reaction against the experimentation of late-sixties rock music mentioned earlier. Slade was the first band to provide this simplicity and they remain perhaps the best of the more 'commercial' pop groups of the last few years. The Osmonds, of course, filled a gap left by the break-up of the Beatles and certainly, and deservedly in some senses, along with David Cassidy, created a comparable wish-fulfilment/hysteria syndrome without at any time surpassing it by moving on into mass acceptance by all ages and classes — that so far remains the prerogative of the Beatles.

Musically though, a point of stasis seemed to have been reached by 1975. The Osmonds and the Bay City Rollers, amongst many others, were eminently capable of producing very fine copies of previous pop styles. But there must lie the criticism; very often they were only copies, albeit often enjoyable and mostly highly successful. Queen, Cockney Rebel and 10cc on the other hand were beginning to show the way forward by having fully assimilated what had gone before, and, from that base, cleverly fashioning new approaches.

But these last three bands appeal to a slightly older age-group than that of the Osmonds. The point is, as Greil Marcus noted some years ago, that youth has

fragmented into little groups of age, taste, politics, geography, and self-conscious sophistication. (1971, p. 39)

Soul music will appeal to one particular age-group and class, the Osmonds to another, Led Zeppelin and Bob Dylan to yet others. In the main, this has always been true of the different forms of pop music. Separate musics, stances and styles will always appeal to separate sets of people: in many ways pop acts thus as a two-way mirror.

Paradoxically, despite this fragmentation, there exists in the best pop music a universality which transcends such differences. It is not easy to explain, for partly it goes against sophisticated canons of analysis, even lying somewhere in an intuitive understanding that a technically poor pop record can still be a good one if 'it's got a beat and you can dance to it'. Pete Townshend understands this well:

The great rock classics are very, very simple, and the reason is that the message is in the simplicity. The idea, the mood of the song, comes across despite the simplicity — something sophisticated and subtle has come through this almost animalistic dance music. (Interview in *The Listener*, October 1974)

It is its immediacy, rough edges and integrity which give a good pop song its meaning, feeling and universality. It has an ability to speak to the audience, and, at the same time, to put into sound their stances, moods and thoughts. This is one of the strongest attributes of pop music, and always comes from the performer himself; it never arises successfully from the intervention of the music industry. In this way, pop becomes personal to each listener, defining with an accuracy that is more than mere nostalgia the particular mood, time and place, identified by the listener, from which the record sprang. It is this summing-up that is universally understood:

Once, overcome by the Drifters' 'There Goes My Baby', we stopped our car and pulled over, just to listen. Four friends drove by while the song was on, and all did the same thing, as five radios blasted out the same song. (Marcus, 1969, p. 13)

Even trivial events in people's lives occur to a constant backcloth of the pop records of the time, and it was faithfulness to this aspect of life which contributed to the realism and success of the films *That'll Be The Day*, *Stardust* and *American Graffiti*.

At first glance it might seem that I have now contradicted any claims I may have made concerning the musical advances of pop. But I do not believe so. Pop is an amalgam, and musicality, or its lack, is but one ingredient. Youth styles, modes of dress and behaviour, stances towards authority and one another, are all inextricably linked in its meaning. Musically, huge advances have been made as the power and range of possibilities open to musicians have increased. Those Teddy Boys jiving in the aisles to Bill Haley in 1956 could not have known what it was to be, but they knew they were in at the beginning of something. Eldridge Cleaver, at the end of *Soul on Ice*, called the Beatles

soul by proxy, middlemen between the Mind and the Body. A long way from Pat Boone's White Shoes. A way station on a slow route travelled with all deliberate speed. (Cleaver, 1969, p. 183)

His meaning was more political than musical, but, to take up his metaphor, the pop music train has now come so far that Jerry Garcia's comment may one day prove not to sound so fanciful after all:

Communication is getting so good, so much music is available on records and it's so easy to hear anything you want to hear, that in another twenty years, every musician in the world will be able to play with every other musician in the world with no problem at all. (Gleason, 1969, p. 328)

References

Belz, C., *The Story of Rock* (Oxford University Press, 1969).
Booker, C., *The Neophiliacs* (William Collins, 1969).
Cleaver, E., *Soul on Ice* (Jonathan Cape, 1969).
Frith, S., 'A Year of Singles in Britain' in Gillett, C. (ed.), *Rock File 2* (Panther, 1974).
Gleason, R., *The Jefferson Airplane and the San Francisco Sound* (Ballantine Books, 1969).
Gunn, T., *Poems 1950–1966: A Selection* (Faber and Faber, 1969).
Jones, LeRoi, *Black Music* (Apollo, 1968).
Mabey, R., *The Pop Process* (Hutchinson Educational, 1969).
Marcus, G., 'Who Put the Bomp in the Bomp De-Bomp De-Bomp?' in Marcus, G. (ed.), *Rock and Roll Will Stand* (Beacon Press, 1969).

Marcus, G., 'Rock-A-Hula Clarified', *Creem*, June 1971.

Melly, G., *Revolt into Style* (Allen Lane, The Penguin Press, 1970).

Millar, B., *The Drifters* (November Books, 1971).

Nuttall, J., 'Techniques of Separation' in Cash, A. (ed.), *Anatomy of Pop* (BBC, 1970).

Rolling Stone Editors, *The Rolling Stone Interviews*, Vol. 1 (Straight Arrow Publishers Inc., 1971).

Rolling Stone Editors, *The Rolling Stone Record Reviews*, Vol. 2 (Simon Schuster, 1974).

Smith, D., Luce, J., and Dernburg, E., 'Love Needs Care: Haight-Ashbury Dies', *New Society*, Vol. 16, 1970.

Wale, M., *Vox Pop* (Harrap, 1972).

Wenner, J., *Lennon Remembers* (Penguin, 1973).

Winner, L., 'The Strange Death of Rock'n'Roll' in Marcus, G. (ed.), *Rock and Roll Will Stand* (Beacon Press, 1969).

Wolfe, T., *The Electric Kool-Aid Acid Test* (Bantam, 1969).

2 Definitions of serious music

GRAHAM VULLIAMY

The school music teacher is naturally concerned with the practicalities of his work and may therefore question the value of discussing 'definitions of serious music'. But it must be stressed that any form of teaching is based on assumptions and beliefs concerning the worth and aims of what is being taught — this is as true of music as it is with any other subject. However we may not always be fully aware of the nature of our beliefs and their effects upon our actions. In this respect an examination of the historical and sociological background to school music teaching is revealing.

I will show that hitherto this teaching has been based on music in the European serious tradition (including both classical and avant garde music as defined in the Introduction). This reflects the music establishment's assumptions about what constitutes 'serious' music, which I shall review critically in the light of its reactions to the development of a new musical tradition. This new tradition, the Afro-American, covers those types of music (jazz, blues and rock are examples) which can be traced, at least in some of their aspects, to the merging of an African tradition of music with that tradition, European in origin, which thrived in the southern states of America in the nineteenth century.

My main purpose in this chapter is to show that the attitudes which I illustrate historically are still current, and that they remain invalid. Such attitudes perpetuate an unnecessary division between 'serious' and popular music. This in turn prevents music teachers from exploring areas of experience which would add impetus and freshness to their work. Having explained my own theoretical views on the values of music, I then continue in chapter 3 to consider some practical suggestions for a change of approach to school music teaching.

At the beginning of the present century the teaching of music in all schools (except the public schools), whether at elementary or secondary level, was confined entirely to class singing. This was a reflection of the fact that in the nineteenth century all the great music educators were concerned primarily with vocal music in schools. Rainbow (1967) suggests that this emphasis on vocal music resulted from the belief of music educators at that time that the main benefits to be derived from school music teaching were religious and moral. Although singing has remained an integral part of the music teaching in most schools to this day, the scope of 'class'

[33]

music has increased enormously since the turn of the century. A major influence was the development in the 1920s and 1930s of the 'music appreciation' movement, which emphasised the importance of guided listening to music in addition to its performance. The reorganisation of secondary schools with the 1944 Education Act resulted in an increase in the specialist teaching of music in schools and an acceptance of the principle of general music classes for all. Running parallel to the growth of music as a class subject has been the increasing importance of extra-curricular musical activities in schools. Since the late 1940s when local authorities began to accept responsibility for providing instrumental tuition in state secondary schools there has been a rapid expansion of such tuition, resulting in a vast growth of extra-curricular orchestral music.

Until quite recently the main components of class music (as opposed to extra-curricular musical activities in the school) were some combination of singing, history of music, music appreciation, the teaching of notation and theory, and in some cases the playing of a simple instrument like a recorder or a harmonica. This conception has, however, been challenged by a group of music teachers who stress the importance of practical creative music-making in the classroom. One of the early influences on this recent approach to class music was the work of Carl Orff, the German composer. His particular interest in music education led him to develop the use of simple, tuned percussion instruments (such as the glockenspiel) which would be cheap to manufacture. Not only has such a development enabled large numbers of children actually to play a wide variety of instruments in the classroom but also the emphasis which Orff placed on the role of improvisation has led to the possibility of children composing their own music. Such an approach has been extended in different ways by recent music teachers who reject the main aims and emphases of traditional class-music teaching. Many of these teachers are themselves composers of serious music (in the field of what is generally referred to as the avant garde) and they are concerned to acquaint pupils with the serious music of today:

The aim of this book is to form a link between contemporary music and instrumental work in the classroom . . . Pupils so often leave school with little knowledge of even the existence of the serious music of their own time. (Self, 1967, p. 2)

Emphasis is therefore placed on the different techniques that today's avant garde composers themselves use. An attempt is made to get away from the traditional approaches to notation, harmony and melody. A simplified form of notation has been developed which has something in common with that used by a number of today's avant garde composers, and the shift in such an approach is away from teaching pupils to play instruments the 'right' way and towards the actual composition of music and the creative manipulation of sounds:

Simple methods — which are often complex in terms of their overall results — are given by which the individual pupil can create his own music. Creativity is encouraged to the utmost degree — a creativity whose roots lie in our own environment and in the work of present day composers. (Dennis, 1970, p. 3)

Thus school music teaching is characterised by a variety of approaches (ranging from what might be called, purely for convenience of comparison, traditional approaches to the more recent emphasis on practical music making in the classroom) but what is common to all of them is the fact that the content of the music lesson tends to be restricted to one particular type of music -- namely music in the European 'serious' tradition. This, one might suggest, has unfortunate consequences in view of the increasing interest of young people in forms of music other than those in the European 'serious' tradition – broadly speaking in various forms of 'popular' music which are derived partly from the Afro-American tradition. Much of the responsibility for this situation lies with the music establishment and its reaction to these latter forms of music, and it is to this that I now turn.

The origins of Afro-American music are best illustrated by considering the early development of jazz in the Southern states of America at the turn of this century. With jazz came the development of a new musical language – a language that was to shape not only jazz but much of the popular music of the twentieth century. Thus Pleasants argues in his stimulating book *Serious Music and all that Jazz* that up until the birth of jazz there was an idiomatic unity which had made it possible for the greatest composers to write popular music and performers to play it. But with the rise of jazz-based popular music:

The Serious musician could no longer play or sing Popular music . . . Only the transition from Renaissance to Baroque and the present transition from European to Afro-American have effected such elaborate changes of vocabulary, rhetoric and syntax that one must speak of new languages, however much each new language has retained of the old. And only these two transitions have represented so drastic a shift of aesthetic base. (1969, pp. 33 and 101)

Since jazz was the product of the fusion of two musical cultures – the European and the West African – it is not surprising that in our predominantly European musical culture the qualities that make jazz and other Afro-American musical derivatives sound different are African in derivation. The relationship between the musical values of jazz and those of African music are explored in a number of works of which Schuller's *Early Jazz* (1968) is generally considered to be the most authoritative. In the latter the links between African music and those aspects of jazz which differentiate it from music in the classical tradition are explored at length in the first chapter.

Perhaps the most fundamental difference between jazz and music in the classical tradition is the differing conceptions of rhythm in each. Schuller suggests that the uniqueness of jazz rhythm derives from two primary sources: the quality which jazz musicians call 'swing', and what Schuller calls the consistent 'democratisation' of rhythmic values. By this he means that in jazz so-called weak beats (or weak parts of rhythmic units) are not underplayed as they tend to be in classical music. Though it is immediately recognisable to any jazz musician the quality of 'swing' is, as Schuller notes, beyond verbal description. He does nevertheless attempt to describe it, whilst admitting that his definition can only take on its full meaning when the thing defined is also experienced. He suggests that 'swing' signifies the accurate timing of a note in its proper place, together with two characteristics which do not generally occur in classical music. These are, first, a specific type of accentuation and inflection with which notes are played or sung, and secondly, the continuity — the 'forward propelling directionality' — with which individual notes are linked together, a result of the tension between the European-based harmony and the African-based rhythm.

Schuller traces these peculiar rhythmic characteristics of jazz directly to the rhythmic basis of African music. Here he draws mainly on A.M. Jones (1959) and notes that prior to Jones's analysis all previous attempts at analysing African rhythmic usages had made two mistakes: 'The African music was approached by way of European music, and no knowledgeable African was consulted who could, in one way or another, verify or refute the results of the findings' (Schuller, 1968, p. 10). The most important aspects of Jones's research may be summarised as confirming that 'African music, including its drumming, is wholly contrapuntal and basically conceived in terms of polymetric and polyrhythmic time relationships' (Schuller, 1968, p. 11). He also found that African rhythm is based on additive rather than divisive principles and that African music is improvised within a most complex and rigorous set of musical disciplines:

The African conceives his polyrhythm in a much more extended, more complex, polymetrically organized basis, where phrases rarely, and sometimes never, coincide vertically. In fact his overriding interest is in cross-rhythms, the more subtle and more complex the better. (Schuller, 1968, p. 11)

Schuller concludes therefore that African music is rhythmically highly complex and, having considered an example from the second volume of Jones, suggests that 'when one remembers that this example of African music is improvised within a highly disciplined framework, one can only wonder at the connotation of "primitive" usually given to African music' (p. 13).

Another important feature of jazz was the extensive use of the 'blues scale', derived from the vocal blues, which had developed amongst the Negro ex-slaves shortly after the latter's emancipation in 1865. The most striking characteristic of the blues scale lies in the optional flattening (or more accurately bending) of the 3rd and 7th notes (and sometimes the 5th) to give what we now call 'blue tonality'. The precise origin of blue tonality is still a matter for debate but its importance can hardly be overemphasised, since the blues might be viewed as the universally and predominantly influential style of Afro-American music.

The earliest blues contained another feature which was to become central to the Afro-American tradition of music and that was the role of improvisation; a simple twelve-bar harmonic structure was usually taken as a structure within which the performer composed his melody (and originally the lyrics as well) as he actually played or sang. Such improvisation means that Afro-American music is essentially

S.BEND-LINCOLNWAY/BENDIX
3030 LINCOLNWAY WEST
SOUTH BEND, IN 46628
US USA

NYSTROM, TAMALEE
415 S FILBERT ST
NEW CARLISLE, IN 46552

BLOCKBUSTER™

WE'VE BEEN LOOKING FOR YOU!

WE HAVEN'T SEEN YOU FOR SO LONG.

Stop by today with this card and enjoy a **FREE VIDEO RENTAL** on us!

Store Manager

OFFER EXPIRES 4/30/92

512PC26

Rent one movie, get a second movie rental of equal or lesser value **FREE!**

Store Manager

OFFER EXPIRES 5/31/92

5610PP00008

an art of performance (the performance entailing spontaneous composition), whilst a classical composition, leaving aside nuances of interpretation, possesses essentially the same kind of identity whoever happens to perform it.

A final important feature of jazz is the sonority of the instruments; as Schuller demonstrates, the sonority of real jazz is traceable directly to African singing and indirectly to African speech and language. When the Negro ex-slaves in America first came into contact with European instruments, they used these instruments in exactly the same way as they used drums (the most important instrument in African music), to imitate the human voice. For the musical consequences of this it is worth quoting Schuller at some length:

The African quality of jazz sonority can be heard in the individuality and personal inflection of the jazz musician's tone. His is not basically the cultivated and studied tone of Western art music, nor a tone that is bought in the music store along with the instrument. Jazz's strength and communicative power lie in this individuality, which comes from inside the man; indeed a jazz musician without this individual quality is not a jazz musician in the strictest sense.

By contrast, a symphony orchestra player performs a different function in which great individuality is not a prerequisite. Indeed, it is more likely to be a liability, except in the case of certain solo players and then only in moderation, since improvisation and creative involvement are not part of the symphonic orchestral picture. Under these circumstances, qualities of extreme individuality must be curbed and subjugated to the style of the composer being performed. The jazz musician, by contrast, must control his individual approach only in terms of his own conception, not that of another composer. This crucial difference between the two idioms is frequently misunderstood on both sides.

This element of individuality is then another African characteristic carried over into jazz. It is so strong in quality that it has survived despite the fact that jazz developed almost entirely on instruments that came out of the tradition of European art music. (1968, p. 57)

The musical criteria on which jazz is based are fundamental to an understanding of popular music of the first half of the twentieth century, since much Tin Pan Alley music consisted of a dilution of the essential ingredients of jazz. But studies of popular music have shown that whilst influenced by jazz, such popular music was not in general characterised by the specific criteria of Afro-American music considered earlier; that is, improvisation gave way to the playing of 'memorable tunes, played without much alteration and with a sweet tone, a saxophonic equivalent of the most maudlin violin tone' (Lee, 1970, p. 140) and rhythmically there was an almost total absence of 'swing'. The somewhat tenuous links which existed between jazz and popular music during the swing era of the 1930s were finally severed with the evolution of 'modern' jazz; as a result of the development of bebop and cool jazz in the 1940s and 1950s, and later with the jazz avant garde, jazz became a self-conscious art-music.

The 1950s, however, saw a revolution in popular music which was ultimately to reinstate the musical criteria of Afro-American music in the forefront of popular music to such an extent that Keil, writing *Urban Blues* in 1966, noted that:

It is simply incontestable that year by year, American popular music has come to sound more and more like African popular music. The rhythmic complexity and subtlety, the call and response pattern, the characteristic vocal elements (shout, growl, falsetto and so on) blues chromaticism, blues and gospel chord progressions, Negro vocabulary, Afro-American dance steps — all have become increasingly prominent in American music. (1966, p. 45)

This revolution was rock'n'roll and the ensuing developments in rock music where the latter term is usually used to identify the wide variety of post-1964 derivations of earlier rock'n'roll. There is general agreement amongst writers on rock music that this 'rock revolution' necessitates a thorough redefinition of the concept of popular music. As Eisen has put it:

Rock music is now much more than music for its devotees, it is a sub-culture in the strictest sense of that word — and the term 'pop' must be redefined radically. (1969, p. xi)

What the 'rock revolution' has done is to place the blues at the forefront of today's popular music; the main influence on early rock'n'roll was the Negro rhythm and blues which had existed since the Second World War on 'race' recordings made primarily for the Negro market in America. As Gillett notes:

In almost every respect, the sounds of rhythm and blues contradicted those of popular music. The vocal styles were harsh, the songs explicit, the dominant instruments — saxophone, piano, guitar, drums — were played loudly and with an emphatic dance rhythm, the production of the records was crude. The prevailing emotion was excitement. (1971, p. 12)

Gillett describes how during the early 1950s young people in America turned in increasing numbers to rhythm and blues music and to the radio stations that broadcast it and how this culminated in white musicians like Bill Haley popularising this form under the guise of rock'n'roll; the latter then evolved into the wide variety of idioms which make up contemporary rock music. This is just one illustration of how Negro rhythm and blues has been transformed into the variety of Afro-American musical forms (e.g. soul, Tamla Motown, progressive rock) which dominate the music of young people today.

It is when we observe the variety of musical styles in the field of so-called pop music which are directly influenced by Afro-American musical criteria, together with the international scope of these styles (rock'n'roll is not infrequently referred to as the only international language!) that we can see the force of the views expressed by Henry Pleasants in the book mentioned earlier. Himself a music critic trained in the classical tradition he believes that this century will be seen by future historians as dominated by Afro-American music, in the same sense as one might associate the Romantic period in music with Germany or the Baroque with Italy:

In each case, or epoch, we have the music and the musicians of a single nation or culture proving to be so irresistibly attractive to other nations and other cultures as to determine the musical physiognomy of an entire civilisation or age. (Pleasants, 1969, p. 91)

Pleasants makes some poignant comments on the debate which has been raging within the music establishment during this century concerning the exhaustion of possibilities of further development within the traditional framework of tonality and the responses of serious composers to this situation ranging from the twelve-tone and serialist developments of Schoenberg to aleatoric music and electronic music. The terms of the debate, as discussed by serious musicians, have been such that the future of music can only be thought of in terms of serious music in the tonal idiom or music in an atonal idiom. Pleasants suggests that serious musicians have been led to such a view only because they have been blinkered by their own terms:

Historians, critics and composers have made the mistake of thinking of the main stream of musical evolution solely in terms of serious music, as if there were a serious music and a popular music instead of simply various qualities of music. (1955, p. 167)

The important change of this century is not to be seen, Pleasants suggests, as the move from a tonal to an atonal language, but rather as the change from a music based on theme and harmony to one based on melody and rhythm. The latter change has however gone unobserved by the musical establishment because it has taken place in an area of music (jazz and popular) which was not, until quite recently, normally recognised as music at all.

How then did the music establishment react to the growth of Afro-American musical forms? The reaction to the growth of jazz in America from the 1920s onwards has been well documented by among others Berger (1947) and Leonard (1962). They both agree that the spread of jazz was resisted because of its identification with the Negro, a low status group in the society, and of further identifications with crime, vice and greater sexual freedom (probably because the earliest jazz was played in brothels, for want of anywhere else where the Negro musicians were allowed to play). Traditionally trained classical musicians opposed jazz because it appeared to violate both classical music standards and classical cultural standards since it was not performed in concert halls. Analysis of British music journals and literature on music education suggest similar reactions to jazz; in 1924, for example, an editorial of the *London Musical Times* stated:

They claim that it [jazz] is a new force that will revitalise the poor old jaded art of music. What has it to offer? Nothing in rhythm, for its rhythmic peculiarities are merely developments of something music has already. It has nothing new in melody or harmony. (Quoted in Scholes, 1947, p. 519)

And in 1933:

Those who pretend that jazz makes any great demand on the intellect are deceiving themselves; they would however have a straight case if they stated that jazz is sexually exhilarating . . . Jazz is essentially an aphrodisiac and should not pretend to be other than such. (Quoted in Scholes, 1947, p. 519)

More recently a pamphlet concerned specifically with the music education of young people had the following to say:

The musical ideals of jazz are in general of a low order. It thrives on distorted tonal values; both the instruments and voices are encouraged to make sounds which are not just different from what we are used to, but definitely less beautiful, less pure and noble. It appeals mostly to the less civilised part of one's nature — the purely physical, the more violent emotions . . . Rhythmic vitality is its foremost attraction, allied to a basic simplicity of form which enables the most untrained to understand it. (SCAM, 1957, p. 38)

The reactions of the musical establishment to the 'rock revolution' were similar in that not only was 1950s rock'n'roll seen as a gross violation of traditional musical values, but also as a moral threat to the young people who represented the greater part of its audience (a point well illustrated by Dave Rogers in chapter 1).

My argument so far has been that we have witnessed during this century a momentous musical revolution associated with the rise of Afro-American musical forms; this revolution, however, was not taken seriously by the music establishment for various historical and sociological reasons. One important consequence of this is that the music establishment, in judging the worth or seriousness of music only in terms of classical music standards, has made highly misleading assumptions concerning the nature of other forms of music, notably Afro-American forms whose alternative musical criteria, derived from an African tradition of music, are not recognised.

Thus musical criticisms of Afro-American forms are made from the perspective of classical music, a tradition concerned primarily with harmony and which largely as a result is notated in scores. This can be very misleading because it needs to be stressed that non-European musics, including all Afro-American forms and so-called 'primitive' music, cannot be notated with any degree of approximation using Western European musical notation:

Melodic ornamentation and systems of rhythm occur which make the notation of a simple primitive chant into a formidable score, from which the transcriber himself is often unable to reproduce the music. (Lomax, 1959, p. 927)

There is, of course, no one-to-one relationship between notation and expression in a classical score since a score leaves room for interpretation. However, the differences in the difficulty of accurately notating European and non-European musics are those of kind rather than degree; blue notes, for example, simply do not exist in classical music and therefore cannot even be approximated using European musical notation. The same applies to marked variations in instrumental and vocal tone and to the rhythmic swing already mentioned. A good example of how standards of musical criticism which are unwittingly drawn from the European harmonic tradition fail to do justice to other forms of music is illustrated by Keil's excellent journal article (1966). This is both one of the best verbal analyses of the concept of swing in jazz and a strong criticism of the views of Leonard Meyer as expressed in his book *Emotion and Meaning in Music* (1956) and also in his article on what makes music great (1959). Keil argues that Meyer, in evaluating various types of music, makes the mistake of using criteria which are only relevant to the European tradition of composed music. Specifically Meyer argues that 'music must be evaluated syntactically' (1959, p. 496) — that is, it must be looked at in terms of its structure or, as he puts it, the 'embodied meaning' of a piece of music. Keil notes that this procedure assumes that 'for analytic purposes music can be fixed or frozen as an object in a score or recording, and it implies not only a one-to-one relationship between form and expression but a weighting in favour of the former factor to the detriment of the latter'. Keil accepts that Meyer's equation of form and expression, which for Meyer equals 'embodied meaning', yields good results when applied to the generally through-composed and harmonically orientated styles of the European serious tradition in music; he shows, however, that when applied to predominantly improvised music, namely music in a performance tradition, syntactic analysis, whilst a necessary condition for understanding such music, cannot be sufficient in itself. In addition to 'embodied meanings' we must consider aspects of the musical process that can be grouped under the general heading of 'engendered feeling'. Keil illustrates aspects of this 'engendered feeling' by looking at the concept of swing in jazz; to do this he focuses on the interplay between bass and drums and develops a schema for analysing the tap of the 'ride' cymbal beat in relation to the manner in which the bass player plucks the strings of his double bass. Using this schema he analyses the particular rhythmic qualities of famous 'modern' jazz rhythm sections. He notes, for example, that Thelonius Monk's groups often combine a drummer (e.g. Roy Haynes) playing 'on top' of the pulse, attacking the cymbal so close to the pulse as to appear to be ahead of it, with a 'chunky' bass player (e.g. Abdul Malik) who plucks low down on the strings with a heavy percussive feel. The early Miles Davis groups, on the other hand, tended to combine 'lay-back' drummers (e.g. Philly Joe Jones), slightly delaying accents on particular notes, with 'stringy' bassists (e.g. Paul Chambers) who pluck higher on the strings, with a light sustained feel.

In the course of his analysis Keil illustrates the vital contrasts between music where 'embodied meaning' is predominant and that where 'engendered feeling' predominates:

It follows that we must be willing to employ two sets of criteria in evaluating music, depending upon whether the processual ('engendered feeling') or syntactic ('embodied meaning') aspect is dominant. In classical Indian music, to use a difficult example, syntactic criteria seem most applicable to the initial phases of a raga's development, whereas the accelerating rhythmic interplay between sitar and tabla during the concluding portion calls for a processual evaluation . . . In music where good process and spontaneity are the avowed goals it seems unfair if not ludicrous to frame an evaluation exclusively in terms of coherent syntax and architectonic principles. (1966, pp. 346, 347)

Unfortunately these are precisely the terms in which varieties of both jazz and pop music have frequently been criticised. Wood, writing on the subject of music education, accepts Meyer's theory in arguing that 'the truly significant factor, as Meyer suggests, is the lack of suspense in primitive music, and in that way it is exactly like most Western popular music' (1969, p. 102). What Keil's critique points to is the fact that 'lack of suspense' is interpreted here entirely within the framework of the European compositional tradition and, as such, imposes a criterion of 'suspense' (namely suspense with reference to a harmonic framework) that is inappropriate to improvised music where it is 'engendered feeling' rather than the 'embodied meaning' which is dominant.

Keil, therefore, in his analysis of jazz swing alerts us to the need to develop alternative criteria for the analysis of forms of music other than those of classical music. The same argument forms the basis of Chester's excellent article 'Second Thoughts on a Rock Aesthetic: the Band' in which the author raises some of the questions which need to be asked if we are to attempt a critical musical analysis of rock music. In proposing a framework whereby we can make 'an appraisal of rock as music' (p. 78) Chester suggests that while a necessary basis of all significant aesthetic expression is adequate space for formal musical elaboration the equation of 'rock = simple, and classical = complex' often made by classical musicians and by some critics of rock music is in fact one constructed on the basis of the specific mode of complexity of classical music itself. At this point he introduces the important concepts of 'intensional' and 'extensional' development in music. These concepts are so germane to many of the themes of this book that, although Chester's prose is at times somewhat difficult to follow, it might be best here to allow him to define precisely what he means by these terms in an extended quotation. After noting that classical music is characterised by the extensional form of musical construction, he continues:

Theme and variations, counterpoint, tonality (as used in classical composition) are all devices that build diachronistically and synchronically outwards from basic musical atoms. The complex is created by combination of the simple, which remains discrete and unchanged in the complex unity. Thus a basic premise of classical music is rigorous adherence to standard timbres, not only for the various orchestral instruments, but even for the most flexible of all instruments, the human voice. Room for interpretation of the written notation is in fact marginal. If those critics who maintain the greater complexity of classical music specified that they had in mind this extensional development, they would be quite correct. The rock idiom does know forms of extensional development, but it cannot compete in this sphere with a music based on this principle of construction.
Rock however follows, like many non-European musics, the path of intensional development. In this mode of construction the basic musical units (played/sung notes) are not combined through space and time as simple elements into complex structures. The simple entity is that constituted by the parameters of melody, harmony

and beat, while the complex is built up by modulation of the basic notes, and by inflexion of the basic beat. (The language of this modulation and inflexion derives partly from conventions internal to the music, partly from the conventions of spoken language and gesture, partly from physiological factors.) All existing genres and sub-types of the Afro-American tradition show various forms of combined intensional and extensional development . . . The 12-bar structure of the blues, which for the critic reared on extensional forms seems so confining, is viewed quite differently by the bluesman, for he builds 'inwards' from the 12-bar structure, and not 'outwards'. (p. 78)

Here Chester's concepts of 'intensional' and 'extensional' development are analogous to Keil's references to the 'engendered feeling' of music and the 'embodied meaning' of music; like Keil, the essential point Chester makes is that critiques of rock music which judge the latter from the standpoint of extensional rather than intensional development in music completely miss the point and therefore fail to do justice to the music concerned. This Chester neatly demonstrates in the latter part of the article where he considers the work of a number of rock groups, the Band in particular, in the light of his extensionality/intensionality polarity (at the end of chapter 3 I illustrate some of the differences between extensional and intensional development with reference to the Beatles' *Abbey Road* album). To many critics, including those rock music critics who value either the more experimental forms of rock or groups whose lyrics reflect critical social comment, the music of the Band seems extremely limited. They do not use extended structures for their songs, they are not very highly gifted instrumentalists in the purely technical sense and their lyrics often echo the sentimentality of the country music industry rather than spring from the life concerns of the Band themselves. But this is to judge them with criteria foreign to their genre. Chester, by examining their music from the standpoint of intensional development, shows why he would consider them to be one of the finest rock groups around. When considering their lyrics he is critical of those who analyse rock lyrics in isolation to the music itself. Almost inevitably such an approach fails to find anything of importance to say about lyrics; any evaluation is usually unfavourable. However we need to realise that those who do this are in fact applying a critical method which is appropriate to poetry (the lyrics of Bob Dylan have suffered particularly in this respect), but which fails to take sufficient account of the relationship between lyrics and music. Chester illustrates this difference with a simple example:

In 'Long Tall Sally' Little Richard sang: 'well long tall sally she's real sweet she's got everything that uncle john need'. Once written, this couplet is immediately banal. But in the song the fact that the vocal line is broken after 'got' and not after 'sweet' produces an aesthetic charge that depends precisely on the tension between the verbal and musical messages that a sung lyric carries. (p. 76)

I have been arguing that in its reaction to various types of Afro-American musical forms the music establishment has used inappropriate criteria and critical techniques, which have led them to highly restricted notions of serious music. In particular it has operated with an assumed dochotomy between 'serious' music and 'popular' music where all varieties of Afro-American music are grouped under the latter label. Thus the whole field of Afro-American music is dismissed as non-music by Routh (1972) in his lengthy survey of contemporary British music since 1945 in the following manner:

The term music is taken to include as many aspects of the composer's work as fall under the heading of art-work. An art-work is one which makes some claim on our serious attention. This implies a creative, unique purpose on the part of the composer and an active response on the part of the listener; it implies that the composer possesses and uses both vision and technique, and that the listener in return is expected to bring to bear his full intelligence. This excludes non-art music, such as pop music, whose purpose is chiefly if not entirely commercial. Pop groups are big business; they are socially significant; there is no question that they form a remarkable contemporary phenomenon — but this does not make the result into an art-work, and to consider it as if it were is an illogical affectation. (p. x)

Such a view embodies a number of assertions which reflect what I believe to be the prevalent establishment ideology concerning the nature of pop music, an ideology shared also by many left-wing critics, for example Parker (1975). In particular, three assumptions are frequently made by critics of pop:

(i)   Pop music is a homogeneous product.
(ii)   Pop music's sole motivation is a commercial one.
(iii)   The musical tastes (and emotions) of young people are thus manipulated by commercial exploiters who aim their product at a mass market.

Here I want to cast doubt on the validity of such assumptions. Concerning the first point, it must be emphasised that the term 'pop' music is a thoroughly misleading one, in that it covers many different types of music, some of which are popular and some of which are not, some of which are found on LP records (which since 1968 have outsold singles in absolute terms) and some on singles records. Various types of so-called pop music (soul, Tamla Motown, teenybopper pop, rock, folk, reggae, progressive music to name but a few) not only have very different musical origins and qualities but also appeal to widely different social groups, a point upon which I shall expand in the following chapter.

The argument that all pop music is commercial is a considerable oversimplification. Whilst it is true in the obvious sense that most pop records, like books (or most other things for that matter), are sold with the intention of making a profit, it conceals the fact that though some musicians' primary motivation may be a financial one, others want to create what they consider to be serious, artistic music. This explains why there are a number of groups who split up for musical and artistic reasons when approaching the height of their earning power. There is an important sense, though, in which the music establishment's attitude merely provides something of a self-fulfilling prophecy in that contemporary serious music (and much traditional classical music, especially opera) which might otherwise not prove profitable is helped by government grants and subsidies, whereas both jazz and rock music, to survive at all, have to be commercially viable, with the result that the less commercial and more experimental works in these genres are discouraged. Until very recently grants were only given to musicians working in an Afro-American idiom if they happened also to be associated with serious music. Another reason why classical musicians need not be so concerned about commercial pressures is that they are subsidised in another way, namely by extensive exposure on Radio 3. The BBC's policy of excluding practically all serious jazz and rock music from the radio has become something of a national scandal. Carr (1972) notes that the almost total exclusion of contemporary British jazz from the BBC has resulted in a number of British jazz musicians having to emigrate in order to survive at all as musicians to either America or Europe, where they can obtain far greater financial support and media exposure. Radio 1, on the other hand, which is supposed to be the 'popular' music programme, is a constant object of ridicule amongst rock musicians and many young people, geared as it is almost entirely to commercial pop singles, whilst the two categories of music — namely 'progressive rock' and 'reggae and soul' — which a recent Schools Council survey (Murdock and Phelps, 1973) found to be very popular with different groups of schoolchildren are conspicuous by their absence.

Thus, unlike classical musicians, serious jazz or rock musicians who want to create music which because of its complex or experimental nature is unlikely to be commercial get little or no help from the government either in terms of financial subsidies or media exposure. In addition the expenses involved in running a rock group are enormous and it is only the smallest minority of such groups who ever recoup enough money to pay back the initial outlay. Whilst some pop musicians are certainly motivated strongly by commercial factors, many others try to make no concessions to the commercial pressures of recording companies even to the extent of living at income levels which would be considered an outrage by any trade union. The further assumption, implied by many critics of pop music, that popularity or commercial gain inevitably leads to inartistic results is also quite untrue. Who would suggest, for example, that Mozart's symphonies are less artistic simply because they were composed in order to make a living, or that Benjamin Britten did not compose some fine works after becoming both rich and internationally famous?

The questionable nature of the third aspect of the music establishment's ideology concerning the nature of pop music follows largely from what has already been said. Those who argue that pop music exploits the tastes of young people never make clear what type of pop music they have in mind; nor do they make clear who is supposed to be doing the exploiting. For instance, those who say that the exploiter is the record industry, conceived presumably as some large monolithic block, show themselves to be ignorant of the nature of this industry. The major record companies who have attempted to impose pop music tastes have been continually outflanked by smaller independent companies who have reflected the pre-existing tastes of different groups of young people. All surveys of the rise of recent pop music forms demonstrate this. Gillett, for example, suggests that 'audiences or creators can determine the content of a popular art communicated through the mass media. The business men who mediate between the audience and the creator can be forced by either to accept a new style. The rise of rock and roll is proof' (1971, p. 1). His survey of the rise of rock'n'roll shows the resistance of the major recording companies in America to this new music which they neither understood nor appreciated. As a result of such resistance they increasingly lost ground to small recording companies who were fulfilling the teenagers' demands for rock'n'roll. It was only after a number of years that the major recording companies finally capitulated to the demand for this music. Gleason's (1969) survey of the rise of West Coast rock illustrates the same process whereby the content of records put out by recording companies was drastically altered by young people's demands for the 'new' music. Rather than the recording companies imposing their tastes on young people, there is now a tendency for record companies to do as much as they can to identify the tastes of young people and then reflect them back in their records — hence the rise of the 'company freak' (see Fields, 1970), whose job it is to provide a liaison between the young audience and the older record company executives.

Other critics see the exploiter as the radio (usually Radio 1), but this fails to recognise that, as I suggested earlier, this programme is not an accurate reflection of the musical tastes of young people. Consequently many commentators are unaware that young people are listening to good music — termed 'popular' music despite the fact that in many cases it is not of mass popularity at all — which rarely finds its way on to the radio (or TV).

I have been arguing that the music establishment's ideology concerning pop music contains many highly misleading assumptions. These assumptions are perpetuated, not only by selective financial subsidies and by certain media policies, as I have mentioned, but also by means of the educational system, where both jazz and rock music have been almost completely neglected in music education. Academic music in this country is totally dominated by music in the European serious tradition: neither 'O' nor 'A' level consider Afro-American music at all in any of its forms, whilst an examination of the syllabuses of university music degree courses and music conservatory diploma courses shows the same pattern. Since most class music teachers have their initial training either in a university or in a conservatory, at no point in their training will they have been required either to listen to or to play any form of music other than European serious music. Such an educational background is likely to produce not only ignorance of the musical criteria of Afro-American musical forms, but also the kinds of attitudes to such music that have been shown to be held by members of the music establishment. Thus Brocklehurst, in a popular book used in the training of music teachers, argues that:

The primary purpose of musical appreciation is to inculcate a love and understanding of good music. It is surely the duty of teachers to do all they can to prevent young people falling ready prey to the purveyors of commercialised 'popular' music, for these slick, high-pressure salesmen, have developed the exploitation of teenagers into a fine art. (1962, p. 55)

What is ironic here is that Brocklehurst is also the compiler of the excellent *Pentatonic Song Book* (1968) which draws extensively from Negro spirituals and folk music material but fails to recognise the link between the pentatonicism of the latter and the fact that much pop and rock music has evolved out of this pentatonic tradition.

If this chapter has gone some way towards providing a critical re-assessment of attitudes towards pop music displayed by many classical musicians and music teachers, it will have served its purpose. More positively, in the next chapter I will consider the implications for school music teaching of taking so-called 'pop' music much more seriously than has hitherto been the case.

References

Berger, M., 'Jazz: Resistance to the Diffusion of a Culture Pattern', *Journal of Negro History*, Vol. 32 (1947).

Brocklehurst, J.B., *Music in Schools* (Routledge & Kegan Paul, 1962).

Brocklehurst, J.B., *Pentatonic Song Book* (Schott, 1968).

Carr, I., 'Down in the Cultural Ghetto, Something Stirred', *Cream*, July 1972.

Chester, A., 'Second Thoughts on a Rock Aesthetic: The Band', *New Left Review*, No. 62 (1970).

Dennis, B., *Experimental Music in Schools* (Oxford University Press, 1970).

Eisen, J. (ed.), *The Age of Rock: Sounds of the American Cultural Revolution* (Random House, 1969).

Fields, D., 'Who Bridges the Gap between the Record Executive and the Rock Musician? I do' in Eisen, J. (ed.), *The Age of Rock*, Vol. 2 (Vintage Books, 1970).

Gillett, C., *The Sound of the City* (Sphere, 1971).

Gleason, R.J., *The Jefferson Airplane and the San Francisco Sound* (Ballantine Books, 1969).

Jones, A.M., *Studies in African Music*, 2 vols. (Oxford University Press, 1959).

Keil, C., *Urban Blues* (University of Chicago Press, 1966).

Keil, C., 'Motion and Feeling through Music', *Journal of Aesthetics and Art Criticism*, Vol. 24 (1966).

Lee, E., *Music of the People: A Study of Popular Music in Great Britain* (Barrie and Jenkins, 1970).

Leonard, N., *Jazz and the White Americans* (University of Chicago Press, 1962).

Lomax, A., 'Folk Song Style', *American Anthropologist*, Vol. 61 (1959).

Meyer, L.B., *Emotion and Meaning in Music* (Cambridge University Press, 1956).

Meyer, L.B., 'Some Remarks on Value and Greatness in Music', *Journal of Aesthetics and Art Criticism*, Vol. 17 (1959).

Murdock, G. and Phelps, G., *Mass Media and the Secondary School* (Macmillan, 1973).

Parker, C., 'Pop Song, The Manipulated Ritual' in Abbs, P. (ed.), *The Black Rainbow* (Heinemann Educational, 1975).

Pleasants, H., *The Agony of Modern Music* (Simon and Schuster, 1955).

Pleasants, H., *Serious Music and all that Jazz* (Gollancz, 1969).

Rainbow, B., *The Land without Music* (Novello, 1967).

Routh, F., *Contemporary British Music* (MacDonald, 1972).

Standing Conference for Amateur Music, *Youth Makes Music* (National Council of Social Service, 1957).

Scholes, P.A., *The Mirror of Music*, Vol. 1 (Novello and Oxford, 1947).

Schuller, G., *Early Jazz* (Oxford University Press, 1968).

Self, G., *New Sounds in Class* (Universal Edition, 1967).

Wood, T.E.B., 'Thoughts on the Teaching of Music', *Journal of Aesthetic Education*, Vol. 3 (1969).

3 Pupil-centred music teaching

GRAHAM VULLIAMY

I argued in the previous chapter that for various historical and sociological reasons the content of school music teaching has been restricted to music in the European serious tradition. This has resulted in the development of a considerable conflict between the musical culture of the school as represented by its music teachers and that of many of the pupils which is centred on the world of so-called 'pop' music. However much we may abhor such a conflict, it would be naïve to deny its existence; in fact, such a conflict is often seen as the root cause of many of the problems that music teachers experience in schools. Thus the Schools Council working paper (1971) has commented:

That there are problems cannot be denied. To put the situation plainly many teen-age pupils, especially those in the 14—16 age group, are indifferent and even hostile towards curriculum music . . . To call these pupils 'unmusical' is merely an evasion . . . It is better to use 'rejection' as a convenient term . . . Part of the answer (an explanation for this rejection) may lie in the very prominence of music in the teen-agers' own sub-culture and the conflict between the values of that sub-culture and those of the school. (pp. 8 and 9)

The reactions of music educators to such a situation have been various and hardly need documenting here. Many dismiss pop music altogether believing it to be an unhealthy influence on pupils which should be counteracted at all costs, whilst others are prepared to use pop music as a starting point, a stepping-stone to the enjoyment of 'good' music (interpreted as classical music in the widest sense). Both these reactions illustrate in different degrees an assumed relationship between serious and popular music which, in my opinion, is fundamentally misguided and on which I commented at some length in the previous chapter. Here I wish to discuss the problems and possibilities of a very different reaction — one which recognises both the positive features of much of the musical culture of the pupils (which is not to deny that there are some more negative features of the latter as well) and especially the positive educational implications of using such music. Such a view, where the use of pop music is encouraged for its own sake with no invidious comparisons being made with other forms of music, has very rarely been expressed by music educators — a notable exception being the useful series of articles by Burnett

(1972) on how music teachers can incorporate varieties of pop music into music teaching.

The benefits of what might be called a more 'open' approach to music teaching were first suggested to me in a *practical* context by my observations in the music section of Twickenham College of Technology in London, although I also recognised that there were problems, to be discussed later in this chapter, concerning the viability of incorporating such an approach at the school level. In the college, music was taught in the context of class music (as a non-optional part of courses from craft apprentice to degree level) and as an extra-curricular activity. What was unusual about the music in the college was that it seemed to be the aim of the Director of Music not to lay down a musical policy based on his own preferences. Instead he would start with the interests of the students, whom he then encouraged to follow whatever directions they found most appealing; there seemed to be no attempt to 'sell' any particular type of music. The musical activities of the college were as a result a very close reflection of the types of music most often associated with young people today. A very large number of music groups took part in the extra-curricular musical activities of the college. During the period of my observation these groups included two rock groups, a large jazz-rock group, a rock'n'roll group, a modern jazz trio, two folk groups, a solo folk singer (in the style of Bob Dylan — guitar and harmonica), a large dance band, a traditional jazz band and a seventy-five-voice choir (then rehearsing Mozart's *Requiem*). There was no attempt to teach musical notation unless the students themselves wanted to learn it in connection with the particular instruments they were learning. The Director of Music, D. Cameron McNicol, stressed in conversation with me that trying to teach notation to students who had not learned it earlier was 'at this stage' most likely to 'just put them off music altogether'. He felt that if a student wanted to master a particular instrument he would want to learn the notation and would then find it quite easy. He explained that 'there's no point in teaching it if they're unmotivated, and anyway some instrumentalists don't need it or want it — they can perform exciting creative music without being able to read music'.

Class music lessons placed much emphasis on listening to music to illustrate certain aspects of its construction, and most of the music selected to illustrate these points (during the period of my observation at least) was from the field of pop. The very large record collection contained, in addition to extensive classical and jazz sections, numerous pop records covering a very wide field from soul music, through folk-rock to 'progressive heavy rock' bands. The main music room was equipped with a very expensive hi-fi system and, in addition, twelve Garrard SP25 record turntables each with their own pair of stereo headphones. The Director of Music explained to me that this system not only allowed students to hear their records at whatever volume they desired (and he recognised that much contemporary rock music has to be played loud for full effect) but also allowed them to hear whatever music they liked without disturbing other people.

Many of the music groups rehearsed on a Wednesday afternoon in the 'music block' (consisting of two 'special' rooms and a number of ordinary classrooms). What was most apparent to me on attending such afternoon sessions was that the conventional barriers both between different types of music (for example, jazz and rock) and between teacher and taught were to a large extent broken down. Lecturers from both the music section and other departments were members of different music groups and musicians of different types (for example, jazz and rock musicians who are often very snobbish towards each other) 'jammed' freely with each other. Criteria of success were not measured in terms of playing instruments 'correctly' or being able to sight read well, but in terms of whether the musician, either playing together with other musicians in a group or playing by himself, created music that communicated with other people (and the Director of Music could judge this by the reactions of other students who were watching the groups rehearse). In this context the primary purpose of the teacher is to organise the groups rather than to give technical instruction.

These points are well illustrated by one particular incident at which I was present. A student lead guitarist attending one of the Wednesday afternoon sessions asked if he could play and so he 'sat in' with one of the rock groups (he had not previously attended any of the college music activities). They started playing a heavy blues number at his request. It was immediately apparent that the guitarist was technically very proficient and within a short time the group had attracted quite an audience of fellow musicians and other students. The Director of Music (who was wandering around observing the different groups rehearse) immediately commented, 'That guitarist is very good', and suggested to the teacher who was in charge of the rock groups that they find him a good bass player and drummer as soon as possible. This was despite the fact that the guitarist's playing, especially in terms of loud volume, use of feedback, blue notes and so on, violated the classical criteria of good musicianship with which the Director of Music had had his own training in music. In fact a number of the section's most talented musicians, particularly guitarists and drummers were, like this guitarist, students who had left the lower streams of their schools having been defined as both 'unmusical' and 'less able'. Like most rock musicians they could not read music and had learned all their music outside the school by playing in apprentice groups with friends and by listening to rock records, thus confirming a view expressed in the Newsom Report that 'out of school adolescents are enthusiastically engaged in musical self-education' (1963, p. 139).

My observations in this technical college were made in the course of research into varieties of approach to music teaching. As an alternative to both the traditional approaches and the avant garde stress on practical music making, which were referred to in the last chapter, it seemed that the more open policy of the technical college's music section had advantages in some respects, whilst also creating further problems in others. In contrast to the traditional approaches to music education the open approach resulted in strikingly different assumptions concerning criteria of success and the number of people who are potentially 'musical'. An examination of the literature on music education suggests that music educators with the traditional approach make the assumption that only a limited number of people are 'musical' and that as Long puts it:

The paramount aim in grammar school music is to discover the talented and to provide the conditions in which they can develop their talents as fully as the school pressures will allow. (1963, p. 148)

Here the criteria of success are the conventional ones of mastering musical theory and notation and/or developing a high level of proficiency on one of the traditional instruments of the orchestra. The problem with such an approach is that this definition of what counts as music and musical ability excludes large numbers of pupils who are potentially highly 'musical' but whose creative musical abilities are harnessed to another tradition of music, namely pop music. By changing the criteria of success the open policy of the technical college recognises the musical abilities of many students who had previously been described as totally 'unmusical' at school. Piers Spencer makes the same point in chapter 5, especially with his detailed analysis of the work of Dene, a pupil who in many more traditional schools would not have been recognised as potentially musical at all.

One positive feature of a more open approach is, therefore, a questioning of the assumption that only a limited number of pupils can make significant musical contributions. In this respect it is similar to the work of recent music educators stressing the more avant garde approach whose criteria of success are also very different from the more traditional approaches. In the avant garde approach the importance of learning conventional notation or facts about music and music history are also played down, whilst the main emphasis is on developing pupils' musical creativity, the assumption being that all pupils, not just a select few, are potentially musical. For example, Carl Orff, one of the pioneers of 'creative' music in the classroom has said:

I do not think of an education for specially gifted children . . . My experience had taught me that completely unmusical children are very rare and that nearly every child is at some point accessible and educable. (quoted in Horton, 1969, p. 25)

Similarly Chisholm states:

It is the contention of my paper that creative ability — the creative instinct — is denied to no one. The astonishing thing to me about Mr Maxwell Davies' unique demonstration of yesterday (he had talked of his experiences using 'creative' music with all his classes) is that we should find it astonishing or unique — for . . . he is only doing in a musical field what is a commonplace in the field of art education. (1963, p. 188)

The avant garde approach and the open approaches to music teaching therefore share a rather more optimistic view of the number of pupils who are potentially musical, because they have different criteria of success to the more traditional approaches. Where the former two differ, however, is in their content. The principal musical influences behind the pedagogical approach to the avant garde style of music teaching lie in the world of contemporary serious music. Pupils using, for example, the simplified notation developed by the contemporary composer George Self will be producing music in the classroom which is similar in many ways to the works of certain contemporary serious composers. However, this music is often likely to prove foreign to the pupils' conception of music in that avant garde serious music uses compositional techniques, such as rhythmic irregularity, which are alien to or uncharacteristic of either traditional classical music or jazz and pop. Despite increasing use of some of these techniques for dramatic effect by film and TV composers, such music does not constitute a significant part of pupils' musical experience.

Thus two obvious positive features of the open approach to music teaching (as exemplified in the technical college described above) seem to be, first, that it taps the musical interests and abilities of large numbers of students and, second, that it does so utilising forms of music that many of the students both appreciate and understand. The Director of Music was quite explicit on the latter point; when asked whether the main reason for his using so much pop music was because this was in fact the type of music that most of his students liked, he was at pains to make the point that:

I use it not because they *like* it, but because they *understand* it – it's a different thing. The young people of today understand music to a depth and as an art more than any previous generation . . . Young people are interested in the creative area of music . . . The important thing is to show interest in their type of music. They want to communicate that the music they like is good. (His emphases)

Another striking feature of music in this context was that it enabled the relationship between the teacher and taught to be far less authoritarian than is often the case. Once the musical culture of the students had been incorporated into the teacher's work, a situation emerged where frequently the students knew more about the subject than the teacher. For example, I asked the Director of Music how he kept up with recent technical and musical developments in pop and in particular how he selected records for their library in areas of music in which he could not have a wide knowledge. He explained that he selected students in each of his classes who he knew were 'into' particular fields of music, whether this was blues, soul, progressive rock or whatever, and asked them to list what they felt were the most important records in that particular area of music; he would then select records from these lists after discussion with other students. A valuable feature of this situation is that the teacher is constantly having to reappraise the assumptions that he and his colleagues are tempted to make concerning the musical culture of the young. In these circumstances the teacher ceases to be an expert and becomes more a guide and an organiser. Not only does he have knowledge derived from his classical training which might prove helpful to the students (the guitarist mentioned above soon wanted to learn how to play the 'weird' chords a jazz pianist was using), but the student also has knowledge derived from his musical culture which he can communicate to the teacher (how do you use a fuzz box with a bass guitar?). What was clear to me was that this sort of attitude tended to help the teacher break down the usual barriers against learning about 'teacher's music'; put simply, the students felt that if the teachers were willing to learn from them, then they were also willing to learn from the teacher, and consequently many of the normal prejudices against both the teacher and his classical music were broken down.

The reader may well be asking at this stage what relation the music section in a technical college bears to music departments in schools; because clearly the problems of using such an approach at school level are far greater. The major problem can be summarised in one phrase — limited resources. The teachers contributing to this book have found that, when given a totally free choice, the most popular instruments that school pupils choose to play are percussion (drum sets rather than timpani), guitars, bass guitars and keyboards, in addition of course to singing. This was also reflected at the technical college where the music department provided a drum set, bass and lead guitars with amplification and speakers and a PA (public address) system for vocalists. At school level this would necessitate a radical redistribution of financial resources. Far too many schools insist on purchasing, say, timpani because they are a conventional orchestral instrument and then have difficulty in finding a pupil motivated to play them, whilst half a dozen or more are only too keen to learn the drums. Some useful tips on how teachers can set about purchasing such instruments to form the nucleus of a rock group are given by Tony Robins in chapter 7.

Another aspect of the 'limited resources' problem is that of staffing. Peripatetic teachers capable of helping pupils with rock music instruments are often not available even when a school music department wants them. Sometimes this reflects a real shortage, but more often it reflects the local authorities' conservative attitudes in the appointments of peripatetic teachers, often appointed only in the sphere of orchestral instrumental tuition; whilst this may benefit those children who enjoy playing in youth orchestras or brass bands, it does nothing for those who seek other forms of individual or corporate music making. Some progress has been made in recent years and a number of jazz musicians are now employed teaching peripatetically in a few London schools, although rock musicians employed in this way are very few and far between.

Even if, for whatever reason, the head of music cannot get outside help, he can always turn to staff members of other departments in his school. There must be very few schools which do not have a competent folk guitarist on the staff if only we are prepared to seek them out — one of the mainstays of Tony Robins' music department (chapter 7) is just such a teacher. But this willingness to delegate teaching and organisational commitments to other teachers, some of whom are not even in the music department, does run against a widely held attitude of many heads of music, that they should run (and be seen to run) the show almost single-handed. The sharing of curricular teaching and of extra-curricular activities amongst specialist and non-specialist teachers is a well-established tradition in sport and physical education, and there is no reason why this should not be so where music is concerned.

A further problem associated with 'limited resources' is that of providing the time and space for groups to practise. Malcolm Nicholls, who in chapter 6 discusses the problems of running an open school music department in Countesthorpe College, is clearly fortunate in this respect in having a number of practice rooms at his disposal. The volume at which rock groups can play obviously creates problems (though school orchestras and choirs rehearsing are also quite loud!). As much soundproofing as possible is essential; so also is careful timetabling, so that flautists are not competing with rock guitarists next door. Finally, headphones can be used, not only to listen to records, but also for guitarists, organists, etc. when practising.

The whole question of electric instruments raises not only the problem of volume, but also that of safety. A number of local authorities go as far as actually banning the use of electric instruments in schools. This is totally misguided. Strict enforcement of such a rule (clearly many schools turn a blind eye to it) prevents the music with which most young people today identify from being played at all. It is difficult to believe that such a rule reflects more than a widespread prejudice (on both musical and social grounds) against the use of electric instruments – a prejudice that surely must soon be broken down considering the number of both jazz and contemporary serious music composers and musicians who are joining rock musicians in exploiting the full range of electric instruments. Clearly these can be dangerous if not used properly, but certainly no more so than much of the machinery to be found in many school metalwork and carpentry workshops. But given their possible danger, surely it is even more important that the school should give pupils instruction in their correct use, since many of the pupils are in actual fact using such equipment outside the school? It would be absurd to stop one of the best musicians in the school from playing his instrument, especially as he may be playing 'gigs' regularly with a group outside the school. The same goes for the ruling of certain local authorities that if electric instruments are to be used, they must be new and not secondhand. Apart from severely limiting what a school music department can then afford to provide, this restricts the buying of instruments to those types which the pupil himself is unlikely to obtain, for reasons of cost.

The formation of school rock groups has a wider educational value, since it encourages the development of many social skills, including self-discipline. As I have learned from what was occasionally bitter experience as a member of a number of rock groups, it is vital to organise efficiently such practical matters as gathering together equipment, checking that it all works, planning rehearsal times, transport and so on; the group thus has to decide who, if anyone, is in charge, how different responsibilities are to be delegated and how decisions are to be arrived at. Because both involve groups of pupils in self-directed work there is clearly a link between school rock groups and the 'workshop' approach to class music making envisaged by *Sound and Silence* (Paynter and Aston, 1970, pp. 9–23), where children work in small groups on creative music projects. Indeed experience of working in groups on projects of this type might provide an excellent training for a group of pupils who later wanted to start a rock group to be run independently of the teacher.

To be successful with the open approach teachers must have some knowledge of the musical and social differences within pop music. If the approach to teaching is truly open then this will follow naturally, as my illustration from the technical college shows. Tony Robins in chapter 7 also comments on the widening of his musical horizons as a result of listening to the music that his pupils appreciated. Another useful source from which the teacher can gain some insight into the relationship in school between different varieties of pop music and different groupings of school pupils is Murdock and Phelps' book *Mass Media and the Secondary School* (1973). It reports the findings of a Schools Council project which studies the influence of the mass media on the experience of schooling and examines the relationship between teachers' and pupils' attitudes to and use of the media. The book is in two parts; the first concerns the findings of a study based on a questionnaire survey of the teachers in ninety secondary schools of various types, followed by more intensive case studies of ten schools. The second part considers the evidence, again drawn both from a large questionnaire and more intensive case studies of individual pupils and peer groups, concerning pupils' attitudes and behaviour with reference to the mass media. Some aspects of the study, notably the questionnaire used, are open to severe methodological criticisms, but many of the insights gained are very valuable, particularly from the few case studies involving depth interviews into the meanings that various forms of pop music have for different groups of pupils.

One of the main conclusions arising from the survey is that pupils from different social class and neighbourhood backgrounds and with different attitudes to school approach the mass media in different ways, and in particular have very different tastes in pop music. More specifically, it was found that for working-class pupils and particularly the early leavers in the lowest streams of secondary schools, the main preferences were for reggae and soul records, together with Motown performers and 'hard rock' groups such as Slade. Actual and prospective sixth-formers on the other hand preferred progressive rock music (most of which was to be found on LPs rather than singles), having changed their allegiances from the mass pop of the Top Twenty to such progressive rock music some time between the second and fourth years of secondary schooling. Such findings make a nonsense of conceptions of a homogeneous youth culture and also suggest that, contrary to much received opinion, it is the middle-class pupils, including many of the academic high-fliers, who are most involved in the pop media, particularly the world of progressive rock music and its related values. This means that many pupils in the lower streams of a secondary school may be as hostile to the upper stream's liking for 'weird' groups like Pink Floyd as they are to the music teacher's passion for classical music; similarly, sixth-formers may deride the musical tastes of the lower streams as merely 'bopping' music (i.e. music to be danced to rather than listened to). In this respect one might hope that a more open approach to school music teaching would break down not only barriers between classical and pop music but also those *within* pop music itself. Some indication that this might be the case is given by the experience of the technical college already referred to and also, in a school context, by Malcolm Nicholls' experience at Countesthorpe as reported in chapter 6.

Another important finding to emerge from the Schools Council survey is that many of the assumptions made by teachers concerning the negative effects of pop music on pupils were contradicted by the evidence from the pupils' study. In particular, many teachers held the view that 'high culture' was in some sense threatened by the pervasiveness of pop culture and that it was the school's duty to fight the latter. Some of the assumptions implicit in this view — that, for example, pop music is a homogeneous category which is standardised in the interests of mass production and then imposed on young people from above — have already been criticised in the last chapter. In addition, this view assumes that young people are a captive and defenceless audience who are totally uncritical in their response to mass media products, and provides the rationale for many teachers who, whilst themselves hostile to the mass media, nevertheless use mass media material in the classroom with the aim of exposing it to criticism and building up defence mechanisms in children against it. Somewhat refreshingly, the evidence from the Schools Council survey shows that, far from being uncritical, many young people are extremely critical in their appreciation of various types of pop music, and approach the latter with clear sets of criteria concerning the relative worth both of various styles and of various records within one style.

I will conclude by commenting on some of the more widely-voiced criticisms that have been made of the open approach to music teaching that is being advocated here, and in the process I hope to make my own position clear on a number of crucial issues.

First, in suggesting that the musical culture of the pupils should be taken seriously and incorporated into the teaching process I am not arguing that this should replace the use of classical music. To concentrate solely on varieties of pop music to the exclusion of other types of music would be as educationally limiting as the reverse procedure where pop music is entirely rejected. The process of musical education should be concerned with expanding pupils' horizons and the best way to achieve this is by encouraging all forms of musical expression without as far as possible holding preconceived ideas about which forms of music are intrinsically better or worse than others. One of the striking aspects of the open approach in both the technical college and the school music department described by Malcolm Nicholls in chapter 6 is that many pupils are led to enlarge on their musical interests (in many cases to areas of classical music) as a result of their present musical tastes being taken seriously and made use of in teaching.

Another worry many teachers have is that pop music in some sense 'belongs' to the pupils and that consequently the latter may well resent the teachers' encroachment into this area. Whether there is such resentment depends on the approach the teacher uses; if he approaches pop music in the spirit advocated here, the evidence suggests that far from provoking resentment amongst pupils it increases their involvement and generates a situation where both teachers and pupils can genuinely learn from each other. If, on the other hand, the teacher uses pop music as a motivational device in the spirit of 'Let's use the Beatles as a stepping-stone to Schubert' and without any genuine interest in pop music itself, then such a patronising attitude will be immediately apparent to the pupils and they will understandably be hostile.

Another vital issue concerns the question of 'lowering standards'. Many teachers think any dabbling in the area of pop music necessarily involves a lowering of standards; a recent handbook on teaching musical appreciation argues that:

The 'pop' disease is so widespread these days that no child seems to escape it . . . To show disgust at the sounds of these records (and they are mostly undeniably disgusting) will achieve little. Better to keep a calm face and insist on your pound of flesh. It is, after all, a music period and not Housewives' Choice . . . One good defence is to say to the pupil who asks for 'pop': 'What has it to do with a music lesson? Do you ask your English teacher for Superman comics? Do you expect to play marbles in P.E. lessons? (Dwyer, 1967, p. 115)

It is true that the allegiance that many pupils give to pop is an extra-musical one; pop is much more than a purely musical experience, a feeling well captured by Dave Rogers' historical and social perspective on varieties of pop music in chapter 1. It is not therefore the case that every pop record which has mass appeal can be justified on musical grounds. On the other hand, it is a central theme of this book that using pop music in schools does not mean an abdication of standards in teaching; critical standards (in a musical sense and a more general sense) not only can be applied to varieties of pop music but are applied daily by the millions of pupils who listen to and buy such records. One general critical dimension that is widely used by pupils is the authenticity or sincerity of the musician: rock music lovers in particular are concerned that the music and the lyrics of a record should be a reflection of the values and attitudes of the musicians or of young people generally rather than being the processed outpouring of some middle-aged song-writer or production man. This illustrates a crucial difference between contemporary rock music and earlier forms of popular music. Prior to the 'rock revolution' there was usually a rigid division of labour between the composer and the performer — a singer would sing lyrics that had been written and set to music by someone else. In rock music, however, the originators of the material tend to account for the total product: not only do groups now write, orchestrate and play their own material, but in many cases they also produce their own records thus eliminating the possibility of outside control over the finished product. The use of such criteria to differentiate varieties of pop music is akin to Richard Hoggart's proposal that 'all cultural artefacts should be ranged along a continuum marked "authentic" at one end and "phoney" at the other' and that a successful cultural artefact is one 'which embodies a deeply felt and authentic experience and which strikes genuine chords in the audience' — our job, he argues, is 'to separate the Processed from the Living' (quoted in Murdock and Phelps, 1973, p. 40).

When we come to evaluate pop music the important point, as developed in chapter 2, is that the criteria of musical excellence so far applied by classical music critics fail to take sufficient account of the nature and value of the Afro-American elements in pop. When these elements are considered we find that musical analysis tends to support the intuitive judgements made by the pop audience. Whilst many rock music lovers are interested in the purely musical aspects of records, this is not generally the case for those interested either in the Top Ten singles type record or disco music such as Tamla Motown or the Philly Sound, to which teenagers' response is likely to be at the level of 'It's got a great beat to dance to − that's why I like it'. Yet if one analyses the musical content of many disco 'classics' such as 'I Heard it through the Grapevine' (Marvin Gaye) or 'Love Train' (the O Jays) from the perspective of Afro-American musical criteria, one can see why they are not only good to dance to but are also excellent records musically, though there is no reason why the teenagers who appreciate such records should see it in these terms.

These arguments show that standards are applied by the young audience to the music, but the mature reader may demand more explicit, rationally supported analyses. But when these have been produced by critics they have often been accused of 'intellectualising pop'. There seem to be two ways in which this phrase is applied. The first rejects all rational and analytic approaches to the music, whereas clearly the fact of my writing here shows that I believe that, within certain limitations, writing about music is a valuable exercise. In this I would furthermore agree with Wilfrid Mellers' argument in the Preface to his book on the Beatles (Mellers, 1973) that in as much as the discussion of any music is a worthwhile activity, this must apply equally to all varieties of music.

The second possible meaning of 'intellectualising pop' is the application of criteria which fail in some way to account adequately for the work under discussion. Possibly the commonest failing among critics is the failure to take sufficient account of Afro-American musical criteria. Thus Mellers' book on the Beatles, to which I have just referred, is to my knowledge the best and most sympathetic critical appraisal of a pop group's work by an academically trained musician; as such it plays the very valuable role of communicating to the music establishment that, even by the latter's criteria, the Beatles were fine musicians. However, the musical criteria used are expressed in the accepted musical terminology which, as Mellers puts it, 'has been evolved by professional musicians over some centuries' (Mellers, 1973, p. 15) (i.e. they are those that have been derived from the European compositional tradition). Thus his study leads us in Chester's (1970) terms to an analysis concentrating mainly on the extensional, as opposed to the intensional, forms of musical development. Such an orientation leads to an overemphasis on the harmonic structure of the Beatles' songs and on those musical elements which are derived from classical music at the expense of an analysis of those aspects of intensional development derived from an Afro-American tradition of music. In the process many facets of the Beatles' music, which the rock music lover untutored in academic music finds the most musically satisfying, tend to be neglected. For example Mellers, in discussing the end of *Abbey Road*, suggests that:

This last number, having asked its question, abandons words for a furious hammering of percussion: which leads into a long instrumental section, all dominant sevenths in rumba rhythm, but rocking a tone lower than the starting point, getting nowhere. Suddenly the hubub stops; there's a tinkling of A major triads on a tinny piano . . . (1973, p. 122)

Now the long instrumental section referred to in this quote is for many Beatles' fans the finest ever guitar solo in their work and the high spot of the album. The problem is that Mellers' 'getting nowhere' is viewed entirely in extensional terms; if viewed in intensional terms the guitar break is a masterpiece. It is a beautifully flowing and very exciting blues-based guitar solo, which in the context of the Beatles' work is highly unexpected because the Beatles (unlike, for example, the Rolling Stones) were never very strongly blues-influenced and therefore rarely had lead guitar breaks of a blues-based nature. In addition, the tone of the guitar is totally changed after each phrase to give the illusion of literally eight or nine guitarists playing in the solo. The preceding drum solo by Ringo Starr sets up a deceptively simple rhythmic pulse which is then carried on by the bass guitar behind the lead guitar solo, whilst the soloist uses highly effective cross-rhythms against the basic pulse.

The above comments do not, of course, invalidate the analysis that Mellers gives us, but they do provide a further musical perspective from which the work of rock musicians can be viewed. Such a perspective can not only deepen our understanding of groups like the Beatles who owe a considerable debt to the classical tradition, but might also provide us with the *only* way of evaluating the work of other major rock music artists, such as Jimi Hendrix, whose inspiration is derived almost exclusively from the Afro-American tradition.

Another important limitation of some commentaries on pop music is exemplified by the work of the critic, Tony Palmer. He begins from a highly restricted definition of culture, regarding the latter largely in nineteenth-century European terms, and fails to take account of the existence of other self-contained valid cultural systems. He thus attempts to force the popular Afro-American based culture into a European high cultural mould. For example he makes the following comment on pop music:

Unfortunately the evaluation of pop in aesthetic terms is usually held, derisively to be the 'intellectualisation of pop'. But by 'intellectualisation' critics tend to mean the use of nasty words like Schubert and Beethoven, forgetting thereby that pop music, if it is ever to achieve any respect at all, has to be made to stand on its own feet alongside such as Schubert and Beethoven. If it does not wish to, then it cannot expect to be taken seriously. (1970, p. 19)

But the result of this view is simply to reclassify the work of a few pop groups as 'art' or 'culture' (yesterday it was groups like the Beatles, today it is groups like

Yes), whilst in no way challenging the basic assumptions on which the division between high culture music and pop culture music rests. It has been one of the main
arguments of my two chapters that such a challenge can be made on rational
grounds and, further, that when such a challenge is made, understanding is enriched
and musical education can be given a new and valuable dimension.

References

Burnett, M., 'Coming to Terms with Pop', *Music Teacher* (1972).
Chester, A., 'Second Thoughts on a Rock Aesthetic: The Band', *New Left Review*,
    No. 62 (1970).
Chisholm, E., 'Creative Education in Music' in Grant, W. (ed.), *Music in Education*
    (Butterworth, 1963).
Dwyer, T., *Teaching Musical Appreciation* (Oxford University Press, 1967).
Horton, J., 'Carl Orff', *Music Teacher* (April 1969).
Long, N., 'Some Problems of Grammar School Music' in Grant, W. (ed.), *Music in
    Education* (Butterworth, 1963).
Mellers, W., *Twilight of the Gods: The Beatles in Retrospect* (Faber and Faber,
    1973).
Ministry of Education *Half Our Future* (Newsom Report, HMSO, 1963).
Murdock, G. and Phelps, G., *Mass Media and the Secondary School* (Macmillan,
    1973).
Palmer, T., *Born under a Bad Sign* (William Kimber, 1970).
Paynter, J. and Aston, P., *Sound and Silence* (Cambridge University Press, 1970).
Schools Council, *Working Paper No. 35: Music and the Young School Leaver*
    (Schools Council Publications, 1971).

PART TWO

A note on conventions of notation in Afro-American music

ED LEE

For the most part, Afro-American music is notated in the same way as classical music, but it also has a few important conventions of its own, which are listed below. In order that these conventions may be understood for what they are, it is worth pointing out that the relationship between the music and notation as evidenced in classical music and Afro-American music is rather different. Most Afro-American music tends to be created and passed on orally, and to lay particular stress on such factors as improvisation, alteration of tone and variation of accent; these aspects of music are, of course, less amenable to notation. On the other hand, even though there is always scope for interpretation, it is nevertheless true to say that classical music is *defined* by the score (see Greene, 1972), and that there are very strict limits outside which deviation from the score is not permissible (this latter point does not apply to some recent approaches in avant garde music). If, therefore, the classical musician who looks at the following notational conventions regards them as a little 'loose' or 'inaccurate', he must bear in mind that they aim to fulfil a rather different function from the notation with which he is familiar.

1. Pitch and melody

Most writers have used conventional notation, leaving any alteration of pitch of less than a semitone unspecified, and to be made at the discretion of the performer. However, some transcribers of 'free jazz' have attempted to be more precise:

Example 1

note plus harmonic
(saxophone)

[62]

Example 2

note sharpened

Example 3

note flattened

Various attempts have been made to indicate 'blue notes':

Example 4

E flat guitar blue note

Example 5

use of asterisk

Example 6

∞ = bend note

In order to indicate 'blue notes' some teachers might find it useful to adopt the following convention which Alain Daniélou (1968) used to indicate the microtones of Indian music:

Example 7

microtones

However, none of these are really of much practical value, since the degree of inflection in blues-based music is so varied; such subtleties are most easily and effectively acquired by ear.

Guitar notation needs a special comment. Single note work follows normal classical conventions; chord symbols are mentioned below. But the notation of finger-picking *solos* has been altered from classical convention, usually in favour of simplification — it is assumed that the ear of the performer will guide him to a correct interpretation. Thus a passage which would be written traditionally:

Example 8

(i.e. with the movement of parts indicated) will be notated in an album of folk solos:

Example 9

(i.e. giving notes in the order in which they are struck, and as though they were a single line of thought).

Tablature is also frequently used (cf. the practice of Flamenco musicians):

Example 10

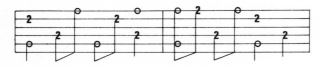

Since editors have often evolved their own individual systems, the best policy is to deal with these only as they arise.

2. Harmony

Conventional notation is used for full band scores. The chord symbol system (of which some idea is given below) is used in parts for rhythm instruments, and as a harmonic guide for a soloist, when he is required to improvise. The main principles underlying the naming of chords in Afro-American music can be deduced from the following examples:

Example 11
MAJOR GROUP

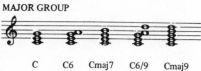

    C   C6   Cmaj7   C6/9   Cmaj9

Example 12
MINOR GROUP

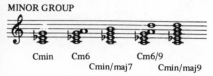

  Cmin   Cm6   Cm6/9
           Cmin/maj7   Cmin/maj9

Example 13
DOMINANT SEVENTH GROUP
(dominant of F major or minor)

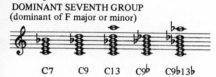

   C7   C9   C13   C9♭   C9♭13♭

For a full account of the use of chord symbols the reader should refer to any manual on popular or jazz harmony (some suggestions are given in the Bibliography).

For the guitar, the system is used as follows:

Example 14

        Dm7   G7

or

Example 15

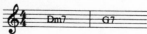

A given rhythm is written:

Example 16

Dm7   G7

Because it is possible to play many chords in more than one way on the guitar, with consequent changes of tone, and also because of the marked tendency of pop guitarists to think in chord 'shapes', arrangers frequently specify their requirements in one of several ways:

(i)   by chord 'windows':

Example 17

B7

(ii)   by an indication of position:

Example 18

(iii) by giving the top note of the required chord, together with its chord symbol:

Example 19

It is worth mentioning that the term 'inversion' is often used for such chordal variants. This is probably because the chord moves or changes in some way, and is, of course, a less precise usage than in classical harmony, in which a change of inversion can only come from a change in the bass note.

   Help is often given to poor readers by combining chord symbols with conventional notation:

Example 20

G7

Parts for the string bass or bass guitar may be written out in full, or the player may be left to improvise from chord symbols, written as in Example 15.

Except for special effects (e.g. a set figure) the piano is given virtually total freedom within the conventions of the style being performed. Its harmonic role may be indicated just by chord symbols (see Example 15), but in many jazz scores these are combined with a written bass part; this is not meant to be duplicated, but is given so that the pianist can avoid unhappy clashes:

Example 21

Piano

In older dance band scores the basic part is notated:

Example 22

Piano

This *can* be played as written, with the left hand duplicating the bass part, but most players prefer to use such a part as a harmonic guide, to be interpreted freely.

3. Tempo, phrasing, dynamics

These follow the normal conventions. The extent to which they are indicated varies greatly, since these matters are frequently left until rehearsal.

4. Orchestration, tone colour, timbre, effects

Again these follow the normal conventions, but add some terminology peculiar to the idiom. For example, the following indication of the tone required is given to the guitarist in 'Spinning Wheel', by Blood, Sweat and Tears:

Example 23

The following example comes from Glenn Miller's 'Cradle Song':

Example 24

These examples illustrate well how little idea of the sound of instruments can be conveyed practically on paper. Though a classical conductor can, of course, conceptualise the sound of a piece fairly well from a score, it is only possible for him to do so because of the relative standardisation of tone, which is part of an instrumentalist's training. In contrast to this, subtleties of timbre, and the cultivation of an *individual* tone are among the major concerns of Afro-American musicians, and thus communication by ear takes on a special importance for them.

A knowledge of the various brass effects is best acquired from the various manuals of jazz orchestration, and most of all from working with brass players. This is also true of their preferences in notation, for instance the fact that some players prefer this:

Example 25

to this:

Example 26

on the grounds that it helps them to visualise more easily what they have to do, despite the cumbersome nature of leger lines in manuscript parts.

Examples of some common effects are:

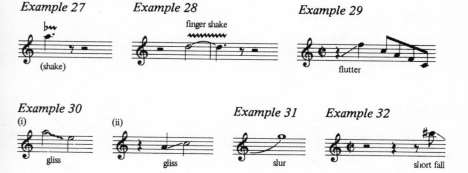

The notation of one effect, that of placing a hat or plunger over or away from the bell of the trumpet or trombone:

Example 33

might possibly be adapted for the 'open' and 'closed' sound of the wah-wah pedal (though I have not seen this done as yet), but normally the details of the use of guitar effects are left to the player. If it is desired to specify closely the amount of treble or bass on an amplifier, the volume setting, and the speed of tremolo or vibrato, it is often useful to adopt a system of clock diagrams of the controls, rather like those used by meter readers of the Electricity Board!

5. Rhythm

Especially in older scores (e.g. those by Jimmy Lally), the rhythm section parts have an apparently ludicrous simplicity but are in fact reinterpreted through improvisation into something much more complex. For instance Example 34 might become Example 35.

Example 34

Example 35

In the above example the drum part is given on two staves for the sake of clarity and accuracy; but though there is nothing to stop the arranger who wishes to specify his requirements in detail from using this method, it should be noted that in actual practice only *one* stave is used. This is made possible without undue complication by the following facts:

(i)   The hi-hat cymbal is so persistently used on the offbeat that its presence is taken for granted and therefore not notated.

(ii)   Unless a special effect is needed, the use of the bass drum is left to the drummer's discretion and is not indicated.

(iii) Though arrangers can and do request particular sounds, e.g.:

Example 36

Tom-tom

this is left largely to the drummer's discretion. This is also true of decisions on how and where to strike the drums.

(iv)   Drum rudiments (e.g. the flam, drag etc.) are never indicated except in drumming manuals.

(v)   The many subsidiary strokes with which a drummer fills in a rhythmic outline such as this:

Example 37

are not indicated and are left to the player's discretion.

The above omissions reduce the number of notes to be indicated in a drum part to two at any one time; they can thus be written on one stave. Also, as a result of these omissions, the drummer's part can be and is restricted to simple rhythmic outlines, rather than giving a detailed indication of what is required. Such rhythmic figures are most commonly used in the following ways:

(i)   instruction to improvise a conventional rhythmic accompaniment:

Example 38

(ii)   instruction to strengthen brass or *tutti* figure using full kit:

Example 39

(iii)   instruction to continue regular rhythm while a rhythmic figure is brought out on another part of the kit:

Example 40

(iv)   instruction to sustain regular ride cymbal rhythm while rhythmic figure is brought out by the other hand, or on the bass drum:

Example 41

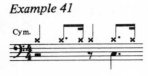

For all instruments, rhythms are notated according to traditional conventions, with one important group of exceptions. These are concerned with the subdivision of the beat into quavers and triplets. In the past, the fact that the crotchet beat can generally be subdivided into a duple or triple metre

Example 42

was often obscured by accentual variations, phrasing and rapid movement from one subdivision to the other. These factors seem to have confused arrangers whose musical training was limited, and strictly traditional, and which therefore gave them inappropriate expectations of what notated Afro-American music should look like. There may therefore sometimes appear to be a disparity between what is notated and what is performed. The problem has been particularly acute in forms such as jazz, which use the triplet subdivision, and is dramatically illustrated in the score of *Improvisations for Jazz Band and Symphony Orchestra* by Matyas Seiber and John Dankworth. The violin and tenor saxophone parts are written:

Example 43

and are accompanied by the following footnote:

Example 44

According to jazz convention the rhythm  is played approximately  Therefore,

these bars are in unison with the jazz band in

spite of the different notation.

Taking a range of popular scores, it would seem that the following rhythms

Example 45

are interchangeable. This apparent illogicality arises again from a lack of standard-isation of interpretation, relative to classical music, especially in matters of accent-uation and rhythmic interpretation. However, the quaver notation seems to be preferred:

(i)   at faster tempos (when the notes inevitably become more even),
(ii) in more modern scores (reflecting a change in inflection by performers),
(iii) in syncopations, when

Example 46

is used, rather than

Example 47

References

Daniélou, A., *Ragas of Northern Indian Music* (Barrie, 1968).
Greene, G.K., 'From Mistress to Master: The Origins of Polyphonic Music as a Visible Language', in *Visible Language*, Vol. 6 (1972).

4 The blues: a practical project for the classroom

PIERS SPENCER

The number of different styles derived from jazz and other Afro-American musics is today so vast that they would seem to have little in common. What connection can a band of the 1930s, such as Benny Goodman's, have with an electric rock band of the late 1960s? What connection can Chuck Berry have with Miles Davis? Yet there is a musical form which links these diverse styles — the blues. Nearly every musician who plays or sings jazz, or music in a style related to jazz, whether he plays boogie piano or sings rock'n'roll, whether he plays in a precise and tightly disciplined big band, or indulges in the wild flights of fancy of a Charlie Parker, has at some time improvised over the twelve-bar pattern of the three primary triads that is known as 'the blues'. Many of the greatest jazz instrumental numbers have been blues, from Duke Ellington's 'Black and Tan Fantasy' to Miles Davis's 'Eighty One', and blues singers have produced some of the most expressive folk poetry of our time, from the raw directness of Bessie Smith to the literate sophistication of Bob Dylan. The blues has great prestige among musicians, who regard the ability to play or sing the blues well as a touchstone of musical feeling. Yet the simplicity of the form is such that anyone can learn to perform it, and by doing so will enhance their understanding of this important contemporary idiom.

This chapter puts forward a project for a class of mixed ability pupils, few of whom will have had experience either of musical notation or of the playing of an instrument. However, there may be one or two musically able and experienced pupils who could tackle more difficult work such as playing a guitar or a drum kit. Essential to the project are plenty of easy-to-play classroom instruments: glockenspiels, xylophones and recorders. It is unfortunate that the tone colours of these instruments are so foreign to the 'dirtier' sounds associated with traditional blues, such as are obtainable from the harmonica, kazoo or banjo — but these could perhaps be introduced by the pupils themselves. It would be useful if there were at least two instruments available whose tone colours are characteristic of pop, namely the electric bass guitar and a drum kit. Both are invaluable classroom instruments, as we shall see. The aim of the project is to get pupils with little or no previous experience of practical music making to perform, compose and improvise both the words and music of simple blues pieces within one term. The course proceeds from the simple *riff* (ostinato), via pre-blues pentatonic songs such as worksongs and spiritual to the twelve-bar blues form and the chord formations that go with it. The making up of words for a blues will be covered, and possible links with English teaching will be discussed. The early stages of the project are envisaged as formal class lessons; later work would be better tackled by pupils working in small groups. The project is designed for classes of mixed ability, and could be undertaken equally well by the top class of a junior school, or by a sixth-form general studies group.

Before beginning the project, however, a debt must be acknowledged. Readers familiar with Carl Orff's 'Schulwerk' will note that this method has influenced both the planning of the course and the way the blues has been broken down into what, it is hoped, are teachable units. 'Schulwerk' is now widely used in schools, and the project should fit comfortably into a music syllabus related to Orff, or indeed any other form of practical classroom work.

1. The riff

The first element of the blues style is the riff (ostinato), a constantly repeated melodic phrase which forms a stable background to the main melodic line. A good riff has a satisfying melodic shape and a stimulating rhythm. A simple riff, using just two notes, might be:

Example 1

(*n.b.* The key implied most strongly here is E minor. I have kept to traditional key signatures throughout the chapter.)
This could be played with ease by a beginner on guitar or bass guitar, and most of the riffs in this course are so designed. Remember, however, that although they sound best on bass instruments, riffs are perfectly satisfactory on any instrument, treble or bass. When we divide a class into groups, there may well be not enough bass instruments to go round.

A riff can also be purely rhythmic, e.g. two sticks beaten together in a pattern such as Example 1. It can also have elements of tone colour, if we use sounds from different parts of the body:

Example 2

This riff could be performed by one person, or split between a group. It could also be transferred to percussion instruments, split between three pupils, or performed on the drum kit by a single player, if he has sufficient coordination. When they can play and repeat simple riffs, pupils should try to combine different rhythms:

Example 3

Many standard dance band rhythms, such as Bossa Nova, cha-cha or medium rock, are useful patterns to learn.

When pupils have mastered some of these rhythmic combinations, it should be possible to make a start on creative work. The class can be split into small groups, making up rhythm patterns of their own, and choosing the tone colours that they wish to combine. Simple resources, such as hand-clapping and finger-snapping, are, as I have suggested, just as effective as percussion instruments, and home-made percussion can also be used effectively. (Some manuals on the construction of simple instruments are listed in the Bibliography.) The polyphonic effect of several percussion instruments playing different riffs simultaneously can be exciting and intoxicating.

Pupils can then try to combine melodic riffs either with other melodic riffs, or with rhythmic riffs. It is a good idea to confine the riffs to the E minor/G major pentatonic scale, as this scale is so suitable for guitars and recorders.

Example 4

Here is an example of a combination of melodic and rhythmic riffs (readers unfamiliar with guitar notation should note that it sounds an octave lower than written):

Example 5

It may be helpful at this point to suggest some music for listening as 'follow-up' to this preliminary work on riffs. Pop music, especially rock'n'roll, is rich in riffs of all shapes and sizes. One has to look no further than the simple, bare pentatonicism of Gary Glitter to realise this. Soul music and reggae, as well as African 'Hi-Life' are characterised by riffs which are often very subtle, making Gary Glitter seem stodgy by comparison. In particular, reggae bass-guitar players show great economy, making much use of rests, and often putting them in quite unexpected places:

Example 6

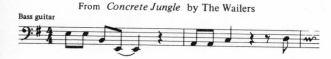

In the above example, the low syncopated E in the first bar is heard as an accent. This creates the expectation that there will be an accent in the same place in the following bar. The avoidance of such an accent by the deliberate placing of rests on the third and fourth beats of the second bar is delightfully surprising, and gives the riff a feeling of spaciousness. The whole number is worth hearing for the bass guitar line alone. It appears on the LP *Soul of Jamaica* on HELP 15, Island Records.

If you want to add some African pop to the school record collection, a good buy would be *Afro-Rock Festival* (Contour 2870–311), a cheap anthology featuring groups such as Assagai and Osibisa. ('Osibisa', incidentally, means 'cross-rhythms'.) There are many fascinating combinations of riff patterns on this record, and pupils will hear the connection between traditional African music and present-day pop. African music, and indeed folk music all over the world, uses repetitive patterns in combinations which belie the description 'primitive'. For at least one school, (Steward's Comprehensive School, Harlow) the performance of African music and dance is a popular and much valued extra-curricular activity.

There are, of course, many riffs or ostinati in classical music, used by composers from Monteverdi to Britten. The four-note bass ostinato from Monteverdi's motet

Laetatus sum is easily recognisable as being similar to a riff, and pupils with greater listening experience will hear similar principles at work behind Purcell's *Dido's Lament*, Bach's Organ Passacaglia in C minor, and the storm music from Britten's *Noye's Fludde*. Recent American composers, such as Terry Riley and Steve Reich, have used riffs as the basis of entire pieces. Listening to *A Rainbow in Curved Air* by Terry Riley, and *Clapping Music* by Steve Reich would provide excellent follow-up material to the practical work done so far.

2. Rhythmic imitation and improvisation

The next stage is aimed to make pupils fluent and confident in building phrases of their own against established riffs. The first step towards this is *rhythmic imitation*, followed by *rhythmic improvisation*.

Against a melodic riff, ask pupils to imitate, either by clapping, or using percussion, short rhythms improvised by the teacher.

Example 7

Vary the lengths of the phrases to be imitated, according to the age and ability of your class. Older (or more able) pupils could easily imitate two- or even four-bar phrases. Vary the dynamics:

Example 8

and the tone colour:

Example 9

It is important also to vary the metre. $\frac{3}{4}$ is not common in blues and Afro-American music generally, and pupils often experience difficulty with this metre because they lack listening experience of it. By the same token, immersion in pop gives children an acute feeling for syncopation, and they usually find no difficulty in picking up patterns such as

Example 10

Compound metres, $\frac{6}{8}$ and $\frac{12}{8}$ are much more common, especially in the blues, and are stimulating rhythms in which to work.

Another very important point about the rhythm should be borne in mind: the element of *swing*. This is manifested both in stressing the beats which in classical music are normally weak (e.g., beats 2 and 4 of a $\frac{4}{4}$ bar), and in the characteristic subdivision of the beats themselves. The use of heavy stresses on weak beats is a characteristic of blues pieces in compound metres, and the tambourine part of Example 9, with its accent on the second beat of the $\frac{6}{8}$ bar, and its omission of the first beat, is intended to intensify the swing of this exercise.

Critical opinion is agreed that rhythmic figures such as ♫ are performed in a special way in order to obtain swing, but authorities differ in their analyses of what happens exactly. Such uncertainty has, as one might expect, resulted in some problems of notation — as are explained by Ed Lee in his 'Note on conventions of notation in Afro-American music'. As I see it, the figure ♫ should really be performed as something halfway between ♪♪ and ♩♫ . In my chapters I have indicated that quavers should be swung in this way by the following indication at the head of a musical example:

Example 11

When pupils are fluent in imitation, we can make a start on rhythmic improvisation. This time, the teacher invites the pupils to answer his rhythmic 'question' with a *different pattern of the same length*:

Example 12

Always make each phrase, whether 'question' or 'answer', follow the preceding one without a break. Here is a plan for a short 'question and answer' piece for pupils to compose in groups of three or four:

Pupil 1	'Question' 2 bars		'Question' 2 bars	
Pupil 2		'Answer' 2 bars		'Answer' 2 bars

Pupils 3 and 4 provide a riff accompaniment throughout; the two riffs should preferably be contrasted rhythmically.

3. The beginnings of melodic improvisation

Now it is time to explore the melodic possibilities of the available instruments.

Again, it is best to confine ourselves to the E minor/G major pentatonic scale. This can be done on pitched percussion by removing the Fs and Cs from the diatonic instruments. With beginners on descant recorder, it is a good idea to teach them the notes B, A, G, E, D and D' first, as this gives them the pentatonic scale. This scale is also easy to find on the guitar. However, no child who introduces notes outside the scale should be thought of as necessarily 'wrong'; it is simply that by confining one-self to the scale, one can find attractive melodic shapes with ease, and these shapes are more likely to relate to the blues idiom. What we are after here is involvement and imagination, rather than correctness. However, once a pupil has started to show musical aptitude and fluency, we can then be more critical of careless playing or inappropriately chosen notes.

With melodic work, one should start with improvisation. Imitative playing, and indeed the playing of 'set tunes', is much more difficult, and should not be attempted until pupils have found their way around the instruments both by teacher-directed improvisation and their own explorations.

Here is an example of teacher-directed improvisation. Against a short melodic, and/or rhythmic riff, the teacher invites pupils to improvise melodic 'answers' to his 'questions'.

Example 13

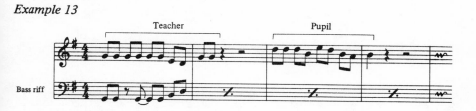

The sense of tonality can be developed by encouraging pupils to end on the key note suggested by the riff. G major is implied by the above, E minor by the following:

Example 14

Pupils should be allowed to explore the melodic possibilities of the instruments either individually or in small groups. The 'conversation piece' structure given earlier would make a good starting point for this type of work.

4. Two Negro spirituals

Before tackling the twelve-bar blues, it is a good idea to work on simple Negro spirituals, which are stylistically related to the blues. Spirituals can help in teaching pupils to play in time, to add riffs, and to paraphrase the original melodies. A good tune to start with is 'Standing in the Need of Prayer', since it is confined to just three notes:

Example 15

This piece could be played by beginners on the recorder. It is constructed simply and symmetrically, and yet it has a stimulating swing to the rhythm which can be offset by the simple 'walking bass' riff in the accompaniment. The riff can be played with ease by a beginner on guitar or bass guitar.

When a group or class has managed to play this piece with reasonable accuracy, the following approach to improvisation could be tried.

Example 16

In this, the whole group plays only the second half of each phrase, while the soloist improvises a paraphrase of bars 1—2 and 5—6. The improvisations could be more elaborate, or indeed more simple than the original melody. The tune could be used as the subject of a rondo with eight-bar episodes improvised by soloists. Here the riff would be continuous throughout, accompanying both subject and episodes:

Bars 1—8	9—16	17—24	25—32	33—40
Theme and riff	Solo improvisation (riff continues)	Theme and riff	Solo improvisation and riff	Theme and riff

One could vary the orchestration by lightening the percussion during the episodes. This would also enable soloists to be heard clearly.

The above improvisations are suitable for a formal teaching situation, and can be played by a whole class, if necessary. The following exercises are best done with the class divided so that the children are working together in small groups:

(i)   adding a counterpoint to the melody:

Example 17

(ii)   making a different arrangement of the theme: adding a percussion accompaniment, and varying the riff:

Example 18

The rhythmic character of the spiritual can be altered considerably by changing the accompaniment. The following should be played with even quavers and not swung:

Example 19

Another useful spiritual is 'Didn't My Lord Deliver Daniel', which is in the E minor pentatonic scale:

Example 20

This piece can be used as a basis for improvisation in exactly the same way as 'Standing in the Need of Prayer'. It sounds effective whether or not the quavers are swung. Performing it first without and then with swing will clarify the meaning of the term to pupils.

There is a suggestion of subdominant harmony in bars 3 and 7, and the accompaniment will sound better if the riff is transposed up a fourth in these bars:

Example 21

This kind of riff I call a 'sequential' riff, that is, a riff transposed to fit in with the harmonic implications of the melody. It is a useful exercise to find out which pentatonic riffs do work sequentially. To help discover this, one should look at the way in which an octave of the pentatonic scale splits into two symmetrical halves, from which sequential riffs can easily be derived:

Example 22

Example 23

It is worth noting that sequential riffs are particularly easy to find on the guitar and bass guitar (for further information see Bibliography).

5. The blues

Before tackling the musical side of the blues, it is useful to deal with the words.

Here is Sonny Terry's 'Dark Road Blues':

Well, my baby left this morning when the clock was striking four
Well, she left this morning when the clock was striking four
Well, when she walked out, the blues walked in my door.

Well, she's gone, she's gone, she won't be back no more
Well, she's gone, she's gone, she won't be back no more
Well, what hurt me so bad, she's gone with Mr So-and-So.

I looked down the road far as I could see
Well, I looked down the road far as I could see
Well, a man had my woman, the blues sure had poor me.

Well, I walked and I walked, my feet got soaking wet
Well I walked and I walked, till my feet got soaking wet
Well, I ain't got my baby and I ain't stopped walking yet.
(Folkways Records)

The structure of a traditional blues lyric consists of three lines: a first line, which is repeated, followed by a third line, containing a new idea, but rhyming with the first and second lines. Readers familiar with the formal aspects of poetry will recognise that the essence of a blues lyric is a series of iambic pentameters, rhymed in couplets. Here is a blues lyric, 'Prison Blues', composed by two fifteen-year-old girls after their class had listened to and discussed the verse-structure of 'Dark Road Blues'.

Well, I came out this morning, and I have nowhere to go
Well, I came out this morning, and I have nowhere to go
I've been roaming round the streets, and I feel so very low.

I've been stuck in a prison, and I can't think straight no more
I've been stuck in a prison, and I can't think straight no more
Well, my baby wrote to me, and she don't want me no more.

Well, the colour of my skin, and the smell of my clothes say no
Well, the colour of my skin, and the smell of my clothes say no
I've been in that prison and I'm not going back no more.

After they have tried to write blues lyrics (on any subject) on the lines of the above models, pupils can be introduced to the musical structure of the blues.

By far the most common framework is the twelve-bar blues. In this form a theme is created over a sequence of primary triads, which is twelve bars in length. Variations then follow; but however free these may become the pattern and length of the basic harmonic sequence remains unchanged.

One way of familiarising pupils with the twelve-bar sequence is to play a simple accompaniment while listening to an actual recording of the blues. Sonny Terry's 'Dark Road Blues' (Folkways Records, FA2327) is ideal for this purpose, but any recording of a similar medium tempo blues will do. Given below is a simple one note to the bar piano accompaniment to fit a twelve-bar blues in E. Note that though the fundamental harmonic pattern is a simple progression of the primary triads, all the chords given take the form of dominant sevenths, even though only B7 actually acts as a dominant chord. The dissonant sevenths on E and A are however so character-istic of the idiom that it is probably best to introduce pupils to them at once. Note also that the harmony is *major*; the amalgam of the 'African' minor pentatonic melody with the 'European' major primary triads is one of the most striking musical features of the blues.

Example 24

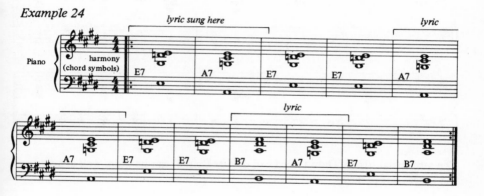

Many blues use a slightly more elaborate chord sequence, like this one. For in-stance, we often find a subdominant chord, in this case A, in the second bar of the twelve-bar sequence. Further information about blues procedures is best obtained from the various blues instrumental tutors listed in the Bibliography. Two things should be pointed out to the pupils: that this twelve-bar pattern is a *recurring* one, and that each bar is based on a *chord*. Once pupils are familiar with the basic struc-ture of the twelve-bar form, the accompaniment can become more elaborate. The harmonic voicings given above might thus be given a simple rhythmic shape as follows:

Example 25

The sequential riff to 'Didn't my Lord deliver Daniel' can be quite well adapted to the twelve-bar pattern:

Example 26

The melodic structure of the twelve-bar blues is as follows (see Example 24):

Bars 1–4: A simple phrase of limited range, corresponding to the first line of the blues lyric, over static tonic harmony (or chords I–IV–I–I).

Bars 5–8: A repeat of bars 1–4, corresponding to the repetitive second line of the lyric, over chords IV–IV–I–I.

Bars 9–12: A new phrase, corresponding to the third line of the lyric, over chords V–IV–I–V.

Here is an example of an instrumental blues, arranged to be played by a class-room group:

Example 27

After the class has played the theme invite individuals to improvise a paraphrase of bars 1—11 over the riff and harmonic pattern. Retain bar 12 in its original form as a 'framework' for the improvisation. The above blues could be used as a basis for further creative work. Given below, for example, are transcriptions of arrangements of Example 27 made by some eleven-year-old boys. These boys were asked to add a riff, trying if possible to make it fit in with the chords, to add a percussion accompaniment, and to find some way of filling in the gaps in the phrasing in bars 3—4, 7—8 and 11.

Example 28 is a pleasing arrangement, and the xylophone player shows musicality in his harmonisation of the theme and in the witty ending on a tonic octave. The texture is uncluttered — the rhythmic pattern on the sleigh bells provides the 'fill-in', and contrasts attractively with the recorder.

Example 28

Example 29, though rather more primitive, shows interesting differences of approach:

Example 29

There is a two-bar introduction for percussion, whose riff is constant throughout. The 'fill-in' consists of a phrase on a second recorder, which is stylish in its shapeliness, swing and syncopation. Perhaps the second recorder player could be encouraged to make more variety by improvising a different 'fill-in' for bars 8—9. Note, too, how the two extra introductory bars are balanced by the omission of the final bar.

Another group of pupils produced an arrangement without 'fill-in' phrases, and with a repeated one-bar accompanying figure, as follows:

Example 30

Although this example is the simplest of the three, it catches the essence of swing by the way the woodblock accents the weak fourth beat of each bar. This little riff is so compelling, even on its own, that we do not feel the absence of 'fill-in' phrases to be unsatisfactory.

Example 31

Example 31 is another blues arrangement to be performed by a class. It, too, could serve as a basis for improvisation and other creative work; for example an improvised solo could begin in bar 12 and finish on the first beat of bar 12 of the next 'chorus'.

6. Composing the blues

Pupils might now try to compose blues melodies of their own, using the following structure:

Bars 1—4: simple pentatonic phrase
Bars 5—8: repeat of bars 1—4
Bars 9—12: new concluding phrase.

Try the following exercise in both imitation and improvisation. The teacher sings or plays the initial phrase over tonic harmony, and the class imitates this over the IV—IV—I—I sequence. The final phrase is improvised by a solo pupil. The exercise should help fix the structure of the twelve-bar blues in the minds of the pupils. A typical result might be:

Example 32

Pupils' first attempts at composing blues melodies will seem very rudimentary. Do not be discouraged if this is so. Fluency will develop with practice. Here is a first attempt at composing the words and music to a blues made by a fifteen-year-old girl:

Example 33

Well, I love Tim Bell, and I still think I love him — Well I

love Tim Bell, and I still think I love him — Well, he's

got an-oth-er woman and his heart ain't mine no more.—

Having composed a lyric and a tune, pupils should work in groups to arrange an accompaniment, and plan an overall performance. It is very important that pupils should learn to plan performances, so that they have some conception of the shape of a piece as a whole. Here is the plan of Sonny Terry's 'Dark Road Blues':
Introduction (4 bars)
Verse 1 (12 bars)
Verse 2 (12 bars)
Harmonica solo (12 bars)
Verse 3
Verse 4

7. Follow-up and conclusion

The educational implications of the project described above are not just musical. In English, the blues as a literary form could be explored further along the lines only briefly touched on here. Many blues lyrics have the quality of poetry, in their stark imagery and complete lack of sentimentality. To quote Charles Fox:

Boll weevil, black snake or morning star — the images were close at hand, the themes nearly always personal, the singers at first anonymous: cotton pickers, stevedores, railroad men. For them the Blues became an emotional release, a way of facing up to life by singing about it. (Fox, 1969, p. 14)

Blues lyrics can be found in many books on American folk and Negro music; interested readers should therefore consult the Bibliography. But it is perhaps worth mentioning a few books here. Paul Oliver's *The Meaning of the Blues* deals with the way blues lyrics were inspired by the American Negro's harsh environment. Charles Keil's *Urban Blues* redresses the imbalance caused by the emphasis on *rural* blues in many other studies. This book deals both with the music, words and social backgrounds of the urban blues, and there are many quotations of blues lyrics. The pervading influence of the blues in pop music has been well documented by Richard

Middleton (1972). The blues, and the people who created and are still creating them, would provide plenty of material for a course in English or social studies integrated with music.

More literary examples of blues-inspired poetry can be found in the work of poets as diverse as W.H. Auden ('Roman Wall Blues', reprinted in Summerfield, 1970) and Adrian Henri (1967). The lyrics of the singer Bob Dylan are often cast in the blues form, or in forms closely related to the blues. The LP *Bringing it All Back Home* (CBS 62515) has several blues lyrics showing great ingenuity, from the display of rhyming virtuosity in 'Subterranean Homesick Blues' to the mysterious and poetical imagery of 'She Belongs to Me'.

Musically, this project was designed to fit into a traditional syllabus, hence the emphasis on group teaching, and the abundance of notated examples. However, one should be aware of the limitations of such a project dealing with the material of folk music, for it can only pick out those aspects which are amenable to classroom work and which can be transcribed into standard European notation. (This remark applies also to the Kodaly method and its relation to Eastern European folk music.) In a way, the project stops where the blues style really starts. It is impossible to notate or teach in traditional manner the real essence of the blues which is its highly developed art of ornamentation — the bending, shaping and colouring of notes which are characteristics of the blues shared with many other non-Western musical traditions. Indeed the word 'ornamentation' is a misnomer — it carries the implication of something subsidiary to the main musical argument. In the blues as in the classical music of India and China, it is the ornamentation of the blues which forms the main musical argument, and has the same function of building up and releasing tension that harmony has in European classical music. Harmony plays its part in the blues, but it is subsidiary, and by European classical standards it would seem primitive and conventional.

When you have finished working through this project, you may well find pupils who show a flair for this music, and you may want to help them develop their playing and singing further, to awaken their interest in the art of blues ornamentation. But an ear for the bending, shaping and colouring of notes cannot be developed by further class teaching, or reading from a notated score. It can only be developed in an informal way, ideally by joining in with and emulating the performance of an experienced blues musician. If you play the blues fluently yourself, who better to serve as a model for your pupils? If you do not, perhaps there is a senior pupil or colleague on your staff who plays or sings the blues? Otherwise, records provide plenty of material for study.

The amount of blues on record is indeed vast. What follows is only the beginning of a collection. For traditional rural and urban blues, Paul Oliver's *The Story of the Blues* on CBS(M)66218 is an excellent double LP with which to start a collection, for it covers both a wide range of styles and a considerable span of time: from the 1920s to the 1960s. The record is a companion to the book of the same title (Oliver, 1969). The twelve-bar blues has permeated rock'n'roll, from Bill Haley's 'Rock

Around the Clock', through Elvis Presley and Chuck Berry to the Beatles' 'The Ballad of John and Yoko'. Among the leading performers in styles derivative of the blues are Ray Charles, B.B. King, Eric Clapton and John Mayall, to name but a few.

Many classically trained musicians are particularly interested in styles in which the blues ceases to be a purely folk form, and interacts with those elements of music, such as harmony, which have been of special interest to European serious musicians. The most important music of this type is that of the great jazz instrumentalists, from Louis Armstrong to John Coltrane. If you are teaching older pupils, say, a sixth-form general studies group, the following discography may be of interest:

CBS BPS 6447. *The Genius of Louis Armstrong*. Contains some of the finest blues-influenced trumpet playing on record.

AHC 176. *Prez*. Featuring Lester Young on clarinet and tenor saxophone. The tracks 'Pagin' the Devil' and 'Countless Blues' show two contrasted approaches to the twelve-bar blues sequence.

CBS 52131. *Charlie Parker Memorial Volume 5*. The four different 'takes' of 'Parker's Mood' are of particular interest if you are discussing jazz as improvisation. Charlie Parker's solos on each 'take' of this number show important differences.

BLP 2460152. *Something in Blue* by Thelonius Monk. Blues-influenced piano playing by one of the most idiosyncratic of jazzmen. Monk's experimental approach to dissonance shows an affinity with twentieth-century composers such as Ives and Schoenberg.

The list could be extended indefinitely. The above is merely the beginning of a 'follow-up' to this brief practical exploration of one of the most important musical forms to have emerged in the twentieth century.

References

Fox, C., *Jazz in Perspective* (BBC, 1969).
Henri, A. *et al.*, *The Mersey Sound* (Penguin, 1967).
Keil, C., *Urban Blues* (University of Chicago Press, 1966).
Middleton, R., *Pop Music and the Blues* (Gollancz, 1972).
Oliver, P., *The Meaning of the Blues* (Collier, 1963).
Oliver, P., *The Story of the Blues* (Barrie and Rockliff, 1969).
Summerfield, G. (ed.), *Junior Voices: The Fourth Book* (Penguin, 1970).

5 The creative possibilities of pop

PIERS SPENCER

Musical education in this country tends to emphasise the European classical tradition. Although performing and listening to classical music has great educational value, there are serious limitations in a music curriculum restricted to this tradition. It is important that music teachers have some knowledge of the musical possibilities of other traditions.

The European classical music tradition is a *literate* one. This literacy has resulted in a division of labour between those who originate the music, the composers, and those who perform it. Music may also be originated by improvisation, but this art fell into decline during the nineteenth century, causing the gap between composition and performance to be widened even further. Performing was, and still is, regarded as a less 'creative' activity than composition. But which musical activities are 'creative' and which are not? As White (1970, p. 132) says, the word 'creative' in common usage tends to imply the value of something, instead of merely labelling a process. When we say that Beethoven's last ten years were his most 'creative', we probably mean that he produced his greatest music during this period. However, I want to use the word 'creative' in this chapter in a more workaday sense, to mean a thinking process which makes decisions about the kind of sounds or rhythms being produced in a piece of music. A composer making an electronic tape piece by himself is, in theory, in control of every aspect of the sound, and his creativity operates in every channel open to him. In most other kinds of music making, however, there is a distinction between a piece as it exists in either notation or oral tradition, and actual execution of the sounds on a particular occasion — in other words, the distinction between composition and performance.

In classical music, the control a composer exerts over a piece depends on how accurately the different musical factors can be notated. Pitch can be transcribed accurately, and, to a lesser extent, so can rhythm, tempo and dynamics. Timbre, in the sense of orchestration, can also be notated, but each individual singer or instrumentalist is responsible for his particular sound. The composer tends to take responsibility for as many areas of music as can be notated accurately, while the performer's interpretation tends to be confined to the relatively narrow areas of dynamic shading, balance of chords, phrasing, and flexibility of rhythm and tempo. Even ornamentation, which eighteenth-century composers had, to a certain extent, left open for the performers to show their improvisatory skill, had, by the time Chopin was composing his piano music, become notated right down to the last detail. This is not to say that interpretation cannot indeed be creative, and no pianist trying to make sense of a piece by Chopin would be able to do so without some mental resourcefulness and decision making and, it goes without saying, a great deal of sensitivity. Yet even here it is the composer and not the performer whose creative thinking predominates. European avant garde music since 1950, under the influence of American composers such as John Cage and Earle Brown, showed a revival of improvisation and a more flexible attitude to the relationship between the composer, the score and the performer. But it is largely true to say that before that date this relationship had remained rather inflexible in classical music.

The traditional conception of the composer's role has had implications for music education, particularly for non-specialist pupils. Creative work tends to be thought of as the preserve of the gifted few, instead of being regarded as something in which everyone, musically trained and untrained alike, should engage as part of their general education. This is because the European tradition has tended to equate creativity with the specialised art of composition. So music making in schools tends to emphasise performance, but even here original interpretative ideas are not encouraged. So much classical music is not the music of childhood. It would be rare to hear a youngster give an original yet valid interpretation of, say, a Mozart sonata. The only music a child (or anyone else) can interpret is music which he understands thoroughly, either because he knows the style, or because he has composed it himself. Decisions about the way children sing or play pieces tend to be made by their teachers, either in their capacity as conductors, or as private instrumental tutors. Initiation into the European tradition, the learning of vocal and instrumental techniques, and principles of style, is a long process. For the average person, it can last through the whole of childhood and adolescence, and often into the early years of adulthood. With such a long initiation, the encouragement of original thinking about sound can easily be neglected.

In recent years, music educators have become aware of this neglect, especially in music courses which form part of the general curriculum in schools (as distinct from specialist studies). The work of Carl Orff, with his pioneering of instruments on which it is easy to improvise melodies and rhythmic patterns and to build textures, has introduced children to music making in which they can make decisions themselves about using the materials of sound. More recently, creative music making related to twentieth-century forms and styles has been introduced by educationists such as Paynter and Aston (1970), Self (1967), and Dennis (1970), and this too has revitalised music curricula, making them more on a par with English, drama, and the visual arts, subjects in which creative work has been an integral part for many years. However, there is another source of musical inspiration to stimulate creative work in sound — the use of Afro-American forms and styles, such as jazz, blues or pop. Elsewhere in this book, contributors have stressed the creativity possible through childrens' practical involvement in this kind of music making. This chapter expands on this concept in some detail, and tries to show that, given the framework of an Afro-American style, be it blues, rock or pop, everyone participating can be involved creatively; given the framework of a style, decisions about rhythm, phrasing, sonority, harmony, even the actual pitch of the notes, can be made by individual performers, even those with a modicum of skill. Again, 'creative' in this chapter is not being used as what Swanwick (1974, p. 39) calls a 'value-laden' word, implying that a creative activity necessarily produces good results. What is being stressed here is that creativity in music education is an area which remains neglected and misunderstood, and the potential of Afro-American music for creative work is well worth exploring.

One of the reasons why musicians are less inhibited about being creative in the Afro-American idiom is that there is not the same reverence for the printed note that one finds among classical musicians, and consequently there is not the same split between composer and performer. 'My music is to be "read", to be "executed", but not "interpreted" ', said Igor Stravinsky (Craft, 1959, p. 119) who wanted the performer to play very little part in the creative process. It is interesting to compare this with a remark made by John Lennon in reference to other people performing his songs:

I've heard some nice versions on 'In my life' . . . Jose Feliciano did 'Help' quite nice once. I like people doing it, I get a kick out of it. I think it was interesting that Nina Simone did a sort of answer to 'Revolution'. That was very good — it was sort of like 'Revolution' but not quite. That I sort of enjoyed, somebody who reacted immediately to what I said. (Wenner, 1973, p. 123)

A comparison of these performances with the Beatles' originals will reveal differences in details of tempo, metre, orchestration, harmony and even melody, for there is a totally different attitude to both composer and performer in the world of pop. Compared to Stravinsky, Lennon seems generous in his respect for an executant's creativity, and this freedom to interpret, indeed 'recreate', is normal in the world of Afro-American music. The practice goes back, of course, long before the present-day era of rock and pop. If you hear any two jazz singers or instrumentalists performing the same number you will usually find striking differences. Indeed comparisons between performances of pieces by different jazz or pop artists could form the basis of some interesting music appreciation work for older pupils. A starting point could be the Beatles' two differing interpretations of their song 'Revolution' (side 4, track 1 of the *White Double Album*, PCS 7067-8, and side 2, track 7 of *The Beatles 1967–70*, PSCP 718).

Nearly every performer in an Afro-American idiom improvises as a matter of course, whether it be Bob Dylan providing simple fill-ins on his harmonica, or Coleman Hawkins rhapsodising on 'Body and Soul'. This applies to singers, too, as anyone who has heard Ella Fitzgerald or Elton John will know. Duke Ellington established composition as an important branch of jazz, but by doing so took none of the creative birthright away from those who played his music. 'Concerto for Cootie' (on the LP *Duke Ellington At His Very Best*, RCA 730-565, 1968) is as much Cootie Williams' creation as it is the Duke's. Nearly all jazz musicians have composed material or written arrangements and, since the Beatles, it has become normal for pop groups to compose their own songs, too. Musical creativity is regarded by jazz and pop musicians as a perfectly normal part of any musician's make-up, instead of being a special gift reserved primarily for composers. The attitude is a healthy one, and its implications are significant for music education.

All that I have said so far does not necessarily mean that I am uncritical of certain aspects of pop — the commercialism, the impression of easy material success, and the violation of many social values that seem implicit in the image conveyed by certain groups. But equally great harm is done by schools themselves who, on the whole, ignore pop, and who rarely create opportunities for children to make the music themselves. There is a parallel here with football: the anti-social behaviour of teenage fans at soccer matches, and the conduct of some famous footballers on and off the pitch has no connection with the nature of the game itself, and certainly does not prevent it from being played in schools. There is a clear separation in the minds of physical education teachers between soccer as a social phenomenon and soccer as a game. We must, as music educators, also be aware of a similar separation between 'pop culture' and music making in 'pop' and related Afro-American styles such as the blues, as a valid musical recreation for young people.

The rest of this chapter is a discussion, illustrated with recordings, of some actual examples of music making recorded in secondary schools. They are made by a variety of children, some musically gifted, others of more limited talents. They all have two things in common: they involve some composition or improvisation on the part of the children themselves, and they relate in some way to pop or other Afro-American styles. Some of the pieces were initiated and structured by teachers, others came purely from the pupils' own initiatives. Some use authentic pop instruments, while others use resources more usually available in the classroom, such as recorders and pitched percussion. The intention is that this chapter should be as helpful as possible to those who may not be familiar with pop and jazz, and the reader is asked to listen to the examples on the accompanying recording to give some thought to his own reactions to the music, and *then* to read the commentary. I am not so much concerned that the reader should agree with my views, as that he should be provoked into thought and discussion, and eventually into exploring some of the possibilities raised by this anthology. It should be noted that I have not tried to offer a collection of outstanding pieces; I have included many examples of average work, showing children grappling with skills they have yet to master. Although some pieces are good, and all have good points, I felt that it would be more valuable to give examples of work which is representative of what one might expect to be created by any group of children in a comprehensive school. Where relevant, I have transcribed the examples, explained how the music originated, reported the help and comments given to the children by their teachers, and added my own observations.

The survey will fall into two parts. The first will be a general survey of the range of creative music making inspired by, or directly related to, pop and other Afro-American styles, with examples taken from a variety of children. The second part will trace the development of an individual pupil, a 'non-academic' boy who composed and sang his own songs.

Part 1: General survey

(All examples from this chapter are to be found on side 1 of the accompanying recording and a guide to the latter is given on page 177.)

Track 1 is a blues, performed on assorted classroom instruments by a group of eleven- to twelve-year-old boys. The 'theme' appears as Example 27 in the previous chapter. The performance was structured by the teacher, who provided the piano accompaniment. Most of the boys had been learning the recorder from scratch for one term, progressing from the notes B—A—G to E—D and then D', giving them one octave of the pentatonic scale:

Example 1

This, as you will know if you are familiar with the Orff and Kodaly methods, is an excellent basis for improvisation. The repertoire of tunes learnt before playing this recording was very similar to that of the blues course described in chapter 4, but the boys had learnt songs and pieces in other idioms as well. The teacher had got them used to improvising right from the start, but the solos recorded here (each about twelve bars) were longer than the boys had attempted before. After the opening theme, during which a boy improvised short fill-ins on xylophone, there are seven solos:

(i)   Recorder
(ii)   Xylophone
(iii) Guitar
(iv)   Recorder
(v)   Xylophone
(vi)   Recorder
(vii) Xylophone

The distinctive sound of the blues, compared with that of other pentatonic musics, is created by the 'false relation' between the major thirds of the accompanying chords and notes of the pentatonic minor melodies, e.g.:

| chord: E major | third: G sharp |
| scale: E minor | third: G natural |

The notes so affected are known as 'blue notes'.

The nature of the idiom is such that, despite the changing chords in the accompaniment, the inexperienced player is free to improvise without having to worry whether his notes fit, provided he confines himself reasonably strictly to the pentatonic scale. On the other hand, a more experienced musician could try to make sense of the underlying harmonies. The sequence in bars 9—10 of solo (v), for instance, shows a response to the underlying chords.

After they had made this recording, the teacher played it back stopping the tape at the end of each solo, and making brief comments. Below, I give the teacher's comments on solos (i) to (iv), together with transcriptions where relevant. I have added some additional comments of my own, in brackets.

(i) Recorder:

Example 2

xylophone solo
begins here (1 bar early)

'Watch your tonguing carefully, and although I know you want to use one or two notes other than those we've learnt so far, try to stick to the notes we've learnt, as they will make it easier for you to improvise well.' (Although going outside the pentatonic scale is by no means necessarily 'wrong', a little restriction is helpful here.)

(ii) Xylophone: 'Listen to what the others are doing, where their solos end, and where new ones begin. Your solo began too early, and finished after it should have done; the guitar was quite right to start when he did! There are some good ideas — I like your syncopated rhythms, and you play the xylophone with a nice, soft touch.' (This boy does not have a clear perception of the structure of the blues, and a little help and guidance is needed here. One of the difficulties of getting away from notation, which in the long term is an advantage, is that one is forced to think ahead, to be really clear about where the music is going, rather than merely to read-and-play from one bar to the next.)

(iii) Guitar:

Example 3

'A very interesting solo with some unusual ideas.' (Here is another exploration out-side the pentatonic scale, rather more successful than (i). He develops the rhythmic motif of the theme intelligently, especially in the long shapely phrase spiced with chromaticisms in bars 5–8 of his solo. The flattened fifth, B flat in bar 7, has indeed a 'bluesy' sound, although some of these chromaticisms, like those in Thelonius Monk's piano playing, may well be lucky finds rather than premeditated ideas!)

(iv) Recorder:

Example 4

'Some neat, clean playing, with a nice jazzy rhythm to it. I like especially the rhythm you set up using just two notes at the end of your solo.'

The improvisations in Examples 2–4 were the result of a formal classroom situation, with a firm framework provided by the teacher. As I said, the class had proceeded on the lines described in the previous chapter, with the instruments limited to the E minor pentatonic scale. An interesting difference of approach is given in the next example. Here a teacher got his class of twelve-year-old boys to listen to a blues record and, while doing this, to write down the words. Several hear-ings of the same number were necessary in order to do this, and it ensured that pu-pils absorbed both the musical idiom and the verse structure. The class was then divided into groups, and was invited to compose the words and music of either a blues, or a song in a related style. Resources were very limited, and groups accompanied their singing with just one or two percussion instruments. The results, although rough and ready, are interesting as they show that through listening pupils catch aspects of style which cannot readily be taught.

Example 5

In this example (track 2), the singer adopts a rasping sound to his voice which is entirely authentic, yet in no way relates to the vocal tone a teacher might want for good choral singing! The pupil's approach to intonation is also much more flexible than being merely confined to the equal-tempered pentatonic scale of an 'Orff' xylophone. The fifth above the tonic is frequently flat, and there are several 'bent' notes (portamenti). There is a good feeling for both syncopation and the rhythm of words, and melodically, the rise to the high D on 'sent me to the County Jail' is both stylish and expressive. These details of style can be caught through observant listening, but they cannot readily be taught. It does not follow, however, that the teacher does not have a role. The boys need help in sorting out which way the notes in the bass riff should go. From this recording they seem undecided as to whether they mean

Example 6

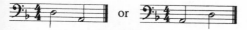

The ambiguity here shows that, despite their ear for the *foreground* aspects of the music, the tone colour, intonation and rhythmic features of the main melodic line, they have not properly worked out the accompaniment. The teacher can help by getting them to think about and decide for themselves exactly what they mean. This will lead to a growth of harmonic awareness, whilst allowing considerably for individual differences.

This recording is encouraging to those of us who work in schools with slender resources for music, for it shows that children will always use their ingenuity. For example, in a piece (not given here) made soon after Example 5, the group had only a suspended cymbal and a temple block, yet the primitive accompaniment they produced had atmosphere, and enhanced the feeling of the words and melody which they had created. Given a complete drum kit, this group might well have sought out more conventional patterns — trying to sound like every other drummer in a pop group, instead of exploring the wider possibilities of sound materials. A marvellous illustration of how primitive resources can give rise to exciting music making can be found on the LP *Savannah Syncopators* (CBS 52799, 1970, side 1, track 6). This is a blues called 'Eloise', sung by a Texas Negro accompanying himself on a set of drums made from oil drums.

Examples 1–5 came from ordinary class lessons, in which the introduction to the blues was meant as a part of the pupils' *general* education. Examples 7, 8 and 9 are the work of a more specialised group, a rock band who took their music making seriously enough to save up and buy their own equipment. The average age of the boys was fifteen when these recordings were made. The teacher 'discovered' them when they brought along a tape they had made of a pop arrangement of Bach's Toccata and Fugue in D minor. The organist, who had master-minded the arrangement, took piano lessons, and was studying for the Grade VI examination of the Associated Board. But the group had developed independently of school or teachers. Inspired by the tape, the teacher composed two rock cantatas for junior choir with an accompaniment for the group, mostly scored in detail, but with some scope for improvisation. In both pieces, we have first a choral excerpt and then an organ improvisation based on the chords of that excerpt.

Example 7

Example 8

ORGAN SOLO (on the chords of Example 7)

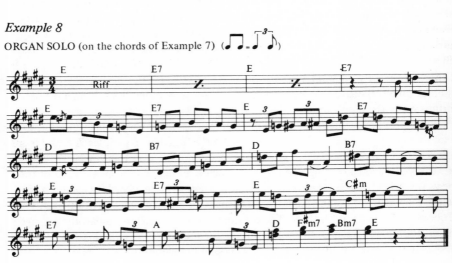

Examples 7 and 8 (tracks 3 and 4) come from a setting of Psalm 107, 'O that men would praise the Lord for the wonders that He doth to the children of men'. It is interesting to compare the improvisation here with the solos on track 1. Again we have the E minor pentatonic scale colouring the predominantly major tonality with blue notes. Since the tuning of the organ uses the equal-tempered scale, sensitive variations in intonation, the 'bending' of notes possible on guitar or voice, are suggested by means of ornamentation: the G sharp to A acciacatura in bar 9, for instance, implies a pitch somewhere between the two notes. There is the added problem here of really having to think out the implications of chord changes and, because of this, the improvising is a little tense and lacking in flow in places. However there are some good, spontaneous ideas, particularly the incisive rhythmic pattern in bars 17–18, which helps bring the solo to a good close in bars 19–20.

Example 9 (track 5) comes from a setting of the poem 'Jazz Fantasia' (Sandburg, 1950, p. 179). With the slower tempo, the organist is more relaxed, and there is space for thoughtful improvisation. Again, pentatonicism, with subtleties of intonation suggested by the ornamentation, is the basis of the style, but this later recording shows a growing awareness of how to handle chord changes. The decoration of the chromatic chord in bar 8 with a Baroque-sounding diminished seventh arpeggio is a striking and imaginative stroke, and equally delightful is the little sequential idea in the last two bars.

The teacher's *educational* aim in composing these pieces was to give the boys a tight yet stimulating framework to work in. The organist was very musical, and he needed to be stretched. It would not have been enough merely to have been satisfied with the free pentatonicism of Example 1. This boy is ready to handle chords and he should be given them. Free improvisation (jamming) over ostinati (riffs) is an important feature of much rock music, but for many young rock groups this can lead to the belief that interminable meanderings over static patterns constitute meaningful music making. The teacher can play an invaluable role by putting talented musicians into situations where they can sharpen their wits on such things as chord changes, and thus develop their musical vocabulary.

For the remaining examples in the first part of this survey I return to the classroom situation, with some compositions that present a very interesting phenomenon: although they show a derivation from blues, pop and commercial musics, they somehow manage to convey a distinctive character of their own. There may be two reasons for this. First, the nature of the instruments used (glockenspiels and recorders are hardly 'pop' instruments, or, at any rate, are only peripherally used in pop music). They may therefore encourage a kind of musical thinking different from the ideas that pop instruments inspire. Second, and more important, I am convinced that, despite their outward conformity to pop culture, the creativity of teenage children remains intact, and they are capable of transforming the raw materials of the music that surrounds them day in and day out into pieces which are often surprising and refreshing. Christopher Searle makes a similar point in dis-

Example 9a

(a) Vocal Line

cussing the influence of pop on children's writing. He acknowledges the commercialism of pop:

> The controllers of this new technology of sound and image, of course, are less interested in the effects of their barrage on the adolescent mind, than they are about the lucrative returns it provides them. (1973, p. 112)

But he shows how some children's poems which take pop numbers as a starting point transcend the crudeness and sentimentality of their models. As he says,

Pop music can be used to create a genuine education experience. We have to work realistically within the media that are inevitably forming the symbolic structure of the children's expression, in order to fight to reverse its pernicious effects. Pop music is having an enormous impact on adolescent experience. If we work against that experience, we work against the formation of the child's identity at its most vital social stage. There are effects which can stretch the adolescent imagination and help the growth of his understanding of others in situations different to his own. A fifteen year old boy takes a Manfred Mann hit song, 'My name is Jack', and creates his own poem, achieving a deep empathy for one of the social rejects of Spitalfields or Whitechapel. He becomes the man through his poem, taking on and confronting a different experience . . . a 15 year old school leaver takes a sentimental song like 'Grandad', and recreates it as a sympathetic insight into the experience of old age, replacing the song's mawkishness with a real understanding. (1973, pp. 112—13)

Searle's sensitive and sensible remarks can apply to music, too, as the next four pieces show.

Examples 10 and 11 are two duets, made by boys from the class who performed in Example 1. The work of this class was based on the two main types of practical class music lesson: a 'rehearsal', where an entire class is involved simultaneously in a teacher-directed activity and a 'workshop', in which individuals or small groups work on projects initiated by the teacher, but shaped and interpreted by the pupils themselves. Example 1 resulted from a 'rehearsal' structure, while Examples 10 and 11 resulted from a 'workshop'. (See Paynter and Aston, 1970, chapter 1, for a discussion of ways of organising 'workshop' lessons.)

Example 10 (Track 6)

Example 11 (Track 7)

Both duets show the influence of the blues style, Example 10 in its syncopations, Example 11 in its general melodic shape. But neither sounds remotely like a blues; their approach is much nearer to that of avant garde music. The witty flutter-tonguings in Example 10 and the atmospheric sound of the cymbals in Example 11 are examples of pure musical exploration without reference to any particular style. Simple though they are, these pieces thus reflect the kind of creative fusion of contrasting insights which can arise when pupils have been exposed to widely varied musical experiences. In this case the insights come from the blues and from avant garde music, as approached, for example, through the *Sound and Silence* projects.

Example 12

Example 12 (track 8) is a more sophisticated composition for glockenspiel, piano, tambourine and tambour composed by four fourteen-year-old girls. The inspiration came from a pop song: Burt Bacharach's 'Close to You' in the version sung by the Carpenters (see the LP *The Carpenters Singles, 1969–1973*, side 2, track 6). The pianist started her explorations by trying to play the piano accompaniment to the song by ear. Although she had a piano at home, she could neither read music nor did she have piano lessons. She had clearly been stimulated by the shape formed by her fingers at the keyboard which, she found, yielded a music sequence providing enough material for an original piece of her own. It is interesting to compare the Bacharach song (Carlin Music, 1963) with this classroom composition. The use of the piano is similar in both. There is a right-hand solo introduction featuring a dotted rhythm, and a reiterated chordal accompaniment to the melodic line. There are similarities in sound — both use suspensions and chords of the seventh. The Bacharach song handles these with expertise and subtlety, sometimes directly resolving, sometimes delaying the resolutions, while the girls, with less technical skill, develop a simpler, recurring pattern of dissonance–resolution in a descending chain of suspensions. (Debussy's 'Clair de Lune' has a similar chord progression at the beginning.) Far from being naïve, this direct, simple pattern is one of the piece's strengths, giving rise to a distinctive overall design. The most striking feature is the way the suspensions move downwards to the climax in bars 25–8, a climax marked by the unexpected, but apt B flat at the end of bar 24, which momentarily opens out a new key, before returning to the C tonality of the final five bars which, almost imperceptibly, are played more slowly and quietly.

Melodically, too, there are comparisons. The four-line verse of the Bacharach song gives rise to a shapely, but conventionally structured melody, while the glockenspiel tune is more improvisatory, with a greater variety of phrase lengths. It does hang together logically, however. The closing section of the piece (bars 21–5) consists of a series of phrases all revolving around a high G. These get gradually shorter until all that remains is a row of isolated, repeated Gs, the essence extracted from the previous phrases. Here we have the instinctive pursuit of musical thought informed by musical feeling, and the effect is gentle and beautiful, and quite different from the sugary sentiment of the song which provided the original inspiration.

Example 13 (track 9) is part of a radio commercial advertising Yardley's 'Moonlight Mist' perfume, made by a group of boys and girls in a CSE music class. They took the opening bars of the 'Moonlight Sonata', and used them as a kind of 'basso ostinato' over which they composed their successive vocal and instrumental counterpoints.

They show commercial music's lack of reverence for great masterpieces, but I cannot help being charmed by the bass guitarist's graceful elaboration of Beethoven's original bass line, and the feeling for mood and orchestration which this piece has. The words were spoken by a teacher, in the absence of one of the girls, but no other help was given. The 'Moonlight Sonata', originally in C sharp minor, appears here in

Example 13

a different key — E minor, which would indicate that the pianist was playing it by
ear, and had not seen the music.

Although this 'commercial', stylistically, does not sound like pop, it is typical of
the pop and jazz view of music, in that instead of performing or even interpreting
an already existing piece note by note, it *recreates* Beethoven's original, altering the
form, texture and orchestration in the same way that a commercial arrangement recreates a pop 'standard'.

Part 2: An individual develops

The examples in the first part of this chapter form a survey of the range of creative
work possible in idioms related to pop. I now propose to trace, in the second part,
the musical development of a single pupil, a fifteen-year-old boy called Dene Gaskin,
who composed and sang his own songs, accompanying himself on the keyboard. He
neither read music, nor had he had any piano lessons. Apart from music, his achievement in other subjects was very limited. I have chosen Dene as a particular case
study, because he demonstrates so clearly both musical creativity and its possibility
for growth and development. First, let us consider a song composed by Dene during
the summer term of 1974. This can be heard on track 10 of the recorded examples.
The song was rather unoriginal and did not seem to hold much promise. However,
bearing in mind that it was an early attempt, the important thing, for the teacher,
was not to point out the derivativeness of the song — Dene's peers had done that
already — but to try and develop any latent musical abilities. The breaking of Dene's
voice had brought with it an ability to improvise an ornate melismatic line, the kind
he sings over the slow chords at the beginning of the song (track 10).

Example 14

Seen her at the club last night ____   Am   I really wan-na hold her tight

She had long blonde hair__   G   And wow the boys did   stare! __ __

Dene liked drawing fancy patterns in sound, and this was a good starting point for
further development.

On the recording, track 11, you can hear four different versions of the slow introduction to the song (which also served as a coda). I feel that the recording may
be valuable in giving the listener some idea of the sort of relationship which existed
between Dene and the teacher, and may thus be more effective than the written
word in giving indications of the sort of practical approaches which are profitable in
this field of music.

One suitable and effective approach was used when Dene's teacher suggested that
he alter the third chord of the corny I—VI—IV—V progression to a minor chord, and
showed him how to play it. He left Dene to experiment in improvising a vocal line
above the changed progression. Dene's first attempt did not work out very well, as
you can hear. The second attempt, however, shows shapeliness and spontaneity. The
two remaining versions illustrate the variety of melodic shapes he was able to extract from the progression. These explorations can be heard on track 11 of the recording. Dene would have benefited from a few more exercises of the same kind.

Example 15, printed for ease of comparison with a revised version, Example 16,
is a sketch for a song composed a few months later: the positive qualities of Dene's
musical invention, his melismatic line, and his response to chords, are here displayed
in a more thoughtful, personal way. He is inventing his own chord progressions too,
and the F minor to E minor sequence in bars 10—11 has a bittersweet nostalgia of
the kind one finds in early songs by the Beatles. Words are clearly a problem for
Dene. But, despite their incoherence, this string of half-remembered phrases is more
genuine than the rather empty verbal formulae of his first song. There is a relationship, too, between the nostalgic mood of the music and the feelings, however inarticulate, that the words seem to want to convey.

The chief musical problem here is one of form. Like many people who are
making their first attempts at composing, Dene sees a piece of music as a stream of
sound, rather than as a self-contained argument needing shape and organisation.
Dene's teacher suggested that he cut out the third, D minor, section for use in another song, and arrange the remaining sections, bars 1—8 and 9—16, in an **AABA**
pattern. The purpose of this was to enable Dene to finish the song, and to teach him
something about form.

Example 15

Example 16

Chords altered or amended by the teacher are marked*

Example 16 is the revision of Example 15, with the amendments suggested by the teacher. It is still rather unsatisfactory, and the G chord at the end is unconvincing. However, notice how Dene has added his own frills to the teacher's alterations!

There is a spontaneous phrase newly improvised over bars 24—5, and a little pentatonic flourish gracing the final chord.

A week later, Dene was composing yet another song (track 14).

Example 17

The texture (an ornate vocal line accompanied by block chords) is the same as that of the last song, but the handling of melody and harmony shows even greater confidence. The opening suspension is a new venture for one who has only previously thought in triads. The opening of the vocal line grows logically out of the suspension, and there are some adventurous triadic harmonies: for example, the alternation of the F and D chords in bars 12—15.

Dene's colleagues were quick to point out that the opening suspension was reminiscent of the beginning of the song 'Pinball Wizard' (by the Who, on their LP *Tommy*). This is a little unfair. The slow rhythm of Dene's chords creates a very different mood from the animated rhythm of the song by the Who. Children are often harsh and superficial critics of their colleagues' original work (they can also be dauntingly perceptive), and it is up to the teacher to be gentler and more encouraging. The teacher is more likely to have an overall view of the progress a pupil is making, and can pick out, through careful and thoughtful listening, exactly where his musical gifts lie.

These twenty or so bars formed the first sketch of the song. It is interesting to watch the progress of the material from this point, to follow both the continuation of the song, and the filling out of the texture with other instruments. First, let's follow Dene's continuation of his material, and the building of a contrasted second section. The above sketch peters out with a half-formed idea — the series of ascending triads in bars 16—19. At first Dene found it difficult to continue this. He was aware that some contrast was necessary, and experimented with two ideas, an animated rhythm of quavers in the accompaniment:

Example 18

and a C major—minor chord progression, over which he improvised a rather clumsy vocal line:

Example 19

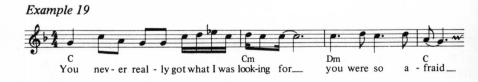

Later, these ideas crystallised into the pattern which can be seen in the final version (track 15).

Example 20

Here, the C major—minor progression was reversed to a C minor—major progression, starting at bar 16. Dene was unsure at first about following the D major
chord in bar 15 with a C minor chord in bar 16, but he gradually realised that the
strangeness of the progression was also rather attractive. The vocal line over this progression had now become more shapely and expressive. The ascending series of
triads, which was the original idea for the continuation, was postponed until bars
24—7, and given the animated quaver rhythm which provides such a contrast with
the solemn pace of the opening. The final bar of the second section makes these
triads descend rapidly in a syncopated rhythm (bar 27), and ends on a chord of C,
to prepare for the beginning of a second verse.

I have gone into detail about Dene's method of working, as I wanted to show that, like many composers, literate or non-literate, he proceeded by a series of insights into his material. The intelligence with which he worked unaided at fashioning this song seems at odds with his modest achievements in other subjects.

The teacher gave a certain amount of help in building up a texture with other instruments. He suggested that two other pupils, an electric guitarist and a bass guitarist, should join Dene to work out an arrangement of the song. He gave some help with the bass line, and suggested that the electric guitarist improvise over the opening chords using notes from the F pentatonic scale. The rest of the guitar obbligato was worked out by the player himself. Like Dene, he proceeded by a series of insights, finding ways of getting round the often tricky chord changes. At first tentative and unsure, he gradually became more confident, and the final result heard on the recording is an inventive counterpoint which is almost continuous throughout.

The main weakness of the song lies in the words, which remain embarrasingly trite. The words of the final version are, if anything, worse than the 'free association' stream of words which Dene improvised in his original sketch (Example 17). At this stage, the musical invention is far ahead of the verbal.

However, Dene was to make a leap forward in the words of his next song, composed a few weeks later, 'Now Summer's Gone Away' on track 16. It is a song about the prospect of leaving school and childhood behind, and of being faced with the big, hard world. Here at last are words which convey a real, felt experience. Dene knows he is still a child, and the sadness and panic he is experiencing at the transition to adulthood come over vividly. There are still clichés, and some lines which do not quite seem to make sense, but the metaphor of seasonal change from the 'summer' of childhood to the uncertain 'autumn' of growing up is sustained very well throughout, giving the words a direction and coherence which were lacking in his previous songs. However, one must not look at the words of children's songs as though they were conceived of as poetry, intended to stand by themselves. They are lyrics, and must be considered in conjunction with the music, which completes the sense and deepens the feelings expressed by the words. It is for this reason that I have decided not to include the latter here and readers are therefore urged to *hear* the recording. The treatment of lyrics as poetry is a common critical error — see, for example, Holbrook (1973); Graham Vulliamy considers this point at greater length in chapter 2.

The incomplete sense and occasional clumsiness of expression in Dene's lyrics should be seen in the light of the responsiveness to the meaning and rhythm of words which he shows in this musical setting. The constantly changing harmonies and the uncertain tonality convey his *unsettled* mood most sensitively. Compare with this the confident, stable tonality of his first song. There are many felicities of word painting. The G chord in the 3rd bar sounds strange and beautiful in its E major context, aptly fitting the word 'fairytales'. The twisting melisma on the word 'realise', early in verse 3, conveys vividly the pain of growing awareness. The rhythm

of the melodic line throughout fits the rhythm of the words perfectly naturally —
there are no longer monstrosities like the 'spread it around, baby' of Example 20.

The sense of overall form shown in this song is also remarkable. The teacher's
help in shaping the earlier song seems to have had an effect, although the organisation here was entirely unaided. The first twelve bars of verse 2 consist of a piano
improvisation over the chords, with the voice re-entering in the 13th bar. The coda
establishes a definite tonality for the first time in the song, and this adds to the
poignancy, for we are made to feel that this C major, like the return of the 'summer'
of childhood that the lyric describes, is transient and illusory. This delaying of a
definite key until the very end, and the clear organisation of the rest of the material,
shows that Dene is now able to conceive of a piece of music as a *whole*.

The improved organisation, however, has in no way been at the expense of
Dene's melodic spontaneity and his tendency to make asymmetrical phrase lengths.
Paradoxically, this song is both more coherent than his previous efforts, and yet
displays greater freedom of melodic invention. As I observed earlier, he was able to
get a great deal of variety from a short, simple chord progression. The song shows
this variety on a larger scale: the melodic line for each verse is different, although
the chords remain the same.

Although the song derives from the styles of Top Twenty pop (one thinks of
Gilbert O'Sullivan and Elton John), both the words and the free, spontaneous line
of the melody show a subtle deviation from the norms of four-square structures and
conventional subject matter more usual in commercial idioms. Indeed, I am convinced that an increase of creative pop music making in schools where, given resources and encouragement, children will find that they are capable of producing
more interesting pop music than is sold to them by the mass media, will lead to
schools creating an alternative teenage musical culture based on *doing* rather than
just listening. This could prove a formidable rival to the 'establishment pop' of the
mass media!

Conclusion

The important thing about pop and other Afro-American musical styles is that
creativity can be involved on every level of music making, and this chapter tries to
show what implications this has for musical education. Music in schools, on the
whole, still tends to be limited to teacher-directed performance. Both pop and the
methods proposed in Paynter and Aston's *Sound and Silence* open up new possibilities of pupil participation in the making of musical decisions. Indeed, there is a
close resemblance between the way children work in groups on a 'Classroom Project
in Creative Music' and the informal way in which pop and jazz groups have always
rehearsed — by group discussion, by trial and error, but without the authority of a
detailed score or a conductor to dictate to them. Despite their immaculately polished ensemble work, even the big bands of Basie and Ellington rehearsed informally,
with a great deal of discussion. Naturally, I am aware that if you are running a big

band in a school, it would be unrealistic to rehearse in quite such a democratic way! Obviously a teacher must be sensitive to what aspect of pupils' music making require direction and guidance, and what aspects can be left to develop on their own with a minimum of supervision. It also depends on the maturity and personality of the individual pupil — some children are natural leaders, some are full of ideas, while others are content to perform the ideas of others without alteration or interpretation. These are, however, matters of teaching strategy and, as such, do not invalidate my plea for a greater awareness of both the creative possibilities of pop and Afro-American music and of the musical needs of young people, which remain neglected in many present-day curricula.

References

Craft, R., *Conversations with Igor Stravinsky* (Faber and Faber, 1959).

Dennis, B., *Experimental Music in Schools* (Oxford University Press, 1970).

Holbrook, D., 'Pop and Truth', chapter 10 of *English in Australia Now* (Cambridge University Press, 1973).

Paynter, J. and Aston, P., *Sound and Silence* (Cambridge University Press, 1970).

Sandburg, C., *Collected Poems* (Harcourt, Brace and World Inc., New York, 1950).

Searle, C., *This New Season* (Calder and Boyars, 1973).

Self, G., *New Sounds in Class* (Universal Edition, 1967).

Swanwick, K., 'The Concept of "Creativity" in Music Education', *Education for Teaching* (November 1974).

Wenner, J., *Lennon Remembers* (Penguin, 1973).

White, J., 'Creativity in Education' in Dearden, Hirst and Peters (ed.), *Education and the Development of Reason* (Routledge & Kegan Paul, 1970).

6 Running an 'open' music department

MALCOLM NICHOLLS

Countesthorpe College, a secondary comprehensive school for fourteen- to eighteen-year-olds, was opened in 1970, and is a part of the Leicestershire Plan of upper schools and age eleven to fourteen high schools. Its catchment area includes pupils from the immediate country area and from a nearby council estate in Leicester. The buildings were designed for the innovatory teaching methods which Tim McMullen had planned and discussed with his new staff before opening. As the first principal of the college, he established procedures of participatory government by the staff and pupils, who in turn established organisational and curriculum policies which still remain largely unchanged. The principle characteristics are:

1. Participatory government: major decisions are made as necessary by the 'Moot', a meeting of staff and pupils. The 'Moot's' rotating standing committee meets weekly to make everyday decisions. Urgent or minor decisions may be made unilaterally.
2. The 'teams': areas of the college are allotted to 'mini-schools' as homes where the pupils spend half of their timetable with their tutor (or 'form-teacher') or one of his team.
3. The remaining half of the pupils' time is spent in 'activities', all of which are optional. All college work is based upon the principle of an individualised, 'pupil-centred' curriculum. Further information on these matters is given in the profile of Dene Gaskin below. I feel it is valuable for a music department to be run on these lines, since each individual, even at the age of fourteen, will have different technical needs and aspirations and unique aesthetic values.

Organisation of the music timetable. In the Countesthorpe 'team/option' curriculum the music teacher has the essential right to arrange the basic constitution of his groups to make each of them include a number of pupils who are self-directing, some who require more attention, as well as some who are compatible in that they can, for example, share guitar techniques or can play a useful combination of instruments. Thus the teacher can at least expect not to be landed with fifteen prospective pianists at one session. However, the flexibility of the team system not only allows these arrangements to be made but also allows the occasional arrangement of 'one-off' and very specialised groups. With advance notice tutors can make arrangements for pupils to change their music time temporarily so that, for example, the music wing and I are left free for a musical afternoon on the theme of 'The First World War' with a group of thirty or so pupils and their tutor. The regular groups, therefore, usually of about ten to fifteen pupils, are the basis of the music provision. On top of this come the 'casual' visitors — pupils who are known to be able to use their time profitably or with particular directions from their tutors as to their requirements. These on average make five to ten extra and include pupils who in fact visit us fairly regularly. Occasionally there may be thirty or thirty-five pupils engaged in various activities in the music wing, without any other member of staff present.

'Friend groups'. One of the most important results of individualised timetabling has been the effect of 'friend groups'. For instance Rob (see below) did not start musical activities without his mates and probably would not have done so. Later in the year he in turn introduced new friends to music activities. Occasionally the process can be reversed and bored friends can press interested pupils to drop an interest — but one can usually see this coming. Particularly curious are the fourteen- to sixteen-year-old 'friend groups' among the girls, which often comprise five to eight individuals. These never seem to split up, but their members are ready to take on anything, whereas individually they would just retreat.

Staffing. Countesthorpe has one music teacher for over 750 pupils aged fourteen to eighteen years, which is obviously inadequate unless there is suitable help from other teachers. My policy has been to encourage this help and to support the prior claim of the team-teachers concerning staffing and allocation of allowances: they have the most difficult job. All the same, the music department heads the list for extra specialist staff. The way in which other teachers can help is best illustrated by a particular case.

Adam T.

Adam is not a pupil but one of the team-teachers who specialises in maths. Like the other team-teachers he helps to teach social studies and English in the general context of humanities, including some drama, science, art and, in his case, music. The team-teachers are the king-pins of the Countesthorpe system and are unusually dedicated and versatile. For the music department to do its job properly it is necessary that these tutors continually encourage their pupils to follow out music activities by making arrangements with me or by bringing groups to the music wing themselves for introductory sessions, usually involving improvisatory activities.

Adam is a bluegrass guitarist, banjo player and singer and has timetabled himself to be in the music wing for one period each week. At this time he encourages some of the pupils in his team who have not chosen other options to join us in the music wing. Obviously because he knows his pupils he has a better chance to find their interests, and in some cases is able to help them himself. Later in the year he may have run out of takers from his own team and he may have to give up his music wing visits. But with luck he can continue to help out, particularly with guitar techniques and his own repertoire of country and western songs. At the time of writing, this arrangement is a luxury but this seems to be the way the music department will expand its teaching force — that is, by timetabling other team-teachers to take responsibility for music activities according to their talents.

The music wing is also fortunate in having a relatively large number of visitors from outside who, like the pupils who have officially left, help the younger pupils with their technical skills and demonstrate their own enthusiasms — as well as enjoying themselves. Relatively insignificant happenings, like two very accomplished teachers playing a sonata for cello and piano, a visiting professional guitarist playing like Django Reinhardt, a visiting saxophonist putting new life into a rock group, all provide the unexpectedness and stimulus for music making.

Example of a busy session

Apart from these occasional arrangements with tutors all teachers are encouraged to visit the music wing regularly, particularly when we are very busy. During one such period last term, I listed the following activities:

Room A (a moderately sized carpeted gramophone room). One pupil listening to a Brahms symphony but researching Groves Dictionary for some information about St Mark's, Venice — work suggested at the large-group lesson.

Room B (a small room with a small electronic organ). Two fourth-year boys reading notation (with some note-names written in) from a duplicated sheet of 'Silent Night'.

Room C (a small room, carpeted and with wall curtains, used for stereo recording, mixing and dubbing). A sixth-year pupil is using acoustic guitar, bass guitar, tambourine and voice to record his own song. He has managed to record voice, guitar and a friend playing tambourine. Now he is superimposing the bass and later will add another vocal part.

Studio 2 (a classroom-sized carpeted teaching room). A team-teacher with his 'A' level English group is making atmospheric music to a Blake poem using, among other things, metallophones, synthesiser, cello, bass and bassoon.

Studio 1 (a very large airy room). Three fourth-year drummers and one fifth-year are taking turns to practise drums. One is using a tuition book, the others are practising a new rhythmic riff demonstrated by the fifth-year pupil. He alternates between this and the following group.

Practice Room 1. A fifth-year team-tutor (Adam), on piano, is leading a group of three quite accomplished guitarists, a boy on string bass and one playing mouth organ in a rendering of 'The Christian Life'.

Practice Room 2. A fifth-year girl is practising flute while two others do some humanities work.

Practice Room 3. Seventh-year Shaun quietly practises a Bach invention on guitar.

Practice Room 4. Three fifth-years and a sixth-year pupil are practising guitar. The fifth-year boys are going through a Beatles book which has 'chord windows'. But for the moment they have persuaded the sixth-year to sing and play a song composed by a friend, and his finger work is the cause for much questioning.

Practice Room 5. Two fifth-year girls are playing an arrangement on the piano of 'Air on a G String' which I have taught them by rote. Next I shall show them a chord sequence and give them some words to attempt a song.

Practice Room 6. Empty.

Practice Room 7. One fifth-year boy is realising the melody and chord symbols of 'Windmills of my Mind' on piano. He incorporates the chords in the right-hand melody and plays a bass line with his left hand.

Further insight into our work can best be given by detailed accounts of the experience of a range of pupils. This should also illustrate the way in which individualised and self-directed activity leads naturally to the more advanced concepts and widening of experience which are the concern of any music course, no matter what its method of instruction may be.

Nine profiles of pupils in the life of Countesthorpe College music department

Dene G.

Dene's family live in a local council estate. They have a collection of pop lyrics going back to the fifties — the *Words/Record Song Book* (Felix McGlennon Ltd). Just before coming to the school Dene and four friends had told their prospective tutor that they wouldn't mind doing some music. So they were timetabled to 'do music' at a time in the week which I had agreed to and when there were few other subject options.

Basic curriculum organisation. Dene came to the department as a member of the fourth year which, like the fifth, was divided into two teams, each of about 180 pupils. Each team with six tutors had a purpose-built area they could call home. The tutors, who in simplified terms were maths, English and social studies specialists, were timetabled together with their own tutor group of thirty pupils for half the week; thus a humanities mini-school operated for half the week, in which tutors could get to know their pupils and make arrangements among themselves for humanities provision. The other half of the pupils' week was a series of optional subjects, courses and occasional activities; as well as this, one or more tutors were always available in the home areas for those not opting for anything. Usually the options at the beginning of the year were varied and attractive but a limited range of options would sometimes arise — perhaps only physical education, parentcraft and music.

First taste of music activities. At such a time Dene and his friends first appeared with fifteen others, mostly new and unknown quantities. Dene's friends, like many new fourth-year pupils, were attracted to the music wing by the cultural image — guitars, drums, amplified equipment and perhaps its reputation for the music produced. They all said they wanted to learn guitar except Dene. He at first seemed a little hopeless standing on the sidelines; but the others were like ducks to water. In the company of the whole group they were given guitars, shown how to play two chords and given three worksheets. One was of simple chord 'windows', another was a selection of verses with directions for rhythmically chanting and strumming an accompaniment and the third was a version of 'Tom Dooley'. An old hand, a fifth-year guitarist, was asked to sit in with them when they went off to practise. The rest, who were new, stayed with me to do a group rendering of 'Spinning Wheel' (by Blood, Sweat and Tears). Each individual, according to his experience, was given a melodic line, chords or bass line, to play. This very repetitive piece is ideal for quick action and achievement. These introductory sessions are necessarily rather hectic and even chaotic but, though they cannot swim, no one is allowed to sink. With the help of duplicated materials and the example and aid of older hands, all the novices will have achieved enough by the end of their session to want to come back next week, and I will have learned enough about their inclinations and talents to make more suitable preparations and timetable arrangements.

Dene's friends stuck together. In another school they could well have found themselves working for examination results but in general regarding school as an irrelevance. Besides following their examination courses, here they were working hard and directing their own learning with the help of a range of materials and the example of a variety of older pupils as well as the guidance of a teacher. But Dene's inclinations did not become obvious until there was some music already going on. At that point he not only sang the tune but began to improvise words and embellish a melody line with considerable musicality. Next he was improvising melody lines to any chord sequence, which made him very popular with the other musicians. His spontaneous words at this stage were a succession of pop song clichés or simply 'doo-bahs'. (An analysis of Dene's musical development is given by Piers Spencer in chapter 5.)

His ability in other subjects was very limited but in music his intonation and ability to use his voice expressively was quite the opposite. Soon he was introduced to playing triads with a doubled bass note on the piano:

Example 1

This he came to hammer out slowly and regularly. Characteristically, he would start singing after the first two beats:

Example 2

The show must go   on _____

and usually moved the triad after two $^4_4$ bars. At first the harmonic movements were governed by their facility on the keyboard, so the most common sequence would be C, D minor, E minor, F, G etc. — to which words and melody would be improvised fluently and musically. These explorations continued, and with some help his keyboard technique became less restricted but remained his own. His improvisations rather reluctantly became a few complete songs. At one stage his mother wrote some words for him and these were used to form the basis of some songs played by his friends who then formed an amplified group consisting of two guitars, bass, drums and organ. This combination provided a boost to the guitarists whose technique suddenly improved dramatically. Unfortunately, 'Moggy' the drummer laid down a beat remarkable for its eccentricity and the guitarists looked around for a new outlet.

Dene has proved a rarity, a confident boy singer who had the common touch and could improvise. He was soon getting requests to join other instrumentalists. He was made the centre of an Elvis-type spoof musical where, with the strong backing of the school's best instrumentalists, he was in his element. The improvisation and composition continued with more adventurous harmony and remarkably, his own quite successful lyrics. He had always been strongly attracted by his heroes, Elvis, David Bowie and many others — in fact he found it difficult not to sound like one or other of them — and so his next 'Sounds' concert performance (see below) included 'Life on Mars' along with his own 'Now Summer's Gone Away'. The eventual line-up was piano, drums, synthesiser, tenor-sax, bass (the only player from the earlier group) and three harmonising vocalists.

Dene has since drawn other friends into the music wing and has generally given singing a boost. He will be leaving this year to become an assistant with the RSPCA but no doubt he will be back, like most of the musicians, in the evenings and holidays.

Joy M.

Joy is a member of the fifth year, the younger sister of a past pupil who did hardly anything in the sixth year but play guitar, piano and organ, and compose music for a very heavy electric rock group which still occasionally visits us. I believe the family has connections with a local church and brother and sister were choristers there. Along with a good proportion of our intake, Joy came to the school in the fourth year from a nearby high school (eleven to fourteen years). At her previous school she had been a leading light in the Gilbert and Sullivan productions and still takes part in local productions and singing competitions. Her brother made sure we knew of her and when the new fourth-years were each interviewed by their prospective tutors in July and told what was offered she expressed her interest in following some musical activity.

Like many academically-orientated pupils she found it difficult to justify to her parents time spent on a 'non-vocational' subject in the school. Joy wanted a course leading to an examination and one that was pretty structured since she was not an initiator of activities like her brother. There are plenty of pupils whose requirements are similar and although activities are initiated by the teacher in individual and small group activities, a large-group lesson is the most economical way of guaranteeing a breadth of listening experience. Joy and the other CSE candidates have therefore to attend a lesson of this type and also, by arrangement, one other period in the week when individualised activities will be followed. Joy plays the piano a little and reads music. During the 'individualised' lesson she has improved these techniques and gained some experience in keyboard harmony. We have made arrangements for two other girls to attend at the same time since all are good singers. Lately she has made up an arpeggio-like right-hand part to the chord sequence of Bach's A minor Prelude in Book 2 of the Forty-eight, invented a rhythm to a chord sequence from Mike Oldfield's 'Tubular Bells', taken part in a group involving organ, metallophones and synthesiser — making music to go with another girl's poem — and joined three other singers in singing Britten's 'Balulalow'. The other ten to fourteen pupils who regularly attend this session work in similar sized groups or by themselves on a wide range of activities in one of the seven small practice rooms or in the recording room; there are ample facilities.

In the fifth year Joy has become more confident and found new musical affiliations. She has found her voice will improvise an impromptu harmonising part and with one or two others she provides a much sought after vocal backing for the various compositions. Casual visits to the music wing have helped her ability to harmonise because she encounters a variety of people with whom she can join in.

The 'Sounds' concerts. Joy is used to public performances and, along with a small group of other girls who provide a vocal backing, has found participation in the 'Sounds' concerts a stimulus to take part in more elaborate arrangements of compositions. These concerts, of which there have been five in the last two years, were originally intended to provide an opportunity for the performance of original compositions in any medium. In fact, they have developed a unique character which must lie somewhere between John Cage's 'Theatre Piece', a school review, the Rolling Stones at the Empire Pool, a recital in the Purcell Room and a New Year's Eve party. Every one was said to be the last. The last three were organised entirely by the pupils with rigid adherence to democratic procedure. Some idea of the quality of the music and of the atmosphere of the concerts can be gained from side 2, track 1 of the accompanying recording.

Keith A.

Keith is out-going, the leader of a group of similar boys in the fifth year, all of whom have done some music activities at some time in school. He has always been an interested listener to whatever music came his way: this has been mostly radio and TV light music. He was introduced to music activities in the school four years ago when the school was still taking eleven- to thirteen-year-olds. Class lessons based on Paynter and Aston's *Sound and Silence* projects were his first experience of music in the new school; these lessons were compulsory in the first and second years. In the third year he opted to spend two periods (half a day altogether) in the music wing following similar activities but with more emphasis on group playing of arranged songs. As I see it, in group music making the style of the music is not so important providing it results in a sound that is good — so that everyone feels he has contributed something and feels the overall sound is really music. Thus Keith joined a group of about eight pupils who would do, for example, 'Everybody's Talking At Me' with everybody singing, two melody lines on piano, two guitars, one playing chords and one a simple counterpoint, string bass, tambourine and chords on electric organ. Later, the same kind of group would try an arrangement with similar instrumentation of, say, Bach's D major Gavotte from the Third Suite. More adventurous group work followed with improvisations of various kinds. The large group eventually divided up.

At this point Keith preferred keyboards, and as in the fourth year the facilities in the wing were made entirely available to the Upper School, Keith made use of the piano, organ and guitar at various times in the week. Usually he kept to an agreed timetable to ensure the availability of instruments and my attention, but he would also appear at other unscheduled times. Such casual visits meant that he was missing something he usually attended. At these times he knew he would be questioned and any suspicion of broken commitments would be taken up with his tutor later. It soon becomes clear who skives and who takes the opportunity of getting in a bit of music when the other work has been finished.

Keith's particular inclination has been to reproduce television advertisement jingles on the piano or guitar. This he manages with great melodic accuracy and is not satisfied with less. His continuous efforts in this direction have gained for him a more precise sense of tonality as well as experience in the use of common modes and the implied chords. He has also gained some insight into the importance of balance of the various elements, of instrumentation and counter-melodies. The influence of television is seen in his asking to be shown how to play theme tunes and current popular music. It was Scott Joplin who provided, in simplified form, Keith's most complete piano piece (apart from Beethoven whose 'Für Elise' he heard me play one day, and was convinced that its first section was worth learning!). It was the accomplishment gained in these activities which gave him the confidence to join our Mode III CSE course for, like many others, he did not previously see himself as a musician.

As a part of the requirements of the Mode III course Keith was obliged to attend the weekly large-group lesson which is vertically mixed, fourth to seventh years, and usually takes in twenty to twenty-five pupils, or about forty different pupils over the year. It is the only regular teacher-centred lesson provided in the department, though I am quite likely to bring together diverse groups occasionally for a teach-in. It was instituted to broaden the pupils' experience and though it is only obligatory for those following the Mode III CSE course, it also attracts most of those who have a strong interest in music.

Despite the discussion in this session and the activities of the group arising from it – such as attempts to imitate Gryphon's 'Pastyme with Good Companye' – Keith still prefers to listen rather than to play a part. Though the session has bred various new combinations of instrumentalists, Keith remains a solitary figure who nevertheless discusses more music now and tries to play more. One of the other demands of the Mode III, to perform a composition, has stimulated Keith into getting together his own guitar piece. This turns out to be a very quiet, sensitive, finger-picked sequence derived from the natural finger positions of the left hand on the guitar and heavily influenced by the 'Some cigars need to be taken seriously' advertisement, which contains a sequence of Bach-like broken chords. Keith will probably leave this year, taking four or five 'O' levels or CSEs. Music will always be quite important to him.

The first 'group harmony' activities. Keith's experience illustrates clearly why we have encouraged all forms of musical interest, including the most commercial pop. At a certain point I came to feel that we could do something about the disparity between the musical lives of the pupils out of school and in school. Since musical education for the over-fourteens was concerned mainly with a preparation for post-school leisure it was unrealistic to ignore the music they were listening to out of school and would continue to be listening to, or at least be bombarded with, after leaving. With the powerful influence of broadcasting media, popular music of all kinds has become a major part of our lives. It is difficult for teachers to touch pop music, not only because they are no longer musically young but also because of certain non-musical characteristics in pop, which are related to the adolescent's need for an independent identity. Also commercial exploitation has made pop — as it has other popular music — disreputable. Yet thanks to the dominance of younger musicians and to the continuing influence of Afro-American musical values, pop and rock music have tremendous vitality. The music teacher's job is to educate and to combat the limiting and desensitising aspects of the mass-media presentation of pop. By no means every pupil is greatly affected by the broadcasting media or by pop music or is a follower of the youth culture, but where they are, as Keith's experience shows, it may be necessary to begin their musical education by starting from what their interest actually is.

Barbara S.

Barbara, one of a prosperous and educationally aware family, is sixteen and now in the sixth year. Her younger brother plays tenor saxophone and is the best improviser we have had here. His approach is 'play as you feel'; he is scornful of 'the dots' and very avant garde in his musical tastes. Barbara does not have her brother's ability to improvise but is an excellent player in the orchestral mould though she does not play in our High/Upper School orchestra. Her attitude to music has become as radical as her brother's, the result of a developing social awareness and a reaction to what she sees as the smugness of the local county orchestra set-up. She has had tuition on the oboe and bassoon for many years, and now plays with a group at the local university. At school she had joined in everything, playing oboe, bassoon, recorder and alto saxophone. For our Mode III examination she chose to play an unusual piece for oboe and piano by John Paynter, of which I knew nothing. To gain its effect the piece employs the electrically amplified harmonics of the piano which are created by the oboe line. Her only timetabled contact with the department has been in the large-group lesson; otherwise she has played with instrumental groups of every kind, playing music from Walton's 'Façade' via a score of trio sonatas to melodic lines in the pupils' arrangements of their songs. It is typical of her approach that after improvising a while she asked for an oboe line to be written for her rather than improvise in the accompaniment to a song composed by a friend. This can be heard on side 2, track 1 of the accompanying recording.

Barbara is happier with the Stockhausen end of the improvisation spectrum; the harmonic kind of improvisation required for more traditionally rooted music requires a special kind of musical development. This can take place naturally but is obviously promoted by early choral experience and musical education such as

Orff's 'Schulwerk'. Although receiving tuition on orchestral instruments it seems that Barbara has missed an important element in her musical education.

The department's image. Perhaps we should take some of the blame ourselves since Barbara has been with us since her second year (from the age of twelve plus, when we still had an eleven to fourteen intake). She received a mixture of Orff, *Sound and Silence* and something of ourselves in her first year of compulsory music education here, but after that she did not opt to do music at all until the fifth year. Although we are getting over this problem, it had previously been noticeable that the image projected by the music wing was keeping some pupils away. Quite justifiably there was a feeling that a lot of the music played there was pop, that there were a lot of 'hard' boys there, that at one point no examination courses were being followed and that it did not seem like school at all. Quite unjustifiably it was sometimes felt that you were not welcome if you liked anything but pop, that only the drop-outs used the music wing and that nobody did any work. In fact it seemed that you had to be on one side of a socio-cultural fence: youth culture/pop/hard boys from the estate, versus orchestral players/GCE candidates/smart girls from the suburbs. It was not until the advent of the sixth year that a less schizoid image was established and the department really began to have its own very catholic identity along with the rest of the school.

But still we have the problems of the passive individual who does not do well in an often self-directing situation and also the exam-orientated pupil who has the ability to take exam courses and sees no other value in education. Both have tended to shy away from the music wing.

Rob G.

Rob, a fifth-year entering the school the year before last, was, like Dene and his friends, introduced into the music wing by his tutor at a rather crowded time of the week. These first weeks are heavily populated in the music wing, partly because the activities have a reputation among the newcomers and partly because music is regarded as a soft option. Later, numbers tend to fall, partly because it becomes obvious that inactivity is only condoned in those who are usually active and also because interest is not sustained and places remain unfilled as a result of bad communications between the tutors and myself. Every pupil has an individual timetable and until he is well known by the specialist teacher cannot change his timetable without his tutor's written approval.

Disruptive pupils. Rob was what could euphemistically be termed a 'disruptive pupil' and used every cunning device to persuade me that he had his tutor's permission to 'do music', whenever he was skiving. His wanting to 'do music' however was not simply a negative choice; it was always a genuine desire to make rather than break — although one had to tolerate both on occasions. In a recent General Inspection I noticed the music HMI jot down on his pad, on appraising Rob's behaviour, 'Impossible boys!' (Rob had a friend with him.)

In the fourth year his efforts to make music or anything else were fitful, vigorous and, as might be expected, demanding of continuous attention. How could this be accommodated in a situation where no one was under constant supervision and where the teacher's time had to be shared between five or six groups each using expensive equipment? The answer lies in the constitution of the total group. Whatever the arrangements, Rob could not get continuous attention but he could be visited frequently, be taken around and be given tasks on a keyboard. It was carefully explained that the keyboard had cost £4 per note and it was demonstrated to be worth every penny. His inclination was similar to Keith's: he would only have to hear a piece of music to plead, 'Teach us it, Malc, show us'. His tastes were wider than Keith's but, like him, Rob would not ask another pupil to show him how; instead he would look on admiringly at anyone playing anything. He would not be satisfied until he got it right and the trick was to leave him when he knew it all but still needed practice. There are not more than a dozen boys as difficult as Rob in the school; if they can be spread thinly there is little problem in integrating them into the department's activities. Indeed, in considering 'disruptive pupils' I would like to make the point that any group of pupils can become bored or inactive when they are directing their own activities with only the intermittent attention of a teacher. Boredom not only means no learning but can lead to minor vandalism with which we were plagued in our early years. It has now become rare, partly owing to the positive atmosphere generated by the older pupils. 'Out of sight, out of mind', sharing out attention, switching from the world of one group's activities to another are all difficulties that the teacher with some experience can overcome.

Rob now also plays guitar quite well and although still not reading music has, like Keith, managed to memorise a good range of music. He is just beginning to get satisfaction from extended keyboard improvisation in which he engages himself very sensitively. I would guess that he will become a guitarist/singer in a few months' time. Finally, I believe it is not coincidental that during his last year Rob's 'illegal' casual visits have been formalised. He is not at all disruptive and his enthusiasm for learning musical 'quotes' has increased.

Jim S.

Jim has had a chequered musical career since he joined us in our first year five years ago. Coming from a family in the prosperous surrounding neighbourhood of Countesthorpe itself, his junior school had a strong tradition of orchestral tuition. He had been taught the violin for a year or two and now wished to take up the cello on transferring to the new school, which at that time was providing for eleven to fourteens. Since then he has dropped cello, started an 'O' level course, though not finished it, taken up guitar playing quite seriously but stopped and for the last two years has concentrated on electronic sounds. Early on he showed a flair for organising unusual musical structures and a strong interest in avant garde compositions.

Jim found no difficulty of course in later years in coming back to ask for help in making music for, say, a poem or around an idea he had. He knew what my reaction would be and he had done it successfully before. But most pupils do not find enough motivation in the idea of making music to a given pretext or structure – e.g. music to describe the aftermath of an atomic explosion – to move themselves to the music wing or even when they are *in* the music wing. These kind of activities are usually teacher-initiated or at least teacher-organised. They are given priority because they often involve pupils who would not otherwise do any music and because they expand the range of the pupils' musical language which for many is restricted to diatonic modes and a folk/pop style.

There are a number of paths to these activities. The teams have been given an extensive list of ideas which I have found stimulate musical activities, as well as a list of the materials in the department. This encourages teachers to bring groups to the music wing and to send pupils to do things. Usually such visitors want to record their own play or poem with music and effects, or to listen to records of music associated with English work. We have work sheets, on such subjects as War, Railways, Fear and Storms, designed for self-directed work including listening to music. There are also suggestions for expressive work in music, words and plastic arts.

Most activities initiated by me which need a pretext or written structure make use of poetry, duplicated sheets or printed material such as Brian Dennis's 'Stars', i.e. a simple structure with directions clearly set out. But on the whole activities arise from a discussion of ideas. Large group improvisations are sometimes planned, occasionally in the nearby windowless drama workshop, on general themes such as 'A Nightmare'. Often they tend towards drama (e.g. a chant beginning with everyone seated round twelve candles), or towards theatre (e.g. a Cage-like piece for transistor radios on the roof).

Electronics and recording. The preponderance of boys doing music here is partly a result of the emphasis placed on composition and improvisation, and it has been pointed out to me that many of the boys that choose to do control technology also regularly do music. Jim is a 'constructor' and has made a keyboard synthesiser of modest performance among other gadgets. His only musical activity during the fifth year was to create some electronic music using radio noise and Philicorda organ as sources and a Revox stereo recorder for echo and editing. At first the result of a lot of work was not impressive but some time later the department got its own small keyboard synthesiser – a 'Minikorg' costing about £300 (1974 price) and widely available. It produces sounds from pure tones which can be coloured to such an extent that a single key depressed on the keyboard can sound like a helicopter landing – but that is just a sound effect. Its real value is musical, for though mastering its technique is painless and stimulating in itself, synthesising music emphasises creative ability. There are no excuses for the player (or rather composer) – he always gets good sounds, but it is up to him whether he gets music. (The synthesiser can be heard on side 2, track 4 of the accompanying recording.)

With this acquisition Jim tried again. Despite discussions he restricted himself to the synthesiser and the very organ-sounding organ. This time the structure was effective if inconcise. All in all, Jim has been left too much to his own devices and has not received enough guidance; this is an obvious danger in our system where self-directing pupils are doing very constructive things but really are making technical progress more slowly than they would be in more usual circumstances of 'the better you are, the more teacher-time you get'. The result of Jim's work can be heard on side 2, track 2 of the accompanying recording.

Most of the serious stereo recording is done to a very high technical standard in a small recording room; the pupils have fitted it out with wall curtains and it contains some modest but good quality equipment. The Revox tape-recorder has proved to be the most essential item of equipment. It is by far the most effective way of improving the standard of presentation of a large number of small group performances. It also enables one person to build up a multi-tracked performance. Examples of this technique are given on side 2, tracks 3 and 4 of the recording.

If Jim did not receive adequate guidance for his electronic tape, at least his equipment was good. The recording side of his music activities is very competent, stimulated by the 'Sounds' concerts which require a sophisticated public-address system as well as recording arrangements. Jim has always been in charge of this and now has apprentices to receive the word. One concert achieved the distinction of requiring fourteen microphones: but it resulted in the production of a record of excellent recording standard.

Since we acquired the Minikorg synthesising keyboard Jim has become a more active musician, joining in with various groups and demonstrating an ear for the apt use of this unique instrument, which requires some conception of the sound about to be made before it is actually synthesised.

Shaun P.

Shaun is also a local boy, aged seventeen, of very high general ability. He is taking three science 'A' levels after a tussle in the sixth year when he wanted to do 'A' level music. In the fifth year he did no music during school time but turned up regularly after school to practise piano. After a few weeks he found a local piano teacher and, doing his practice regularly after school, made rapid progress. He also took up guitar and attended an evening class here. In the sixth year he timetabled himself with a group of other sixth-years for group music activities with the vague intention also of following our CSE course, which I mentioned in connection with Keith.

Examination courses. The Countesthorpe College Mode III music syllabus was devised to fit the particular character of the school. The most important parts of the exam consist of two performances, one in November, one in March, which may be group performances; these are marked on one set of criteria if the music is an original composition and another if not. Also, there is a test of ability to add vocally or on any instrument a second melody line, chords or bass line to a melody played by the examiner and worked on with him. The syllabus was presented to the local CSE Board to give the course extra purpose in the eyes of the pupils, who are used to questioning the reasons for doing activities set them. In music the situation is confused by the element of taste, and the question arises in the pupils' minds 'If I am not enjoying it why am I doing music?' So the introduction of a breadth of musical culture to a large group of individuals in our circumstances requires an interesting presentation, the generation of a lot of good feeling and tolerance and the opportunity for a qualification at the end — otherwise they would eventually vote with their feet.

A further reason for establishing a CSE course was a call from a small but vocal minority of pupils for GCE 'O' and 'A' level courses. Especially with the advent of RoSLA, it is difficult to justify a regular teacher—pupil ratio of five individuals or less and so, after examining the individual's reasons for the request for GCE courses, arrangements have been made as far as possible to provide appropriate activities for these pupils. The CSE course has become more like a Certificate of Secondary Education/Certificate of Extended Education course involving all four years in the joint weekly lesson and at least one other session for individual work. The qualification is in reality insignificant, but the breadth of study is invaluable to any pupil who can find interest in other musicians' techniques, be convinced that a hit is worth a few misses, or be persuaded that it is useful to know about music one does not particularly enjoy yet.

Shaun attends the large-group lesson and also spends as much time as he can joining in freer-type improvisations, reading classical guitar music, making a lot of transcriptions from piano music and doing some compositions. He has, in fact, become not a pianist but an excellent classical guitarist with already wide experience in playing and listening. In this his last year, he pressed very strongly with two other boys who were a year younger to follow an 'A' level music course. Shaun was ready to drop his intention to become a doctor and wanted to become a professional guitarist. He was particularly keen to do composition. With adequate attention, he could have completed an 'A' level course in music quite easily in eight months and it was distressing that I was not able to give enough of my time to provide it for him and the other sixth-year boys. This is as far as mixed-group teaching can compromise; although in other subjects it has proved quite possible to teach 'A' level candidates along with CSE and non-examination pupils, and to teach 'A' level candidates along with well-motivated non-'A' level pupils, in music the disparity between the GCE syllabuses and the requirements of the majority of even musically active pupils is so great as to be irreconcilable. The situation has been somewhat better with 'O' level music courses which have been followed by small groups, mostly in evening lessons; they will continue in the future if numbers are sufficient.

As it has turned out, the other two boys who wanted to do music 'A' level travel to another school for their music 'A' level lessons — an arrangement which, although they hate the change in teaching method, must for most school pupils be inevitable when involving such a very specialised pursuit. Shaun, I feel, has not only made the right vocational choice in returning to his science 'A' levels, but has benefited from the 'activity' approach. However, I must concede that a perfect musical education would provide him with more depth than we are providing at the moment.

Kev H.

Kev is also in the seventh year. He comes from a home on the local council estate and has been with us for just over three years. His first introduction to the music wing was late in the first term when his tutor personally introduced him to me saying that he was particularly interested in avant garde music. This kind of introduction is common enough, though usually it is by note or by previous arrangement: it goes on throughout the year. If I cannot cope with the extra pupils immediately, I at least make arrangements with them to come at another time.

It was unusual however for a pupil already to have an interest in avant garde music and Kev was knowledgeably talking about Stockhausen and Feldman. It was not until much later that I discovered he was as much an authority on pop and rock music. The first weeks were awkward; we talked about modern music and listened to records but nothing got going. I asked his tutor to keep encouraging his attendance. He came again and we talked about the Debussy concert he had been to the previous night at the local concert hall: he obviously regarded me only as a classical musician. His father apparently took him to every concert that was on in Leicester from King Crimson to the Amsterdam Concertgebouw. He began to use the solitude of the practice rooms for his writing which was endless, rather surreal but always sincere and often inspired. Song writing was suggested but Kev's highly self-critical habits have made him reject scores of attempts at songs mostly at the words stage. The one or two he has produced have rhythmic and reasonably conventional accompaniments. However the guitar — which he was attracted to — was an instrument which suggested a language to him that was not suitable for song accompaniment. Kev used the fingerboard like a passionate cellist. Over the next two years he gained confidence and became 'king' of the more avant garde jams.

Jams. He thus fitted in with the more spontaneous musical happenings which frequently occur, often arising from the sixth year. Finding themselves a viable group musically when gathered in the sixth-year area or already in the music wing, they frequently decide to 'have a jam'. This can mean anything from an indulgent but therapeutic mêlée to a very correct rendering of a Rory Gallagher track including 'breaks'; structures range from the twelve-bar blues or a two-chord riff to a descending Aeolian bass line for a structure. More often there is someone with a less conventional idea. Other music will arise from pretexts presented to them by a teacher lately or in times past — structures such as music for Ariel's flight, Stockhausen's

YLEM, a Mike Oldfield or a Purcell ostinato/riff, or simply an instruction like 'Start with silence and play *pianissimo*'. Some jams arise from the situation: everything is way out of tune, the stereo tape recorder is in the room and can provide echo, a recorder mouth-piece instigates swooping-sound ideas, or perhaps everybody has to play very quietly, owing to recording next door. A true 'jam' aims to express feelings spontaneously and though this often develops into 'communicating music' (i.e., it sounds good to the listener), its real purpose is to provide a living relationship between the players. An excerpt from a jam is included on side 2, track 5 of the recording.

Sixth-year influence. Kev's influence on this situation has been considerable. Whereas, on seeing a young newcomer pick up an electric guitar, my first reaction would be, 'Stop, be careful', Kev and most pupils' reaction was more on the lines of, 'OK, join in if you can stand the pace'. Young pupils always seem readily to respect technical ability especially when it is part of their own culture. Kev still does not know the names of the chords he is playing — usually one would find it difficult to give them a name. He has affected the atmosphere of the music wing, as all pupils do to some extent, so that it is more a place for playing what you feel. He has taken advantage of the prevailing atmosphere of constructive freedom and of security, a condition essential for the often very personal nature of musical expression. It is clear that having had time to establish their own culture and skills, the seventeen- to eighteen-year-olds are in a very influential position. Though the younger pupils may make signs of rejection, they closely imitate the life-style of the older pupils. This influence requires some moderation but in the difficult period of early adolescence the stable society of the older pupils is essential. If this unnatural splitting off of age groups must occur it should not occur at the age of sixteen.

Kev's most recent piece of work was very different, and arose with the help of a group of friends in the music wing, from an idea he had talked about months ago. Briefly, Mr Everyman goes into a seedy cinema, whose manager is God. The only innocent characters are the projectionist and the ice-cream sales girl who are in love: God decides to 'cut the goodies', close the show and start again with the sales girl and the projectionist. This was rehearsed by Kev's describing the plot and general format, reading God's part and handing out two short scripts for the major characters, but the music was left entirely to the performers — including bassoon, saxophone, synthesiser, two pianos, electric guitar, bass guitar and beer bottle. The result, performed at the last 'Sounds' concert was untidy but refreshing. The original concept really needed to be in the film medium. Kev will leave this year (at least officially) to become, he says, an office cleaner.

Adrian B.

Adrian officially left the school last spring at the age of seventeen but he keeps his drum set at the school and spends a good deal of time here when he is not working, especially at weekends. He has been the mainstay of a number of rock groups over the past four years or so and intends to become a professional drummer. Lately he has been able to come in during the school day and has given invaluable assistance to aspiring drummers. He has also got a group of them to turn up regularly in the evening for a drum jam and the group recently put on a performance at a concert.

Adrian remembers with nostalgia his days as a choirboy. When he joined us in our opening year he was in the fourth year and had done no musical activity for about three years, except for a short spell learning trombone. His main problem was a common one in fourth-year boys: he could not commit himself to any regular activity without a lot of chasing up. Within a year or so most of his time was spent making music: it was something at which he excelled and to which he gradually became more committed. His fond thoughts for his choirboy days were partly a result of his love for music and partly a longing for a more ordered world than he found in his middle adolescence, a period during which his mother had left the family. I would be deeply disturbed if I felt that this situation might be exacerbated by what Dr Rhodes Boyson has termed 'the pathless desert' of individualised curriculum where pupils are 'craving for order'. Certainly it is just possible that an authoritarian system would have produced short-term results in the form of examination passes. However, in the long term I have no hesitation in saying that his self-directed musical activities in school have given him order for the future in terms of a sense of values and self-respect.

Adrian is one of a number of ex-pupils who regularly revisit the music wing. Though this occurs mostly at weekends, holidays and in the evening, it can also happen during school hours with short university terms, occasional unemployment, half days and part-time attendance at jobs. These ex-pupils are of great help in establishing an adult atmosphere and exemplifying technical standards. Their attendance demonstrates one of the ways a large school can genuinely act as a community college.

Before coming to Countesthorpe I taught music in conventional secondary schools in Birmingham for a number of years; I know how different our organisation here is and how difficult it is to obtain these conditions. The Leicestershire Education Authority were courageous in setting up the school and generous in providing a music wing where individual and group activities could flourish. In my own view it has been successful in some ways, though not in others: we keep trying. I hope more schools, and particularly more departments of music, can find something of value in our experiences.

The last word I leave with Adrian who, after reading the draft of this manuscript, commented: 'It's true, but it's oversimplified. And it's all . . . "good". It doesn't tell you the wrong things.' (!)

7 The presentation of pop music

TONY ROBINS

Introduction

My exhilarating, challenging exploration of pop music was sparked off not by a change of heart or a radical reassessment of taste, but by a change of instrument.

The significance of the change from the keyboard to the guitar is, in retrospect, quite astonishing; it was probably the most important single factor in my musical development. It opened up a whole new world of sound experience and, as proficiency and skill developed, a subconscious but positive affinity with other styles and concepts of musical expression blossomed. In particular, lute transcriptions of Renaissance music gave that period an added lustre, the preludes and studies of Heitor Villa-Lobos disturbed and re-orientated my conception of dissonance and the gravel voice and aggressive playing of Bob Dylan, together with the poetry of his lyrics, fell on a by then fertile imagination and an expanding appetite. From there it was a short step to seek out the best of pop music.

It was fortuitous that my late discovery of the guitar should coincide with the mid-sixties folk boom, spearheaded by Dylan, and that his subsequent development into folk rock carried me along with it. In a very short space of time, I found myself on the inside looking out, and what I found there pleased me — musicians of the calibre of Joan Baez, Leonard Cohen, Ralph McTell, Tom Paxton, Joni Mitchell, Buffy Sainte-Marie, Randy Newman, Carly Simon and James Taylor. The last of these has been remarkably important in my presentation of pop music, since he makes no pretence to greatness. His music, though limited, has been an inspiration to many young, aspiring musicians. It is accomplished and efficient in the folk rock idiom, and though Taylor's lyrics are not comparable in quality to those of Dylan, they often contain a subdued strength, and recognise qualities of the human condition that echo the teenager's own experience. On the guitar, he does simple things well.

A predominant insight which I have gained is that pop music requires a very precise, accurate and disciplined approach. Very rarely will a piecemeal arrangement suffice — one needs written arrangements for larger groups of school musicians, since improvisation is the fruit of acquired skills and years of experience. The only time I omitted to write out some parts and did not attend to the finer details on others, the result was a disastrous recording session, demanding over a dozen 'takes' of the same piece.

An interest in one particular idiom does not mean that other groups, composers or styles have no place in my concept of pop music – quite the reverse, in fact. Pop ballads are occasionally worthy of consideration; Tamla Motown, at its best, has a drive that is infectious and I confess to a special weakness for the 'neo-classical' French composers of pop standards, such as Francis Lai and Michel Legrand. Rock 'n'roll too, has a distinctive beat and style which, if used sparingly, can be an attractive highlight of a performance; in addition, the influence of the very fine Bossa Nova exponents – Antonio Carlos Jobim, Laurindo Almeida and João Gilberto – is constantly evident in many pop rhythms. The subtle and delicate flavour of the astonishing sound experience that some progressive rock contains in groups like Santana, and the characteristic approach and musicianship of groups like Focus, are all there for the listening, and are all elements which will naturally colour one's own approach to pop music.

A brief apprenticeship

My first serious attempt at vocal arrangement started at college with the old 1930s song, 'Pick Yourself Up'. I soon found that the idiom presented great difficulties to the classical music student. This unaccompanied five-part arrangement (SSATB) demanded a strict tempo and, because the performers felt unable to relax and to relinquish the clearly defined interpretative approaches of their classical training, advancing and retarding the beat within the strict tempo framework caused immense problems. Every quaver tied over the bar line had to be analysed before we could attempt relatively simple syncopation – something instinctively felt by the jazz greats. Our stage of rhythmic development was almost back in the pre-Scott Joplin era; his 'School of Ragtime Exercises' could no doubt have been gainfully employed. Then came the problems of chromatic harmony in similar and contrary motion, not to mention intervals of major seventh, major ninth, eleventh and thirteenth. As an introduction to dissonance, we attempted and just about succeeded in doing what Charles Ives' father had his son working at in the 1880s, namely, singing 'America' (the tune of our own national anthem) in C major, with the accompaniment on piano in A flat major. As far as 'Pick Yourself Up' was concerned, after two solid hours' practice it barely got off the ground.

I concluded, therefore, that a traditional background in harmony and musicianship was of no great value in the pursuit of performance of pop music, and that unskilled participants with an intuitive understanding and love of the idiom were probably a better proposition.

And so to school

At my first teaching post (in an eleven to eighteen comprehensive school), I started in a small way to put into practice my central idea — the formation of a choral and instrumental group. For too long, it seemed to me, these two fundamentals of musical performance had been kept apart (except for yearly performances of musicals, Gilbert and Sullivan works and other prestige productions) whereas I wanted this type of music making to become a regular activity in the musical life of the school, and not just a once-a-year event. I was immensely surprised (somewhat naïvely in retrospect) to find that, for attempting to operate in what I considered to be a practical, sensible and worthwhile area of musical expression, I was classified as a radical — either dangerous, mad or both.

The choral and instrumental group needed to employ two basic ingredients — voices in unison, or in two or three parts and a rhythm group consisting of piano, electric lead and electric bass guitars and drums. In addition, I could include, where appropriate and at hand, any other instrumentalist playing a counter melody or harmonic progression as well as solos. This was and still is a fairly onerous task, involving a careful choice of piece (primarily, one good enough for us to live with for any length of time), its arrangement in terms of the musicians at my disposal, and subsequently the problems of getting over ideas and concepts to the performers.

The rhythm group

A rhythm group such as I have outlined is essential, the backbone of the sound one wishes to achieve. Strangely, perhaps, and happily, this has presented no problem so far as recruitment is concerned.

Pianists abound, fortunately, and their participation can be geared, if necessary, to simple chording. The right hand plays a chord in close harmony, with the left hand adding only a simple bass. Once the right hand has got used to such novelties as the augmented fifth and major seventh chords, the left hand can operate quite happily in single notes, octaves, fifths and sevenths. Your pianist, if he has a spark of initiative in him, will complain bitterly however at being fed this relentless and ultimately monotonous diet. So you 'stretch' him and, if the process continues unabated, you will soon be 'stretched' yourself to satisfy his expanding appetite. I am now quite normally writing parts for piano which were initially beyond my own capabilities. (I assess my own standard on piano as approximating to somewhere between Grade VII and VIII of the Associated Board Examinations, though I have never attempted them, and my playing is confined strictly to a utility role.). Any musician should be capable of writing parts superior to the normal sheet music available, though this type of song copy can occasionally be useful as a basis of arrangement. Sheet music is also useful for lyrics that are difficult to write down from records or cassettes.

Exactly the same process applies to the guitar. Your rhythm guitarist will need at least to have acquired a left hand capable of obtaining most of the open-string chords, and a right hand competent in the strumming style. This somewhat limits your choice of music, although it may well be sufficient for the requirements of a folk group; this can in turn serve to provide the nucleus of a choral and instrumental group, which you can introduce to more intricate and demanding styles. Eventually, the guitarist will have to come to terms with the barré in the left hand, and finger-style techniques for the right. At that point, you can then quite successfully employ two guitarists — one strumming the rhythm guitar part, the other developing from finger-style techniques towards lead guitar work. Your Guitar 1 will want lead guitar lines (melodies, counter melodies, riffs, etc.) and you will have to meet that require-ment. Guitar 2, (rhythm guitar), will usually have enough to do to justify his par-ticipation, but both of them will probably astound you with the ingenuity with which they add to and interpret your written part. Chord symbol notation (see Ed Lee's 'Note on conventions of notation in Afro-American music') is usually suf-ficient, for neither guitarist is likely to be a traditional musician. I have taught all my guitarists and bass guitarists myself (at least initially) and the common factor in their development has been an incredible work and assimilation rate, and a strength of purpose linked with immense self-discipline. At the end of this chapter I shall be looking at the development of the whole choral and instrumental group concept through the achievements of one such guitarist.

Drums, in my experience, present no problem — except that of affording them. Once the kit is in your school, and you open up its supervised use to any and every one, you will discover at least one talented pupil who probably had no idea of his own latent ability. Get him first of all to lay down a simple 'oom-pah' beat (feet only) to a pop record, the 'oom' being the right foot on bass drum, and the 'pah' the left foot on the hi-hat cymbals. If he can lay down a quaver pattern on top of that with stick or brush on the 'ride' cymbal, you are half-way there.

Example 1

Drums 'ride' cymbal
       hi-hat
       bass drum

What you are looking for at the beginning is an immaculately strict tempo — the fancy work can wait. I have been pleasantly surprised by the fact that all of the three drummers who have played for my rhythm group have been girls. It is a re-freshing novelty in a performance and adds immeasurably to the image of your group inside the school if she also happens to be reasonably good-looking! Do not underestimate 'image' — you can make or destroy your department on this alone, and certainly its importance in pop music is vital. Fortunately, I have never yet had to write out a drum part, though I have often talked over the piece with the resident percussionist, suggesting a lead-in phrase, beginnings, endings, counter rhythms, what should and should not be hit, when and where. Successive drummers have always found their own rhythmic approach from a combination, I suspect, of emulation and feeling. It is all quite simple as soon as you know what you want — in the words of Bob Dylan's classic 'A Hard Rain's A-gonna Fall': ' . . . and I'll know my song well before I start singing'.

It is not difficult to realise how the bass guitar, with its potentially deafening sound, can make or break a group. It is concerned with two vital roles — that of harmony, providing for the most part the root of the chords, and at the same time, and more importantly, linking with drums to establish a solid rhythm foundation. Because the bass guitar plays the roots of the harmonies, you can really only justify three-part singing, unless you give your bass singers a more diverting baritone role; to double the part is useless and wasteful in this style, as a general rule. The bass guitarist ultimately needs to be something of an egoist, but should also possess the ability to present his contribution with discretion. Initially, one who blends well is infinitely preferable, leaving the ego to emerge in its own good time. For the most part, bass guitar parts consist of obvious standard patterns and, as with some of the other instrumentalists, your only problem as the arranger will be to introduce sufficient variety into their parts by varying note order and rhythm patterns. Make sure you do not duplicate the left hand of the piano too much, otherwise your pianist will wonder why he should use two hands, when only one actually adds anything.

The choral group

What happens if only six regulars turn up to sing? The really nice thing about a choral group within a choral and instrumental group setting is that its size is so flexible. Assuming that one or two soloists emerge in the course of time (it would be more unreasonable to assume that they would not), the chorus can then become a 'backing' group — another pop phenomenon — and your six regulars can pair off in three parts, if necessary. Two-part singing is quite sufficient for a large selection of songs, and often unison is all that is required. Three-part chorus singing (SSA or SAT) is the maximum I would advise in this context. Of course, all this assumes the use of microphones and amplification; I shall be dealing with those important features later.

If your chorus is fairly large, then group songs, rather than solos with chorus backing, are yours for the picking. You can select from the work of the Edwin Hawkins singers and of Burt Bacharach; there are a large number of good standards, such as 'Windmills of your Mind' by Michel Legrand. The Henry Mancini Chorus and the Mike Sammes singers can give you useful ideas, but personally, I always steer well clear of Ray Conniff. I have listed the current repertoire of my choral and instrumental group at the end of this chapter; this should provide some guidance for teachers who are unfamiliar with this area of pop music.

Close harmony is preferable on the whole to wider spaced arrangements, otherwise you tend to clog up the piece for counter melodies and some of your more exotic touches from available woodwind and brass. The chorus, in my view, can often be used as a preferable alternative to strings. In pop music all string players for ballads, etc. are drawn from the leading symphony orchestras and their sound is often added to with echo and reverberation. You have no chance of producing comparable sounds in live performance, and little chance of doing so on tape or disc, even with expert mixing, over-tracking and other technical advantages. They are mainly used to induce a 'mushy, slushy' effect anyway, and I find I can live without them quite happily. 'Oohs' and 'Aahs' are a feature of chorus singing in the pop style, and there is really no need for you or your 'straight' singers to be ashamed of them. If you need them, use them — with liberal discretion — and you will soon find that they are accepted as a normal feature and essential part of your output.

Finally, it may be your personality which will recruit people to your group (never beg or continuously plead for support — you lose all credibility that way), but it will be your music, if it is good enough, that will keep your musicians coming along.

Other instruments

It is certainly beneficial to include the traditional instrumentalist in the group; there would be something drastically wrong if you found you could not. He is, for the most part, pleasantly surprised at the standard and quality demanded from him and works hard to become familiar with the idiom. In my own case, recruitment for the rhythm group (excepting the pianist) and the majority of the chorus, was from pupils without musical experience, and the addition of trained musicians with a classical background was of great social benefit as well as musically desirable. My guitarist laughed loud and long the first time he heard the sound of the bassoon, but the laughter, born of unfamiliarity, was soon transformed into a viable working relationship between the two, each subsequently admiring, using and blending their respective talents. Among the instruments I have or have had in the group are: flute, clarinet, oboe, bassoon, treble and tenor recorder, french horn, trumpet, trombone, E flat bass and sousaphone. They have never all been employed at the same time, unless they sing when they are not playing, but I have used any permutation of those instruments at my disposal. I am beginning to be competent enough to extend those musicians whose instruments I do not play, and the dividend reaped by the incessant demand on skill and expertise is that one's own instrumental proficiency develops in previously untapped areas. Consequently, I find myself a reasonable bass guitarist, have been known to maintain a steady if somewhat unimaginative beat on drums and have even managed to get the odd C major scale on the flute and worked with the flautist to develop flutter tonguing — all important side effects for the arranger.

Amplification

If you employ a drummer in your group — and pop music would usually sound lopsided without one — you are bound to need amplification equipment. If you need it for one instrument, you need it for most (if not all), and here our main problem of financing the venture begins. Also we encounter the important secondary considerations of balance, separation and the plague of 'feedback'.

Lead guitars should be of the semi-acoustic or solid electric types, with good pick-ups and good action. Rhythm or finger-styles can be played on good folk guitars ('jumbo' or plectrum types with lighter gauge metal strings) using a separate, detachable pick-up.* Bass guitars, too, can be semi-acoustic or solid electric models. Semi-acoustic types are more versatile because they can be practised without amplification and some pop guitarists prefer them — models such as the Gibson ES 335 or copies — but I'm afraid that 'image' (there it is again) more often than not demands the more usual solid electric models which are almost universally found in pop groups.

To deal adequately with lead and bass guitar, you need an amplifier rated somewhere around 50 watts, plus a 12, 15 or even 18-inch speaker in a separate enclosure. You may be fortunate enough to find a suitable integrated amplifier (i.e. one with speakers) but only the best models will give good performance in the lower bass frequencies, and a separate bass speaker assembly is recommended. Now, if you place the piano in the foreground and keep sensible levels of amplification, you can balance your rhythm group fairly successfully.

But what about your poor flautist or bassoonist? — he cannot make his presence felt unless he sits in the conductor's lap. I'm afraid it's back to the headmaster for more money. A public address (PA) system is a fair compromise. There will not be great subtlety or quality in terms of output, but a system that incorporates around three to four channels, two inputs per channel, will be sensitive enough to allow the more delicate tones of the woodwind instruments to be heard. Ideally, a third amplifier should be used for the solo vocalist and/or the chorus backing. You can thus not only make do, but work completely successfully with half a dozen singers. To complete your system you will, of course, also need microphones, microphone stands and the very valuable and versatile boom arms to get in amongst the lesser and more awkwardly obtained sounds — clarinet and oboe, for example. Brass, if positioned correctly, need not be amplified, and you can experiment for the most pleasing overall balance, as indeed you will need to. 'Feedback', the result of distortion of sound signals picked up and fed back into the amplification system, is nothing short of a violent and extremely unpleasant assault on the ears and one to be avoided wherever possible. A basic rule to observe is to place your amplified musicians and microphones further back on the stage than the speaker enclosures of the PA system, and as well spaced from each other as possible. With more sophisticated systems you may not encounter this problem or need to take similar precautions, but I am assuming that your school has limits on the amount of money available for your department.

While on the subject of amplifiers, I hope to anticipate two immediate queries, namely — 'How much will this sort of system cost?' and 'Where do I get it all from?'

*See p. 157.

The quick and fairly unhelpful answers are (a) approximately £500 (all prices quoted are at 1974 levels) and (b) amplification specialists, secondhand surplus dealers, private advertisements in the local press, trade magazines, or papers such as *Melody Maker*. Lest the first answer should immediately dash your hopes, there are other factors to consider.

You will almost certainly not be able to afford new equipment, and therefore secondhand and trade-in items are your target. As a musician, you need not expect to have an exhaustive knowledge of electronics, but there is usually some member of staff who understands these things, and therefore your role is to seek out the equipment you think you need and engage his services to check it out. I must add also, that in both schools in which my choral and instrumental group has operated, money has been made available for such items, with the rider that at no time has this exceeded £250 initially. The vital factor is that first purchases should be good enough to form the heart of your system, and that from there on, you buy additional items as and when your case wins administrative approval and funds allow. A PA system can also have useful outlets in other areas of school life where voices have to be heard (e.g. sports days, school discos, outside activities, announcements etc.) and this may prove a useful and valid bargaining lever in obtaining the necessary cash. Do not ignore the role of the PTA: you may well be able to establish financial support from this not insubstantial source, with perhaps the additional benefits of contacts within the trade.

Buying equipment

Amplifiers

I managed to make the initial purchase of a secondhand integrated amplifier at both schools, at a cost of £50 and £60 respectively. Both had two channels, two inputs per channel and could handle electric guitars, voice microphones and bass guitar (just), so my rhythm section and soloist were catered for — not ideally, but as a working proposition. A subsequent purchase of a PA system, consisting of separate amplifier and 'stacks' (i.e. column speakers), gave four channels, two inputs per channel at a cost of £100. Each channel had its own volume control, while treble, middle, bass and presence controls operated on all four channels simultaneously. A useful accessory was a 'standby' switch; this device enables one to leave on the amplifier's supply of current, without passing sound through the speakers. As I mentioned previously, these are the heart of your system, so make sure purchases are of reputable makes such as Fender, Marshall, Hiwatt, Wem and HH. In the secondhand market you are often among the teenage group 'trade-ins' (an enormous number of groups never make it), and your bargaining ability could well save you £10 to £20 and sometimes more, as the retailer may already have made a profit on the deal.

Microphones, stands and boom arms

Microphones, too, can often be obtained secondhand, and a £30 model may well be found at half-price in certain surplus dealers' stocks. Do check it over before purchasing. There is one model (Densei) that I purchase new, because although it is a little coarse, it is extremely sensitive, of the cardioid type, has dual impedance and retails for well under £10. My advice here is to purchase one which is unidirectional (as opposed to the omnidirectional) and which is fitted with an on/off switch. Make sure that the microphone impedance (low or high) matches that of your amplifier.

Secondhand microphone stands are like gold dust to come by, so you need to allow at least £10 for each stand, of the heavy base, extendable type — giving reassuring stability and flexibility of vertical movement. Boom arms are expensive (almost the cost of the stands themselves), yet these can be made with little difficulty and at a fraction of the retail cost by your technical studies department, if you supply them with suitable gauge alloy and weights. A further point about microphones, stands and boom arms is that you have to ensure that all the fittings and accessories have compatible threads. Microphone cradles come complete with new models, or are purchased separately for secondhand items.

Instruments

Instruments should certainly be purchased secondhand. I have never paid more than £25 for an electric lead or bass guitar, with all the strings in good condition. This latter point is important, particularly with bass guitars; the bottom E string alone costs approximately £2 to replace. You should check the action, pick-ups, volume and tone controls. A fine guitarist of my acquaintance picked up a superb electric guitar for £15 from a secondhand dealer, so there are bargains around if you can take the time and trouble to look for them.

Drum kits, too, can be bought secondhand, and my purchases have been in the £60 to £70 bracket. These should include: bass drum and foot pedal, snare drum and stand, one 'ride' cymbal and stand, one hi-hat cymbal unit, bass drum fitting and floor standing tom-toms. Additional items recommended are a proper drum stool, a sizzle cymbal (one with rivets round the rim that produces those pleasant elongated sounds), and wood block and cowbell to complete the outfit.

The problem of the requisition is greatest in secondhand dealers' premises. They do not appear to be over-keen on IOUs, Green Shield stamps *or* requisition forms — cash is what they want. I have performed several doubtful manoeuvres to acquire items of equipment from such places and, incidentally, saved my Local Education Authority and the ratepayer an impressive sum by so doing. But it is imperative that if equipment is acquired outside the normal requisition, that you should make certain that it is properly insured and is always stored under lock and key — new acquisitions with such an attraction for teenagers could be stolen.

A great deal of time and trouble and expense has gone into the preceding build-up. There has to be good reason for it, provided, I hope, by what follows.

The choral and instrumental group in performance

The rhythm group sound

My first teaching appointment afforded me the opportunity, albeit in isolation, of putting the idea of the integrated style of choral and instrumental performance into practice. Most important, the acoustic guitar became the main means of contact both with and between pupils, because of its extraordinary versatility. It is easily accessible and portable, as a symbol it is contemporary and its image is credible. When it is used in its commonest role, as an accompanying instrument, it has no equal as a means of getting pupils to participate — with the added bonus that it aids class discipline.

Because it was used in the curriculum, assemblies, sixth-form general studies and recreation (group singing, entertainment, etc.) and in out-of-school activities such as folk groups, junior and senior guitar clubs and evening classes, the instrument soon became the staple diet of a substantial number of pupils. The wideness of its appeal attracted two or three very promising young musicians, who soon left simple strumming on open-string chords, together with the harmonically tedious 'three-chord trick' — in performance, of course, they employed the simpler techniques with ever increasing accomplishment. One player, in particular, was quickly able to tackle most barré chords and sequences presented to him; these were given in chord symbol notation, whilst for decorative passages, introductions and codas I used staff notation.

There can be no doubt that he was practising not less than three to four hours daily to make such rapid progress though it was never directly asked of him, and he had therefore acquired an inner motivation that drove him relentlessly along the path toward expertise. A non-traditional musician, he nevertheless was able to feel harmonic progressions, and two or three runs through new material made notation redundant. The only traditional notation needed, other than that described above, was the rhythm pattern and figuration for the right hand:

Example 2

The letters in the above example
are taken from the Spanish:

p (pulgar) = thumb   m (medio) = middle finger
i (indice) = index finger   a (anular) = ring finger

This was all that needed to be explained, and so within approximately six months, starting as a complete beginner, the rhythm guitarist — a quarter of the rhythm group — was avidly available and extremely proficient.

At this stage, lest the above should appear an exorbitant claim or just a one-off 'lucky break', it is worth stating that almost precisely the same thing happened the second time around, and has happened again. The apparent difficulty in discovering these young, talented and enthusiastic musicians probably arises from the absence of pop music and guitar playing in the school's musical life. Every year-group must surely have at least one such pupil, probably not involved in more traditional music making, ready and waiting to be taken seriously, to be encouraged and given a vision of just how much there is to be enjoyed and achieved.

Electric bass guitar, though initially a simpler instrument to learn, can be more of a problem to introduce to pupils, primarily because, unlike the acoustic guitar, its normal role is not to function in isolation. Therefore, rhythm guitarist, pianist and drummer should already be working together before the bass guitarist is added to the group, though it is unlikely that things will turn out in such orderly fashion. A traditional or non-traditional musician can adequately fill in with simple parts. For non-traditional musicians, where reading music from the bass clef is still something of a mystery, it is time-consuming though a feasible task to write out at first the letter names of notes, phrase by phrase, and to allow him to pick up the rhythm in his own time. At the same time, he should be familiarising himself with the note names of the first five frets of the four strings:

Example 3

FINGERBOARD CHART

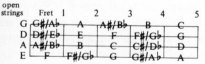

It is also of great benefit to introduce finger patterns and shapes for intervals of the fourth, fifth and octave, since he will be using these frequently:

Example 4

PATTERN FOR CHORD OF C MAJOR

The traditional musician may well be equally unfamiliar with most of the fore-going, but sight-reading from the bass clef and/or the playing of the orchestral bass should prove an advantage. Musicians of both types, however, will need to appreci-ate fully the role of pulse in bass guitar playing, and it could well be that the non-traditional musician will grasp this more quickly. Critics of the regular pulse of pop music may justifiably accuse less worthy examples of monotony, but even these are played with an impeccable precision which is a basic requirement of the rhythm group right from the start.

For the percussionist, there is patently more to be learnt than the straight 'up and down' approach of — if you can remember them — Dave Clark and Ringo Starr' early efforts. And yet a fairly simple rhythmic figure, such as was given in Example 1, will often be considered adequate. A simple development of the bass drum figure gives a more common and authentic pop music 'feel':

Example 5

Delicacy and subtlety have as much place in pop music as in any other form of musical expression. All my percussionists have been very aware of the potentially overwhelming power of the percussive sound, and that it must almost invariably be tempered to avoid wiping out instrumentalists, soloists and the chorus. Yet their efforts must necessarily employ a basic 'drive', a strength and cleanness of approach and confidence — not to be confused with arrogance.

The pianist is almost certain to be a traditional musician and has certain new techniques to master until the style becomes familiar. Since the timbre of the piano is relatively mellow, dynamics are necessarily increased, and *fortissimo* markings are not infrequent. Indeed, with the addition of amplified equipment and the necessity of correct balance, dynamic markings are more easily assessed during the rehearsal. Accenting of single notes, chords and link phrases is common and, although *pianissimo* playing is rarely encountered, this does not rule out sensitivity or negate good tone and clarity, and positively encourages the percussive touch demanded by, for example, much of Bartok's pianoforte music.

As the jazz pianist Oscar Peterson so rightly observed, the left hand can easily be-come lazy and even obsolete in the context of a rhythm group, but if the piano part is substantial enough, the left hand will have more than enough work to do.

It is important not to omit the pianist's role with regard to the tuning of the other instruments, since this will certainly occupy some considerable time initially. Guitarists, like all players, need the ability to tune their instruments, in order to participate. It is wise to insist that they always attempt to tune their instruments even in the earliest stages of learning, and wise also to check the procedure until they are thoroughly competent. The pianist must be a patient ally through all this, since he can help considerably by, for example, incorporating the minor triad built on the note required.

A final pleasing aspect in my experience of choral and instrumental group presentation is that it has always been possible to find a pupil to fill every group place — despite, at times, an abundance of musical talent on the staff of each school. Examples of groups consisting entirely of pupils, and of groups in which the staff also participate, are to be heard on tracks 6 to 10 of side 2 of the accompanying recording.

The choral group line-up

The constitution of the choral group which is to perform publicly is probably the biggest single factor in making a choice of repertoire. It is, I think, fair to assume that the largest number of pupils in the choral group will be drawn from the late-teenage population of the school, from fifth-formers upward. This is especially true of thirteen plus schools (my present school is a thirteen to eighteen comprehensive), where the infectious enthusiasm of the eleven- and twelve-year-old is absent. Practical music making and singing in particular do seem to take a minor place in the interests of the thirteen to fifteen age group, while conversely the sounds and heroes of charts music, discos, juke boxes, singles and LPs boom into extraordinary popularity. But while the interest and appetite of this age group often appear insatiable, they are content, by and large, with a passive role of being entertained and fed a constant and somewhat repetitive diet — pop musical chips with everything. This, quite obviously, does not exclude them from participating, especially those whose instrumental skills are still developing, and there are always the exceptions who come along. But the generalisation is largely true of the average pupil who has no tradition of music making and no specialisation in the subject; this point is relevant only because it is to the non-specialist particularly to whom the choral group seeks to make its appeal.

The consensus of opinion in the group, therefore, is more likely to be that of the more mature and critical teenager, who, whilst unfamiliar with the specialist skills and techniques, will have definite likes and dislikes and be liable to make his opinion known vociferously. Perhaps inevitably, in their late teens, they become the most severe and least tolerant critics of the 'teeny-bopper' culture and the music associated with it. This is proclaimed in no uncertain fashion in a pupil's original composition, 'Fools', which can be heard on side 2, track 10 of the accompanying recording.

In this heady atmosphere, it is obvious that the choice of song comes under the severest examination, and the deciding factor, more often than not, is the content of the lyrics. Obvious banality, triviality and mediocrity are unlikely to find a place in the repertoire of such a group; if a number with a poor lyric is chosen, it usually has other substantial artistic merits. One such song is the Stevie Wonder number, 'You are the Sunshine of my Life' (which can be heard on side 2, track 7 of the accompanying recording). The reasons for its inclusion were mainly centred around its musical content — for instance, the whole tone scale employed in the introduction, the precision and attack needed by the backing group, and the obvious 'send-up' of the lyrics, not least by the composer himself on the original version.

Good songs require no justification and it is for this reason, I suspect, that James Taylor has made such an impact with the choral group. Only two songs sung by him have ever made the singles charts, for instance. (This is another dangerous stream to swim in. If one attempts to emulate singles chart music, while it is still popular and familiar, one only invites disaster, for your version must obviously invite comparison which will very rarely flatter it. Better to leave the song until it has largely been forgotten, when you will be in a position to stage its comeback!) James Taylor's music is in the folk rock idiom I referred to at the beginning of this chapter, and this idiom abounds with good songs. It is the folk element which carries its appeal, in that it contains largely melodious music in a tight musical form. The lyrics combine imagery and symbolism with simplicity of statement. There is no wastage and little embroidery, and the themes are age-old human statements of love, loneliness, dreams, compassion, religious experience, pain and pleasure, war and peace. The rock element sells the song in contemporary dress.

The tone required of the chorus is a harder, harsher sound than generally produced by girls of this age, and is not without its own appeal. Quite often the demands are so severe that they can, perhaps, only be fully answered by the developed, full-toned sounds of the late-teenager. Not only this, but the stamina demanded for a chorus number such as 'Windmills of your Mind' is considerable; if the tempo flags at all, the urgency and atmospheric potency of the song is lost. With the chorus as a backing group, too, the emphasis is almost always on attack, so confidence to lean into the microphone and to hit notes first time, clean and true, in order to support and enhance the soloist, is at a premium. It is not unreasonable to expect soloists to emerge from among those who can meet demands such as these. Thus we have changed over gradually to songs requiring soloist and backing group, so that there are at least as many of these in our repertoire.

For choral group performance with smaller numbers at least three microphones are desirable, and in part singing it has proved beneficial to separate firsts and seconds, positioning them round the microphones in groups of up to six singers. Larger groups can be positioned towards the front of the ensemble to be effectively heard without amplification.

Rehearsal timetables are as vital for a choral and instrumental group as for any other group of serious musicians. There should be ideally at least three a week — one for the instrumentalists alone (until they are good enough, who will want to sing with them?), one for the chorus with a rehearsal pianist, and the third for the two elements together.

Extension and diversification

But is this all that can be hoped for from such a group? Certainly, it has become the focal point of school music for me, but I wanted to see 'spin-off' groups, who found a need to do things other than the larger scale choral and instrumental group arrangements, and who would become sufficiently independent and competent to undertake other music in smaller ensembles with only a minimum of guidance. What ultimately happened far exceeded my expectations.

A percussion group, employing the drum kit, claves, maraccas, tambourine and bongoes, under the direction of our peripatetic teacher, performed a series of pieces based on Latin American and military rhythms; the flautist performed Bossa Nova pieces accompanied by two guitars and simple percussion; and the female vocal soloist joined with the male lead guitarist to sing accompanied solos and duets. In addition another group formed within the main group. They called themselves Wheels and used, by and large, the music of James Taylor, the Beatles and some original material. The main inspiration was the lead guitarist, who also did the lead singing. The group consisted of him and four others on rhythm guitar, vocals, bass and drums respectively. They were particularly impressive because of their attention to detail, and the degree of professionalism they achieved in a relatively short time. Added to this there was the fact that their arrangements were largely intuitively worked out and, more important, were their own.

Initially, the lead guitarist had a difficult problem with singing in public, and we were for some time at a loss as to what to do about it. Fortunately, he wanted to sing badly enough and persevered long and hard enough, so that he subsequently did not dry up when confronted by a microphone and the rest of the group. From then onwards, the problem was to keep up with him.

The name of James Taylor has appeared a few times in this chapter. This is because it was this artist specifically who inspired the lead guitarist to achieve what he did. He had a very special affinity with the musical style and the content of the lyrics of the early Taylor numbers. The techniques this pupil acquired were gained directly as a result of knowing exactly what he wanted to do, and most of these were self-taught. Only rarely was there any need for analysis of sounds particularly difficult to achieve. After a reasonable period of establishing his confidence and vocal and instrumental expertise, I had to point out that there was a limit to how far direct imitation could be taken, however good the artist, and that he really ought to be trying to find his own individual style.

He had already written a few songs in the Taylor mould, and even now his lyrics especially are often derivative of that style, however original their content. He was a fair graphic artist, and currently studies at a College of Art, but confessed that he found the performing arts more satisfying in terms of personal expression — for he really did have something to say that was important to him and, he hoped, to others. So much so, that without any traditional background in music, he decided that he wanted to understand what he intuitively composed, and opted to undertake a one-year 'O' level music course. Starting with only a minimal knowledge of theory and history, he achieved a pass grade in the subject, to his eternal credit and my immense satisfaction.

By now, he was writing songs at an astonishingly high level of output and quality and, in a sense, outgrew his peers. He was thus forced to turn to musicians who had rather more expertise and background in performance and presentation. In the end, the group that emerged contained two teachers on lead and bass guitars respectively, and three other pupils on drums, flute and extra percussion. We then sat down with his lyrics, melody and chordal accompaniment and, as far as possible, put our own interpretation of his music into our individual instruments. Very little was written down, apart from the chord sequences, and we built on these interpretations, incorporating a number of 'mistakes', eventually achieving a mutually satisfying blend.

We have been extremely fortunate in securing the services of our local radio station, BBC Radio Humberside, to record a great deal of the school's musical output, and these original songs were similarly recorded in their studios. Side 2 of the recording uses some of these recordings and thus gives an accurate reflection of the extremely high level of creativity, sensitivity and discipline achieved in performance. He is still writing, and some of the current set of songs have more potential still.

For me, this boy, still only in his late teens, made sense of all I had tried to do — and especially of the original concept of the choral and instrumental group. I do not think his talent is unique (however individual and prolific his output may be), so my concern is for all the others who wait patiently in the wings for their opportunity to contribute — who knows how successfully? — to the world of music.

The choral and instrumental group repertoire

Composer	Style	Title
Burt Bacharach	Ballads	'Don't Go Breaking My Heart'
		'This Guy's in Love with You'
Edwin Hawkins	Religious/Rock	'I Heard the Voice'
		'Joy, Joy'
J.S. Bach	Vocal jazz	'Sleepers Wake'
		'Air on G String'
Traditional	Folk/Rock	'The Grass is Greener Still'
		'Oh, Miss Mary'
James Taylor	Folk/Rock/Ballad	'Brighten Your Night with My Day'
		'Carolina in My Mind'
Carly Simon	Folk/Rock/Ballad	'The Right Thing to Do'
		'The Carter Family'
		'Forever My Love'
Traditional	Folk/Rock	'Mockingbird'
Lyra/Vandre/Gimbel	Bossa Nova	'Take Me to Aruanda'
Ed Welch/Tom Paxton	Folk/Rock/Ballad	'Maybe It's Today'
		'I Couldn't Wait to Tell You'
Ed Welch/Tom Paxton	Folk/Rock'n'Roll	'Smile like a Movie Star'
The Beatles	Ballad	'Something'
Neal Hefti	Ballad	'Girl Talk'
Lynsey de Paul	Ballad	'Won't Somebody Dance with Me'
Stevie Wonder	Tamla/Ballad	'You Are the Sunshine of My Life'
French Traditional	Folk/Rock	'Say I Won't Be There'
		('Au clair de la lune')

Joni Mitchell	Folk/Ballad	'From Both Sides Now'
Michel Legrand	Ballads	'Windmills of Your Mind'
		'I Will Say Goodbye'
Marvin Hamlisch	Ballad	'Nobody Does it Better'
Antonio Carlos Jobim	Bossa Nova/Ballad	'Wave' (vocal version)
Paul Anka	Rock'n'Roll	'It Doesn't Matter Any More'
Chuck Berry	Pop Ballad	'Roll Over Beethoven'
Melissa Manchester/ Carole Bayer Sager	Folk/Rock/Ballad	'This Lady's Not at Home'
Otis Blackwell/ Jimmy Jones	Folk/Rock/Ballad	'Handyman'
Ware, Sawyer	Rock/Ballad	'If I Ever Lose This Heaven'
Stuart	Rock/Ballad	'Queen of My Soul'
James Taylor	Folk/Rock/Ballad	'Let It All Fall Down'
Bobby Gosh	Pop Ballad	'A Little Bit More'

*Separate detachable pick-ups are available nowadays (straight from the factory if required) in models like the Gibson J55 complete with the now famous Barcus Berry pick-up. More significantly, the 'classical' or 'Spanish' guitar can take advantage of micro-technology in the shape of such things as the 'Ibanez' 'Bug'. This minute pick-up — about an inch long and fairly costly (but worth it)— is stuck behind the bridge at the level of the 1st string and simply plugged into a good quality amplifier with superb results.

8 Pop and the teacher: some uses and problems

ED LEE

Despite the spread of innovations of the type described by Malcolm Nicholls in chapter 6, most teachers still spend most of their time on 'class music' — teaching large numbers of pupils in a classroom by traditional methods. However, though class music is the commonest situation in which the music teacher finds himself, it is also the most limiting. This leads me at once to my main contention, which is that class music must cease to be the major outlet for the teacher's effort, precisely because it is so restrictive. Moreover, the difficulties of organising a large number of pupils into a profitable working unit are often aggravated by conditions in which it is impossible to permit even a level of volume far below that which is sometimes implied in this chapter. In such circumstances the music teacher needs not, in the first instance, suggestions for work methods, but a change of working situation. Difficulties of winning attention, keeping discipline or avoiding apathy in the pupils would seem to be almost inevitable when a teacher is not permitted to utilise even the standard range of approaches to his subject; it is as though one were asked to teach typing without typewriters. It is clear that such calls for change are at the moment rather utopian, but it is to be hoped that the evidence provided by this book will help to strengthen the position of music teachers in any attempt to achieve both working conditions with suitable acoustics and the much more desirable 'open' situation, such as that described by Malcolm Nicholls in chapter 6. These observations are in many ways as applicable to the teaching of classical music as they are to that of pop.

Class music: listening to records

No musician of any idiom speaks for long without stressing how essential it is to listen to appropriate masters. Some of the difficulties currently experienced in 'musical appreciation' lessons might well be eliminated simply by taking pop as their subject matter, instead of the classics. Dave Rogers (chapter 1) gives a very full account of the main trends and artists in this field of music. His chapter could therefore easily act as a basic syllabus. But it should be borne in mind that the response of the class may be just the opposite of what is hoped for, particularly if the teacher is unsympathetic to the material he is using. Because pop is so linked with the need for identification with a social group, adolescents especially may well resent what they see as an attempt by the teacher to get under their guard. Alternatively they are often willing to have pop music played (preferably non-stop) while they think of their girl friends, attempt to do homework under the desk or engage in any of the activities usually found in a class which is apathetic, but which recognises the need to keep the teacher happy. But they are then likely to remain obstinately silent when asked to discuss what they have heard. They dislike discussion, querying and the application of reason; the mystery of pop is felt to be too sacred, and rational discourse, with its aim of objectivity, is sensed to be too alien to their emotionally based choice of idiom, a choice which arises from a need for certainty and solidarity. Nevertheless, when the teacher finds an acceptable approach — which will nearly always be based on a genuine concern to understand and exchange viewpoints — listening can be mutually enjoyable, as well as going a long way towards keeping the teacher abreast of new developments.

Class music: performance

If a teacher has to choose, one might well argue that his time should be spent on practical work, on the grounds that we can all play a record player whereas we cannot as beginners engage in group activity without the guidance of an experienced leader. But we are at once confronted with the major limitation of class music, which is the need to keep the whole of a class busy when the needs of the individual involve making a noise, usually disturbing others in the room. Three approaches suggest themselves, all of which are dependent on a fair element of good fortune in the matter of numbers and distribution of talent among the class. These are: a vocal group, a big band and guitar instruction.

A vocal group

This idea is discussed at length by Tony Robins in chapter 7; I need therefore add very little to his account.

Before going on to the more musically satisfying but time-consuming approach of writing special arrangements, the teacher can begin with the approach of the Ray Conniff records, or the various radio 'Singalong' programmes, in which a chorus or audience sing pleasant, well-known tunes to a rhythm accompaniment. Suitable material can be obtained in a variety of ways — from commercial dance music orchestrations, from sheet music or albums of popular songs, or by transcribing directly from records or the radio. Information about these sources is given in the Bibliography. The teacher should find little difficulty in using any of them as a starting point for his own simple orchestrations. Tony Robins also shows how orchestral players can be drawn into the backing group and, more important, he stresses the essential function of the rhythm section. The provision of simple percussion instruments (e.g. claves, cowbells etc.) can solve the problem of what to do with those pupils who are not singing or playing in the instrumental backing group, and the teacher new to this field should realise that percussion parts can be made much more demanding as the player's technical ability and conceptual grasp increase. With a careful selection of pieces one can use a fair number of percussionists, in the manner of groups such as Santana, or the old Afro-Cuban bands. Attentive listening to even the most unpromising recorded material, such as very commercial reggae, will show that added percussion is frequently blended into the basic rhythm accompaniment of pop records. The discovery of these parts is a valuable exercise in listening to music for the pupil, who can then be drawn to perceive and take on a disciplined but acceptable function in a group. The result of such large-scale work will inevitably be top-heavy and crude, because of the impossibility of getting so many people of diverse capabilities to perform really accurately – but it might at least be enjoyable!

If timetabling permits the teacher to select pupils or to offer them a choice of options, as often happens in general studies programmes, the idea of a large vocal group is much more practicable, and one's aims can be much more ambitious. Vocal harmonies (even if parts have to be doubled) or the simpler work of the Swingle Singers can be attempted.

A big band

Another idea for a large group is a big band; it is particularly worth considering in view of the widespread current interest in things dating from before 1945. Such a group can attempt a wide range of music – jazz, dance music, Latin American music, as well as jazz-rock of the type played by groups such as Blood, Sweat and Tears. Big bands are already found in some schools as an extracurricular activity, but provided that noise considerations permit, a big band can also be offered as another possibility in a programme of options. On such occasions the idea is usually acceptable to colleagues since with ten brass, five saxes, four rhythm and, if desired, four or five percussionists, the music teacher takes his share of numbers. A further advantage is that a simplified version of the styles of Count Basie and Fletcher Henderson is accessible to musicians with a very low level of technical attainment. Wherever I have seen such a venture, it has attracted a large and enthusiastic following, especially at dances. Links can easily be forged with the National Youth Jazz Association, who are very glad to supply advice (free) and orchestrations (reasonably priced, and written by first class musicians). Further information is given in the Bibliography.

It is useful at this point to mention 'riffing'. Piers Spencer has already discussed (chapter 4) some applications of this technique in teaching blues improvisation, but this by no means exhausts its possibilities. Modern rock musicians such as Mike Oldfield have shown that new dimensions of the use of riffs are still to be found. In the context of the big band, however, the term refers to the use of repeated phrases, in the style of the period 1930—50. The technique is extremely useful from the teacher's point of view in that

(i)   riffs are easily learned by ear (i.e. little writing out of parts is needed);
(ii)   some listening to big band records will show that the blues approach is flexible enough to deal with a range of chord sequences (i.e. numbers need not only be based upon the simple three-chord progression);
(iii)   a class can be divided into three or four sections, each with its own riff;
(iv)   an exciting piece of music can be created very quickly which, though simple, can nevertheless give considerable insight into such concepts as group interplay and musical economy. Again, the teacher can test this assertion by attentive listening to good big band work.

Guitar teaching

With the aid of a piano to hold the pupils together, it is possible to teach quite large numbers of pupils the guitar simultaneously. Objections can be raised about the possible formation of bad habits, laxness of tuning, etc., but I am convinced that the possible dangers are outweighed by the excitement of playing a piece of music, no matter how simple, and of playing together. A further advantage is that the un-certain pupil can 'hide' in the crowd (or so he believes). The initial enthusiasm can be overwhelming — the teacher can be seen as a miracle worker if he starts with simple but effective techniques. (A list of suitable guitar instruction books is given in the Bibliography. These include tutors on folk music and its derivatives which would make a valuable introduction and support to the kind of work advocated by Tony Robins in chapter 7).

Working in smaller groups

If the music teacher can arrange for his pupils to divide into smaller groups, teaching becomes much more workable and very exciting. The work described by the other contributors is largely in this area. The teacher's first problem is therefore to engage in the often tortuous process of negotiation and persuasion which is necessary to obtain one of several possibilities: selection of pupils on grounds of interest and ability from a larger grouping, smaller teaching groups, more rooms, more staff. In these circumstances it becomes necessary (and in my opinion desirable) for these small groups to work independently of the teacher. When this happens, one effec-tively moves into something like the 'open' situation described in detail by Graham Vulliamy (chapter 3) and Malcolm Nicholls (chapter 6).

At this point the inevitable question of discipline arises. Surely, the teacher may argue, working in this way is asking for trouble? Certainly it would be as foolish to pretend that such problems cannot and do not arise, as it would be to claim to have the definitive answer to them. Current events in education suggest that it is doubtful that there is any one answer; it is certain that if there is one, we have not yet found it. Nevertheless, it would be equally wrong to be totally pessimistic.

The teacher may, for example, argue that, especially in the more difficult schools, the type of pupil who listens to pop is likely to have a lack of respect for property, resulting in, for example, cigarette burns on the piano, damage to equipment or theft. The care of equipment is however a problem which must be faced continually by all teachers, and the experienced teacher has usually developed a range of realistic but not too repressive strategies for ensuring that such care is taken.

Again, it might well be suggested that a lack of consideration for others may manifest itself in such forms as litter, rudeness to maintenance staff and general rowdiness, and that such problems can only be intensified when the music itself requires a volume which in many schools would make teaching in other classrooms quite impossible.

However, noise is a recurrent problem which music teachers have to face. More important, the pupils will presumably be led towards the goal of independent working, rather than be given immediate and total freedom. During this process one would assume that the teacher would stress that the rights and privileges given entail obligations to act in a mature fashion, and that an important indication of maturity is consideration both for the property and feelings of others.

Above all, the success of these approaches will depend upon the relationship which a teacher has developed with his pupils. In more difficult schools this often already involves a degree of informality and flexibility which is well outside the range of the traditional conception of the teacher, and as such may well be unacceptable to some teachers for reasons of personality. Clearly, the teacher who himself feels a need for a very formal pattern of procedure in the classroom will not find the above suggestions acceptable. However, I would wish to stress that, after a period of transition, a situation can emerge which is at least as satisfactory as that produced by more traditional methods, and is often more so. (Malcolm Nicholls makes this point several times in his chapter.)

Let us assume that the teacher feels confident about coping with the above difficulties, and that he is in a position to guide his pupils into musical ensembles of orthodox size and composition, rather than of having to force them into massive groups involving duplication of parts and redundancy of function. He will then have to make decisions about an aspect of education which is undergoing a fundamental reconsideration — who is to be in charge? Three possibilities are open to the teacher: teacher-led groups, groups led by one pupil and corporate work.

Leadership by the teacher is not necessarily a bad thing; it is perhaps the only way in which pupils can work at the very beginning of their musical careers. Teachers should certainly not discount the usefulness of this more traditional approach just because of the possibility of criticism based on 'modern' theories, which the critic may have misunderstood, or which may be inappropriate to the situation in hand. There are many teachers (e.g. Peter Maxwell Davies in avant garde music) who by their energy and the farseeing nature of their vision have presented their pupils with a real challenge, a broadening of horizons, and a real sense of involvement in helping to create a piece of music which the pupils felt to be of worth. There are an increasing number of works, especially school musicals, which are specially written by the teacher in the light of his pupils' particular needs, abilities and tastes. Even if a teacher's talents do not permit him to be so ambitious, there is ample testimony from pupils themselves that firm but sympathetic guidance is not only acceptable, but even desired. Though some pupils will wish to rebel and assert their individuality, many will wish to play a sound and valued part under the teacher's direction in a group doing something which they feel to be of interest and worth; this is particularly true of many 'working class' pupils and 'singles charts' fans. The idea of learning under the guidance of a master has, after all, a very respectable ancestry.

After a period, however, groups should move on to a second stage, in which they work independently on assignments, at first using worksheets prepared by the teacher. This is necessary, since so many secondary pupils find it difficult to plan and carry out independent work for themselves. However, unless a worksheet is very carefully thought out, it can be a very imperfect form of communication, with the result that time given to self-directed work can be inefficiently used, or even totally wasted. It is worth remembering that to appoint a pupil to be in charge of the group will not necessarily resolve this difficulty – generally, if the teacher is taken away, there is no one who has or is felt to have sufficient musical authority to guide others.

Because the preparation and use of worksheets necessitates a good deal of thought and effort, teachers who are used to a very traditional class music situation and syllabus may need some guidance from colleagues who are used to teaching younger children, with whom such methods are widely used. Again this illustrates a recurrent theme of this chapter – the need for a change of role for the teacher – since as things now stand (with a virtually full timetable and constant changes of class) the introduction of worksheet-based teaching could easily involve an inordinate amount of work.

Sometimes, however, a group will spontaneously throw up a natural and acceptable leader, or will turn to an older pupil; much less detailed guidance will then be needed. Malcolm Nicholls gives an example of this process in his profile of Keith A. At this point things can and do happen, but the more traditional teacher is warned that the behaviour of the group can seem relaxed to the point of chaos. Three amplified musicians all playing totally different things at high volume while two others try to talk, for example, is a form of activity likely to produce an intolerable strain on the teacher who is used to a more obviously disciplined learning situation. But he should try to distinguish at the earliest possible point between this apparent lack of organised and systematic activity and plain rowdiness and lack of discipline. The latter cannot of course be tolerated, whereas the former is a necessary stage in the growth of self-discipline and the positive use of time given to creative activities.

This tendency to apparently mindless chaos reflects, I believe, radical changes in our society, which manifest themselves in school as soon as there is no set and obligatory learning pattern. Among the factors involved is the changing social position for young people which leads to a greater unwillingness in many cases to accept external discipline, and combines with a lack of understanding of the need for self-discipline, which is a prerequisite for making really good music. Young people also tend to have an image of pop groups in which success is instantly acquired by a form of divine inspiration; this is often linked with a failure to recognise technical deficiencies in their own performances. Finally, many young people today seem to wish to be engaged in creation and improvisation, rather than in re-creation and learning from an instructor. The older pupil who gravitates to leadership can give shape to this amorphous mixture of feelings, and bring about the necessary changes in awareness of what is needed if the musical activity is to grow in competence and subtlety. But the teacher needs to remember that the pupil will do it in his own way, and that this is likely to be very different from the methods of the trained teacher.

The teacher should also be aware that the type of behaviour described in the last paragraph can contain within it a form of group dynamics, virtually impossible to explain or define, in which interactions between the participants lead to the creation of a *mutually agreed* and acceptable result. This can involve not only creativity but also conflict of a very subtle kind. This approach to music is based on a concept of the nature of art and creative responsibility which is diametrically opposed to the traditional concepts of the insightful composer and the authoritative conductor. The justification of the approach is to be found in the work of groups such as the Beatles. Their film *Let It Be* is largely constructed around a film record of the apparent aimlessness and crosscurrents in the preparatory and creative stages of making new pieces of music. This contrasts strongly with the polished but exciting nature of the finished pieces in their famous 'Concert on the Roof', which ends the film.

It is clear that in such situations one is releasing powerful forces, which must inevitably disturb any teacher whose training and, perhaps, personality dispose him to work from a basis of control, preferably rooted in respect for the controlling authority. Such a teacher should consider the point that what I have been suggesting does not involve the total abdication of authority, but rather the different exercise of it. Though a group of pupils may not be willing to accept detailed and formal instruction on all aspects of their work, they will usually be open to comments sparingly offered, on technicalities and matters of musical skill, and made from a genuine interest to see their work presented at its best. In the technical college discussed by Graham Vulliamy (chapter 3) this was the main approach used by the Director of Music. It was combined with more detailed instruction on work of the students' choice by visiting professional musicians who were familiar with the relevant styles. However, perhaps the most effective form of control is to put on a public performance; groups rarely fail to rise to such a challenge and improve as if by magic.

Creativity in pop

Having discussed how groups might be arranged, I now propose to consider what they do. I have suggested above that some pupil music groups have clear aims, but that others have to be led. However, the suggestion that he should *lead* a group may cause the conscientious teacher to worry about his failure to encourage creativity. Piers Spencer has discussed this concept in chapter 5, but some further comment can usefully be made.

Some of these worries may well arise from a lack of clarity about such terms as 'creativity', 'originality' and 'improvisation' and their application to pop music. Since to foster these facets of aesthetic experience is widely seen today as a valuable and liberating activity, to suggest, as I now do, that many pupils should spend a lot of time imitating records may well seem to be limited and stultifying. In order to answer this criticism, we need to compare avant garde and pop interpretations of the terms, at least in so far as they apply to teaching.

Clearly, a central aim of newer approaches to teaching music (e.g. as exemplified in Paynter and Aston, 1970) is to develop creativity and originality. In the first instance the teacher encourages pupils to relinquish cliché, and to free themselves from obedience to archaic textbook 'rules'. In particular, he attempts to guide his pupils towards the discovery that many contemporary composers see music as the organisation and creation of structures in sound, and that such structures result from the application of thought processes to the basic elements of sound. The experience of exploring music from this point of view ('creativity') is cultivated so as to enable the pupils to make individual and highly personal pieces of music ('originality').

In contrast to this, it is essential to bear in mind that most pop music (including rock) is perceived by its creators and audience as a form with clearly defined characteristics and sub-idioms, which are invested with great significance not only by teenage listeners, but by the musicians and singers themselves. One is thus, for example, not just 'a guitarist', or 'a pop guitarist', but 'a country guitarist'. The major way to pop success was and largely still is mastery of one of these idioms in all its subtlety. This is not to deny the possibility of a meaningful application of the term 'originality' to pop, but we do need to be constantly aware that originality in pop refers to insight and creativity *within comparatively fixed limits*. This makes it inevitable that originality in pop can only normally be acquired after an apprenticeship which is long and exacting, even if it is informal. Such an apprenticeship must necessarily entail close and accurate imitation of accepted models. Pop can thus be seen as a discipline, and has many of the advantages of one; for instance

it leads to an understanding of the need for practice based upon a striving for quality;

it develops the ear and an acute sense of idiom;

it encourages internalisation (i.e. profound and intuitive understanding, arising from practical experience) rather than superficial analysis of the nature, materials, standards and aims of music;

it gives a sense of achievement in the manifest acquisition of a skill which can be assessed by comparing it with existing and publicly valued examples of the form.

The important role of improvisation in both avant garde music and pop is well known. But there is some danger in concluding that as a consequence the aims and potentialities of improvisation in the two forms can be equated. To begin with, the concept of 'improvisation' includes a range of activities, notably:

(i)   playing an unwritten part, of which the nature is clearly prescribed by the conventions of the idiom;

(ii)   flexibility beyond the classical norms over detail and ornamentation, as part of a search for an individual and personal (rather than standardised) style of self-expression;

(iii)   total extempore composition.

It is this third form of improvisation with which the teacher who is interested in modern serious music and the most adventurous forms of rock will be most concerned. In these fields improvisation is encouraged, both as a form of self-expression and in order to avoid premature rigidity of conception, even if successful improvisation is later formalised into a fixed composition. The use of improvisation in most pop and rock, however, is limited to the first two usages above.

In conclusion, it is worth recalling that Tony Robins makes a convincing case for the avoidance of current 'hits' as study material, but it should be noted that this need not always be a problem. I believe that immediate relevance is so powerful a motivating force in secondary school pupils that a teacher should be very cautious about ignoring it. The imitation of artists whom he values can give great satisfaction to the young player, and such imitation usually generates considerable interest, admiration and often competition among his peers. With beginners the achievement of a high technical standard often seems to be less important to both player and audience than the choice of material. Naturally though, this issue is one that should be decided by the pupils themselves, or by the teacher on the spot, sensitively responding to the situation.

Individual work

The first problem here is one of resources and space. Some of the teacher's needs are:

(i)   Record players or tape decks. The noise problem can largely be resolved through the use of headphones.

(ii)   Practice rooms for acoustic instruments.

(iii)   Practice facilities for amplified instruments, involving
        good sound-proofing,
        small amplifiers with headphones,

practice amplifiers with low wattage (note that 'low' still means 'loud' by traditional school standards).

(iv)   Practice rooms for drummers. Drummers *can* practice on a pad or a set of pads, known as a practice kit. In this matter dire necessity (angry neighbours and the like) can produce some ingenious solutions. But at a certain point there can be no substitute for actually thumping a real kit. This is true from both a musical point of view (imagine always playing on a muted trumpet) and as an emotional fact. If one is to grip pop fans used to lavish displays of expenditure, toy instruments and fake situations will not do.

(v)   Tape recorders with parallel tracking facilities (i.e. machines of the language laboratory type, which permit imitation of one track on another, or superimposition). Though apparently a luxury, this facility is certainly valuable, and possibly vital. Some skills, such as playing electric rock guitar or blues styles, can *only* be learned by ear. But it is also often necessary to use the same aural approach in teaching elements of music which are conventionally passed on by notation when one is dealing with pupils who do not read music, whether due to a lack of opportunity, aptitude or interest. It cannot be sufficiently stressed that we are dealing with a revolution of orthodox Western practice, and that learning by ear is as fundamental to this area as is the need to read in the traditional system. This need to follow the tradition of aural communication in Afro-American music is often reinforced by the resistance of pupils to the orthodox system of teaching by means of notation, a system associated in their mind with a culture with which they do not identify. It is thus true to say that pupils will tend to expect and need to learn from records. Again, however, worksheets have an important part to play in guiding them towards effective habits of listening.

It would be valuable if individual study could be linked to guidance from peripatetic instrumental teachers. However, as many such teachers are so accustomed to concentrating upon examination-orientated technicalities, they are likely to be suspicious of many of the ideas I have been suggesting. It is thus important for the full-time teacher to encourage discussion about the problems involved, and to invite comment by peripatetic teachers upon the results being achieved. It is also necessary to stress to LEAs (e.g. through music advisers) the need for and possibility of employing professional but unqualified musicians. Visiting players of non-conservatory instruments such as electric guitar and drums can add very much to the sense that one is engaged in real music making, and they bring with them high standards and a sense of dedication. This has begun to happen in various areas of the country through the engagement of players such as Graham Collier, Ed Harvey and Don Rendell (from the field of jazz), but the principle could be greatly extended, with benefits both to schools and to music in general. Guaranteed work of this sort is the next best thing to a subsidy for the artist and is perhaps healthier for the art; it also offers a mutually valuable solution to the problems of the player who is coming to the end of his playing career.

Pop and girl pupils

The argument is often raised that pop music is a characteristically male activity, and that much of its greatest success has been based on the projection of various forms of male image (e.g. aggressive — Mick Jagger; boyish — David Cassidy) to passive and adulating adolescent girls. Though to some extent this argument is irrefutable, I need to stress again the point made in the Introduction that many criticisms of pop are half truths. Certainly the criticism fails to reflect the rapid and radical changes of role and attitude among women over the past ten years or so.

I am inclined to believe that at present girls *do* tend to shy away from heavier, rowdier, more dissonant and more aggressive forms of music, as well as from music requiring a greater degree of attention and reflection; they seem to prefer the lighter and more immediately accessible forms such as folk songs, ballad pop and sentimental mass pop. But even this would give a wide enough basis for some serious and valid musical education of the type proposed in this book.

Furthermore, it is plain that such assumptions could easily become self-fulfilling prophecies. We are never likely to win our pupils' interest in forms of music which we never offer to them. I see no evidence that any attempt to broaden the area of response to music is any less likely to be effective with girls than with boys.

With regard to the performance of music, one again comes across a recurrent image of 'feminine' and 'unfeminine' instruments. This can be disposed of in a similar way. The work of Tony Robins, for example, indicates that a girl can and will play the drums; her effectiveness can be heard on side 2, track 6 of the recording. Certainly there are many women singers, guitarists and pianists; to this we can add the regular range of classical instruments. Artists such as Melanie, Carole King, Joni Mitchell and Aretha Franklin have shown that women are as capable as men of winning an international reputation. They also present the teacher with an extremely wide range of stylistic approach.

There is therefore no need to assume that work in pop is unsuited to or disliked by girls, or that it is necessarily in some way demeaning or unfeminine. Though there is ample opportunity for those who wish to do so to take on a more assertive role (following the direction of Janis Joplin or Grace Slick), the girl pupil (or woman teacher) who prefers a more traditional role need make no compromises in order to achieve much of value.

The pop syllabus

The reader will have observed that no detailed suggestion for a syllabus has been given; one reason for this is that such detailed guidance is not the aim of this book. There is, however, a more fundamental consideration, which is that once again the teacher has to acclimatise himself to a new situation in which he will be obliged to make his own syllabus, and also to revise or change it frequently. Such a suggestion may come as a shock to the teacher who is used to working from a traditional syllabus prepared by others, based on clearly understood and well tried aims, and containing familiar and even predictable musical material. In such a teaching situation there is clearly a profound and satisfying sense of security, arising from the fact that one is assured of the generally accepted value of one's work, and of one's competence to teach it.

In contrast to this, a significant feature of teaching pop (or any other contemporary form) is that it is never possible to feel this security to anywhere near the same degree, because the processes of development and creation are still going on. The range of records released makes it impossible for any teacher to know the field exhaustively. Rapid changes of fashion add a further complication, so that a list of current 'hits' given here would be useless by the date of publication. The teacher can and should of course acquire a great deal of factual knowledge, technical skill and theoretical insight. To this end, a visit to a large music shop will introduce the teacher to the range and availability of instrumental tutors, transcriptions of solos and sheet music of themes; we have also attempted to give some initial guidance in the Bibliography. But the classically qualified teacher may still feel, with some reason, that as far as pop is concerned, he does not in an important sense *know* his subject.

To some teachers this may be so worrying a thought as to be quite unacceptable. But it *can* make for a sense of freshness, excitement and discovery, springing from real communication between teacher and pupil. In such circumstances secondary education can embody all the openness and vitality currently associated with much primary school work, with the added bonus that, at least with his older pupils, the teacher has little need to make allowances for age.

Links with other subjects

If the music teacher is prepared to forge links with other colleagues, another range of possibilities opens up. These are most suited to the freer environment of the primary school, or of integrated studies in middle schools, but a good deal of liaison can of course exist between teachers in secondary schools, where subjects are more rigidly separated and a strict timetable has to operate. Some useful indications, together with practical examples from different schools, of how music can be incorporated into various forms of integrated studies in the secondary school are given in the Schools Council publication *Music and Integrated Studies in the Secondary School* (1972). Here I merely wish to indicate a few points of contact which the music teacher may find meaningful, together with some suggestions which he can make to colleagues who wish to exploit pop as a teaching medium for their own subject areas. Additional material on these lines is given in the Bibliography.

In making these suggestions, I am effectively asking for the erosion of some of the barriers which the structure of our school system all too often imposes upon. those who work in it. The mutual profitability of cooperation with interested colleagues who are amateur musicians is strongly stressed by Malcolm Nicholls, particularly in his discussion of 'Adam'.

Science and mathematics teachers can very easily lead out into a range of applied studies involving acoustics and electronics. For example, the theory and construction of the gadgets which produce many pop music effects, such as the fuzz box, are within the limits imposed by upper school courses in physics and electronics. Not only these effects but also simple practice amplifiers are possible construction projects. Articles giving the circuitry of such devices appear at regular intervals in the various electronics magazines, which also usually run a column answering readers' queries about technical problems and giving relevant sources of information.

Teachers of *mechanical or technical subjects* can clearly link up with such work. The delicacy and care which goes into electronic construction has to be matched by equally careful thought about how the apparatus is to be protected from the many rigours to which it will be exposed when being moved about. Tony Robins also points out that the technical studies department can be invaluable in the construction of microphone accessories.

A further possibility, of real interest to a minority of pupils, is instrument making. As there is no problem of soundbox construction the solid electric guitar makes a very suitable project, but the more ambitious pupils will inevitably turn to the challenge of building acoustic instruments; the results can be very impressive.

A final idea, but one which can occasionally grip a pupil with almost fanatical fervour, is the study and construction of mechanical instruments (e.g. the pianola, musical box, etc.). A trip to the Piano Museum at Brentford would be a good starter here.

Teachers of *art* have a role to play too, in the exploitation of pop as a subject matter for teaching. Pop music is a performing art and thus swings constantly towards the visual emphasis which we find in opera. As well as assisting with school productions the art teacher can use matters of lighting, dress and stage presentation as starting points for introducing the basic concepts of design. This can come from performances by pupils, visits to concerts and watching films or television. It is worth remembering that many art teachers now find that commercial art has become so sophisticated and draws upon such a range of historical periods that it can be a most valuable source of ideas and material. The study and design of record sleeves has been very popular and successful, wherever I have seen it used.

There are many possibilities open to the teacher of *dance and movement*, and indeed many younger teachers have already begun to exploit this area. It would thus be presumptuous to lecture them on the value of using pop. But I feel that certain questions can nevertheless be put with profit. Is the teacher using the whole range which pop offers? Children in some schools are already being brought to respond to more adventurous music, such as that of Mike Oldfield and Pink Floyd. But is it also possible to use aspects of pop (e.g. reggae, mass pop) which are currently less valued in educational circles? Can we find a place for teenage dances, as they become fashionable — perhaps integrating them into a mixed media production?

Also very important and challenging is the use of rarer metres and changes of metre, such as came into pop music in the mid-60s. Even more fundamental is the cultivation of a sensitive response (in both pupil *and* teacher) to tempo, and the subtleties of the rhythm section. These are not merely academic niceties, but vital to musicians. It is easy to stick to the belief that pop rhythm consists of no more than three or four obvious variants of four-beat time; but this is to miss much of the interplay between the rhythm instruments, and to fail to respond with the sensitivity which the groups themselves display.

This is perhaps also an apt point to mention that pop music is being successfully used in many schools as an adjunct to *physical education*. Pop records with a regular beat can be used for circuit training, doing an exercise for, say, every two beats. Pop has also been used (even at Olympic level) to accompany floorwork gymnastics exercises. It is of no little importance to the teacher that this approach seems to get the pupils to work twice as hard without realising it!

Teachers of *academic arts subjects* can find some useful points of integration with music. Even a subject such as geography can be enriched by drawing upon the popular music of the area studied. Records from the Third World are now fairly easily available. The *history* teacher too can find plenty to help him bring a given historical period to life. In the past ten years or so a range of popular music from before 1914 has become easily available. Folk music, either in its pure form, or given a modern but sympathetic reworking as in the music of a group such as Steeleye Span, can be invaluable, as can the songs of the Victorian music hall. There has also been a rise in the popularity of the music of the period 1914—54, which can be easily linked with studies of modern history. Apart from recorded material, the BBC frequently broadcasts programmes on earlier periods or performers. For instance, they have recently tackled the music of George Formby.

Since a large amount of current pop is concerned with the less fortunate, and in so doing reflects the increasing social concern of young people, one can utilise pop as teaching material in *social studies* or *general studies* lessons as an adjunct to or starting point for the exploration of a contemporary problem. Such work clearly overlaps with some of the work done by many English teachers, but there is also ample scope for the introduction of the methods and perspectives of *sociology* by teachers trained in that discipline. An important possibility (with obvious application to other subjects) is mentioned by Guy (1973) — that of getting pupils to prepare a history of a certain style of pop music (e.g. reggae) and present it in the form of a taped 'radio' show. Such a documentary presentation can be a very valuable exercise, especially when a group of say three or four pupils are concerned with producing it. The group must battle out between themselves such questions as: In what way, if at all, should there be division of labour within the group concerning accumulation of material? What material should be presented, in what order, and why? Finally the purely technical problems of presentation are in themselves involving and valuable. In this respect it has been observed by many commentators (e.g. Murdock and Phelps, 1973, p. 142) that one of the best ways in which to develop a pupil's critical awareness towards mass media products is to engage the pupils in actually creating media materials themselves.

It might at first sight appear that no one could find less use for pop than the teacher of *religious, ethical or moral studies*, but this is far from true. A substantial amount of rock music has been concerned with matters fundamental to any serious consideration of religion and ethics. In the first instance rock songs are often deeply concerned with morality — songs against war and exploitation, or songs of sympathy for the weak and underprivileged. Secondly, there is what for want of a better term one might call a 'mystical' element. Record after record will illustrate the fact that though there is no coherent philosophy behind rock music (despite some interest in Hinduism and Zen Buddhism) there is a pervading sense of the deep longings and aspirations currently felt by many young people. The religiously committed teacher may indeed wish to see this fact as a major explanation of the concerns and modes of expression of rock music.

The lyrics of pop (and more especially rock) can provide valuable starting points for the work of the *English* teacher. The modern poet has been particularly concerned to communicate with his audience through metaphor, symbol and archetype which, as the psychologist Ornstein (1973) describes more systematically, take us directly into the inner life of human beings. Because current pop and rock lyrics have often turned to the same forms of expression, they thus offer a convenient link with poetry. Furthermore, there seems to be little doubt that young people today tend to respond far more quickly and intuitively to such modes of expression than did earlier generations; they seem to be less bedevilled by a concern for immediately perceptible, sequentially and logically expressed meaning. Naturally, since we are dealing with *lyrics*, which are conceived of in relation to music, we should not expect them necessarily to stand up when separated from that music, in the way that a *poem* must; nor will meaning be so densely compressed. But they will offer us some lines of approach to poetry.

The study of pop lyrics in purely formal terms, as an analytical and critical discipline, is difficult to handle, and is probably best approached in connection with creative music making. Inspiration by a particular subject and the desire to experiment with or overcome the problems of a form are surely the major generative forces of creative work. Three main types of pop form suggest themselves:

   (i)   Folk ballads.

   (ii)   Blues. This is a very good starter because one only needs to compose a simple couplet (see also Piers Spencer's suggestions in chapter 4).

   (iii) Older popular forms (pre-war lyrics). These can be a real challenge to a certain type of pupil, because their patterns are often quite complex. Such work can also stimulate related satirical pieces (e.g. the music of Roxy Music and Lou Reed).

These forms all involve rhyme and something like a traditional approach to metre. However, as any teacher who has been involved with creative writing will know, there are many pupils who can enjoy the tighter forms mentioned above, but who are unable to use them. Free verse approaches can be valuable in such circumstances. The use of lines of varying length and rhythmic structure has been a growing feature of pop in the past ten years, with very exciting results. The various texts on creative writing in primary schools (e.g. Rosen, 1973) show a method of approach to the writing of free verse which can easily be modified to suit the older pupil.

A few final points for the English teacher remain to be made; many of these are equally applicable to teaching under the label of 'music'. The possibility of talking about the music (and the possible failure of this approach) have been noted earlier, as have the potentialities of operatic or mixed media work. There is much valuable work to be done when pupils create or select music to accompany a poem which is being studied (Malcolm Nicholls mentions a class which was doing this). I believe also that the teacher should not totally discount the possibility of letters to pop stars and to the papers, handouts and posters for discotheques, project files on favourite singers and so on. Clearly this is a far cry from purely academic work, but with the young or less able pupil it can be a way of inculcating ideas of systematic work, pride in arrangement and presentation — even a crafty bit of spelling correction!

Conclusion

Finally, I would like to sum up the ideas which I have been trying to stress in this chapter. They are:

(i)   Pop music is clearly of great interest to most pupils, and thus is likely to be more effective in motivating them to action and study.

(ii)   The teacher is naturally concerned with the question of value; but as well as asking his pupils to develop their powers of discrimination, he should ask whether there are not some grounds for a change of attitude on *his* part.

(iii)   The music teacher is concerned not only with matters such as 'quality of emotion', but with technical skills. Where apathy or hostility could be the result of using traditional approaches, the teacher may find that he can teach skills which he does value, by means of work whose spiritual quality he feels to be less than that of works which he prefers (I do not suggest that he should utilise material to which he is actually opposed on moral or aesthetic grounds). Put crudely, if there has to be a choice, it is better for pupils to learn the concept of 'harmonic progression' by playing pop guitar, than not to learn it at all.

(iv)   The music teacher needs a change of role. He needs to become the Director of Music, or more strictly, the Initiator of Musical Activities, with a roving commission. Though he must continue to meet the traditional requirements of the music teacher (such as providing music for Assembly), he should not need to be committed to a full timetable of class music. This can still have its uses, as Malcolm Nicholls points out, but the music teacher's main purpose should be to provide a thriving centre of interest, an information service, and an outlet for all who care to take advantage of it. He should be concerned not so much with what music is made, but that it shall be made at all. I believe that every contributor to this book can vouch for the fact that when this happens, the only problem tends to be that of getting the pupils to go home, as many a caretaker will testify.

References

Guy, L., *Pop Music and Working Class Culture* (Liberal Education, No. 25, 1973).
Murdock, G. and Phelps, G. *Mass Media and the Secondary School* (Macmillan, 1973).
Ornstein, R., *The Psychology of Consciousness* (W.H. Freeman, 1973).
Paynter, J. and Aston, P., *Sound and Silence* (Cambridge University Press, 1970).
Rosen, C. and H., *The Language of Primary School Children* (Penguin, 1973).
Schools Council, *Music and Integrated Studies in the Secondary School* (Schools Council, 1972).

Postscript: pop into the eighties

DAVE ROGERS

1

for introduction

Oh, won't you tell me —
Where have all the good times gone? (The Kinks, 1965; David Bowie, 1973)

By the end of 1975 rock music had largely lost the undisciplined excitement and vital audience contact which were part of fifties rock'n'roll and the sixties beat boom. Those roots seemed far away.

There was plenty of good music which was increasingly better-produced. But better production had always been only one element (and not always the most dominant one) in the best rock music. Rock had become a part of the same entertainment industry that had thrown up its hands in horror at the raw, disturbing unprofessionalism of its origins. 'Money, money, money/It's a rich man's world', sang Abba at the top of the charts, while Rod Stewart wasn't the only rock star to make his home in the United States as a tax-exile. Elaborate stage costumes and presentation, as well as extremely costly sound and light equipment, distanced bands further and further from their audiences. Spectacle began to replace excitement.

Tours by big-name bands such as Bad Company were becoming once-a-year affairs at huge impersonal venues like London's Earls Court, with the acoustics of a Concorde-hangar and no possibility of audience participation. You sat and listened as though you were listening to the band's records at home. The excitement of rock'n'roll can only come from being *involved* in the music — and this was increasingly hard to find.

I used to like people like Alice Cooper when I was about thirteen, and you could never get to see them because you didn't really have much money and they played the big places in London and it cost loads of money to get in and you couldn't really go and see them. (18-year-old Tracie, quoted in *The Sex Pistols* — Fred and Judy Vermorel, Universal/Tandem 1978.)

Meanwhile the music itself reflected the new life-styles of the stars — and stars they were in the Hollywood mould of the past. Significantly, the record industry in Los Angeles had by the mid-seventies largely replaced the dying, old-style Hollywood film industry, and was now increasingly allied to films, as the emphasis on soundtrack albums and movies like *Grease* was beginning to show. At one extreme, lyrics penned by expatriate rock musicians living in style on the American West Coast bore scant relevance to the lives of their young listeners in Britain. At the other, such pop music as that of the Carpenters and Abba, though skilfully crafted, dealt in the old traditions of pop — in a cosy, fantasy world quite divorced from the grey reality and lack of excitement of the mid-seventies, with their problems of inflation, growing unemployment and limited career opportunities. Rock had even thrown up its own middle-of-the-road music: in America many rock bands' music was now categorised as AOR (Adult-Orientated-Rock).

In the main, the big-selling bands were the old ones — Pink Floyd, the Rolling Stones, Yes and Genesis — those the record companies were willing to invest safely in and those who, through their success, could afford the outlay needed to play on long tours and in large halls.

This situation was acceptable to the now-settled generation that had begun listening to rock in the late sixties. But for a younger teenage generation there was little to be excited about — little they could feel a part of. With rare exceptions, rock music had become safe, bankrupt in ideas and — yes, it does have a meaning in this context — middle-class. It no longer slashed at your ear-drums, straightened your spine at the opening chords, over-rode everything else and made you want to dance. More and more it was music to sit down to, to appreciate and to discuss. 'Do people actually *listen* to that music? No! it's just background music while they buy their jeans — *flared* jeans. Is that any state for rock to be in?' (Johnny Rotten). Evidently it wasn't — though there was excitement to be found in the biting r'n'b of Southend's Dr Feelgood and in the increasingly popular reggae of Jamaica's Bob Marley and the Wailers.

Into this stagnant scene in 1976 exploded the Sex Pistols and punk rock — with something of the same force as rock'n'roll twenty years earlier and to a lesser extent the Beatles, Stones and Who in the mid-sixties. It wasn't just a rejuvenation; it was a direct, iconoclastic and violent reaction against the meaningless pomp which rock, allied with the multi-million dollar record industry, had become.

2

The future's gleam is a sharpened scream. ('Anarchy In The UK', the Sex Pistols, 1976)

On 25 May 1976 the Sex Pistols were playing for their third consecutive Tuesday night at the tiny 100 Club in Oxford Street, London. A mile away in Earls Court Stadium six thousand people, who'd paid between two and four pounds each for the privilege, were watching the Rolling Stones nearing the end of a week's engagement, the climax of their first British tour for three years. A week earlier Patti Smith and her band from New York had played at the Roundhouse with the

Stranglers in support. Booked at the same venue for America's Bicentennial Independence Day were the Flamin' Groovies and the first British appearance of New York's top punk band, the Ramones.

A strong following had already grown up around the Sex Pistols. Spurred on by them, in London and elsewhere, other new young bands were starting up. In Manchester, Howard Devoto and Pete Shelley, as tired of the redundancy of rock as Johnny Rotten, were already forming the Buzzcocks. It was the first significant upsurge of new bands of the seventies. Clearly, and at last, something was happening which had little to do with much of the audience at the Stones' concerts that week, or with the increasingly distant and much older rock stars of the sixties and early seventies. 'So you know, that's what was good about the Pistols. You always knew they would play in places that didn't really cost much to get in. You could go along, you could say what the hell you wanted, dress how you wanted and no-one cared.' (Tracie)

The music was basic, raw, exciting — and audience-involving. Johnny Rotten's voice was the most original, disturbing and arresting of the decade. This was as obvious to those who saw the Pistols live as to those whose first acquaintance was with their single 'Anarchy In The UK', all the way from the opening demonic chuckle to the final word 'destroy'. (The record was withdrawn within weeks by EMI when, worried by what they had signed, they terminated the band's contract.)

In September 1976 the 100 Club staged a Punk Rock Festival featuring the Pistols and most of the early punk bands — the Clash, the Damned, Siouxsie and the Banshees (it was their first performance) and the Buzzcocks amongst them. By this time the music press had already written at length about the new music and its audience. But, apart from a feature in the *Sun* predictably centring on the bizarre appearance of punk audiences and calling it 'the craziest pop cult of them all', the first national exposure came with the Sex Pistols' appearance on an early evening TV programme at the beginning of December. The show's presenter, Bill Grundy (a peculiarly apt name) deliberately goaded them into using words not normally heard on television. The press outcry which followed was again predictable, if ridiculously vehement, in its condemnation of the band and punk rock in general.

'The Filth And The Fury' screamed the front page of the *Daily Mirror*. 'Punk? Call It Filthy Lucre' pointed the morally agonised finger of the populist *Express*. A country-wide tour by the band was cut to a handful of dates as venue after venue cancelled bookings. Reactions to rock'n'roll in the fifties were echoed:

We feel these programs are not for the good of the community and that's why I ordered them banned. (Local official, USA, 1956)
We feel their act is undesirable and unfit for the people of this city. (Local official, Newcastle City Hall, 1976)

Punk (and by extension the 'cult's' followers) was 'obscene', 'grotesque', and 'anti-life'. To Derek Jewell of the *Sunday Times* punk rock was 'the latest musical garbage bred by our troubled culture'. One newspaper found space to report what Bill

Haley thought of it all: 'I am all for entertainment but I have got a teenage daughter and I wouldn't like her to listen to some of the language these fellows use.' As usual the media had seized on the outward appearance and worked itself into a frenzy of self-righteousness. The models for their stories were those they'd produced in the past when dealing with rock'n'roll and Teddy Boys, and Mods and Rockers. The parameters of punk defined by the media — violence, spitting and safety-pins — were already firmly set in the nation's consciousness. Hopefully, the viewer who kicked in his TV screen ('I was so angry and disgusted with this filth that I took a swing with my boot') later regarded his impetuous destruction with deep regret.

What those who had such reactions failed to see was that a new music and youth style for the seventies and eighties had begun: a 'new wave'. A line had been drawn between all that had gone before and what was to come. The past could at last be seen as out of date. 'Today's Sound Today' was a Stiff Records catchphrase; 'No Elvis, Beatles or the Rolling Stones/In 1977' sang the Clash.

3

Rock'n'roll to me has to sound like a train, madly out of control, going down a mountain side just about to fall off the tracks. (Jake Burns of Stiff Little Fingers, *New Musical Express*, February 1979)

The spirit of the new bands was the rebellion, noise and energy of rock'n'roll. Their music was original, though it took its inspiration at first from earlier groups — sometimes from David Bowie, the Who and T. Rex, in a few cases from Captain Beefheart, but more often from tougher, less well-known urban bands of some years before: Iggy Pop's Stooges, the MC5, the Velvet Underground and the New York Dolls. The keynotes of the new music were commitment, relevance and direct contact with the audience. As Johnny Rotten put it: 'I'm against people who just complain about Top Of The Pops and don't do anything. I want people to go out and start something, to see us and start something, or else I'm just wasting my time.'

The preoccupations of the new bands were with themselves and their position in society. Though much was heard of nihilism and anarchy, the early epithet 'Blank Generation' was essentially a misnomer. For the first time in the seventies here was a music and a movement which, at its best, was constructive and forward-looking. As had happened with British rock in the sixties, and with skiffle in the fifties, the new movement was nation-wide. From in and around London came the Pistols, the Clash, the Damned, the Banshees, the Jam and a host of others. But all over the country new bands began, playing in small clubs and halls, often taking control of the whole process of making and recording their own music, manufacturing their own records at their own expense. The Desperate Bicycles' first single cost them £153: 'Xerox music is here at last', they sang, 'It was easy, it was cheap, go and do it'. From Scotland came the Rezillos and the Skids; from Northern Ireland, the Boomtown Rats and Stiff Little Fingers; from Newcastle, the Angelic Upstarts and their disturbing 'Murder Of Liddle Towers'; from nearby Ferryhill, Penetration; from Sheffield, the Human League; from Leeds, the Mekons and the Gang of Four. The Adverts came to London from the West Country, while Manchester rivalled London's importance with a scene of its own built initially around the Buzzcocks and Rabid Records.

The music itself was as varied as its places of origin. Fast, guitar-thrashing punk, based partly on the music of the New York Dolls and on the minimally-chordal, fast and relentless two-minute songs of the Ramones, was just one aspect, though a vitally important one. The spectrum was wide. What drew it together was that music, performance and life-style were not the manufactured mannerisms of the monopolistic large companies — nor were they pop-sentimental, bland or distant. These new bands were entertaining, exciting, but also of mostly serious intent. In the main, what they sang about was what their audience was also concerned about.

They offered me the office/offered me the shop,
They said I'd better take/anything they'd got.
'Do you wanna make tea at the BBC?
Do you wanna be — do you wanna be — a cop?'
Career opportunities — the ones that never knock,
Every job they offer you's to keep you out the dock —
Career opportunities
The ones that never knock. (Joe Strummer/Mick Jones, the Clash)

Some bands had their feet in camps of the past as well as the present — from the r'n'b-based songs of the Boomtown Rats inspired by the Stones and Bruce Springsteen to the Jam who looked back to the Who and Carnaby Street styles of the sixties. The short-lived Pistols crystallised the energy, drew the outrage and provided the starting-point. The Clash's songs are firmly set in a tough social reality, their music drawing from punk, rock'n'roll and reggae, while their stage performances provoke deserved comparisons with the Who as the best rock'n'roll band of them all. Their energy live makes it seem as if an invigorating high wind is blowing through the hall. Pete Shelley's songs for the Buzzcocks are another dimension of the movement. They have the instant effectiveness, power of delivery, originality and melody of the best songs of the Beatles before their *Sergeant Pepper* album, while in no way resembling them.

A refreshingly new music is that of Siouxsie and the Banshees with its dark and powerful dynamics, intelligent lyrics and the compelling presence of Siouxsie herself. 'You don't think about old forms,' said bass guitarist Steve Severin in a *Melody Maker* interview, 'You pretend that you're the first person ever to put pen to paper and ever to play guitar.' Siouxsie reflects a new and more healthy position for women in this area of music. First, there is a larger number of women than ever before fronting or playing in bands. But, more important, the role which they are willing to play has changed radically. There are still performers such as Debbie Harry of America's Blondie, who fit, to some extent, the established commercial pattern of the sex-symbol with the band behind her. But, in contrast, there are many artists

who present an uncompromisingly different front, more in keeping with the changing social position of modern women. Among them are Pauline Murray of Penetration and Fay Fife of the Rezillos; the Adverts and Talking Heads both have
women bassists, while the Slits began as an all-female band — and this is to mention
only a few. To the traditional audience they are often disturbingly 'unfeminine';
but for the young artists themselves, the new wave is another part of a process of
emancipation, which has been delayed for far too long: 'We're not playing in a
rock'n'roll band in a calculated way. It just comes naturally. I don't understand why
a great many more women don't do it too. I find it quite confusing that there aren't
many more girls in rock bands.' (Viv Albertine, the Slits.)

Thrown up too by the new wave were the brilliant and uncompromising songs
and music of Elvis Costello, who must be counted the single most important writer
and performer to have emerged in the late seventies, as well as the unique music of
Ian Dury, derived partly from the music hall and partly from rock'n'roll. Dury's
stage presence and songs in his pre-'76 band Kilburn and the High Roads were a
major influence on at least part of the new wave. New voices for a new age — and
firmly British.

4

I belong to the blank generation,
I can take it or leave it each time. (Richard Hell)

The American new wave was much smaller and also lacked the social cohesion of its
British counterpart. Notably, with some exceptions, it was based on the East Coast,
growing up around a small New York club called CBGB's. Most of the important
new musicians played there: Patti Smith, Television, Talking Heads, Blondie, the
Ramones, Richard Bell and (before their move to Britain) Johnny Thunders' Heartbreakers. Again energy and new ideas were the watchwords, opposed to the bland-
ness of middle-class American pop/rock.

But the differences between the various groups are very marked. Blondie has
grown into an excellent rock'n'roll-based pop band; the Ramones' machine-gun
bursts of short, sharp, thunderous songs helped fuel the British punk explosion. The
Heartbreakers and Richard Hell's Voidoids were excellent late-seventies rock'n'roll
bands. The Heartbreakers' image sprang from the sleazy glitter and outrageous camp
of the exciting New York Dolls. The latter were managed in their final incarnation
by Malcolm McLaren, who returned to Britain to form the Sex Pistols, modelling
part of their image on Richard Hell. The music of Television and of Talking Heads
is far more consciously and intellectually constructed, while Patti Smith moved
from reciting her poetry to welding it into a rock band.

5

If the kids are united
They will never be divided. (Jimmy Pursey and Sham 69, 1978)

I have given a large amount of space to the new wave because, along with disco, it is the most important development since the late sixties. But there are other youth audiences and other musics. When I wrote chapter 1 in 1975, I quoted Greil Marcus comment on youth's fragmentation into 'groups of age, taste, politics, geography and self-conscious sophistication' (p. 30). The gap between American and British tastes has widened in many cases, and the comment still has some relevance.

For example, remaining sixties bands, and new ones formed in their sometimes unconsciously-parodied images, continue to produce largely unoriginal variations of early-seventies rock music. Thus in this country Queen have lost any edge they once had. In America there is a seventies generation of bands such as Boston and Aerosmith who have turned out flashy but undemanding rock, which has meant little in Britain, though it brought them great popularity at home. Others, such as the Eagles, have taken once-vital styles like country rock unerringly into the middle-of-the-road for older, and in the United States at least, mostly middle-class, salary-earning audiences. American Country music, too, has continued its journey closer to the heartland of mainstream pop, despite the efforts of artists like Waylon Jennings and Guy Clark to lead the way back to a Nashville music which doesn't look to Hollywood for its style.

In Britain, though, there are few hard and fast dividing lines — different sorts of music often have their very separate audiences. As always, however, there is a large degree of overlap. Simon Frith, in an article in *Rock File 5* and in his book *The Sociology of Rock*, goes a long way towards delineating such differences. Some of the new-wave bands — Clash for example — have links with reggae. The principal populariser in this field has been Bob Marley. However, his music, though still good, is at the time of writing showing signs of softening its previously trenchant sound. It is the rhythms, the dub and toasting styles, and the religious, political and social stances of the last half of the seventies which have been the most arresting — finding echoes too in some new-wave music. This type of link has been fostered by the growth of British-based reggae bands like Merger, Steel Pulse and Misty.

Reggae and new-wave bands with this kind of orientation have had an important role to play in the movements to foster racial harmony. 1978 saw the rise of the Rock Against Racism movement and the Anti-Nazi League, which held joint marches and carnivals to combat racism and the activities of the National Front. On these occasions, as a deliberate policy, both new-wave and reggae bands were booked to play free. Their great success, helped by the passionate honesty and determination of such as the Tom Robinson Band, Sham 69 and the Clash, was not only encouraging but another sign of the times. 'I don't care' was a much-misunderstood punk epithet taken at surface value by the media but belied by the best of the new wave. In this sense *New Musical Express* writer Paul Morley's phrase 'realistic rock'n' roll' has a real meaning. Stiff Little Fingers came from Belfast, and their first album 'Inflammable Material' contains the most savagely direct (as well as almost the only) set of songs on Ulster in the seventies.

We've said all along we're not giving solutions. We're just telling people all around us what's going on . . . We never set ourselves up as being politicians or anything . . . Even when I'm on stage saying this killing is wrong to these kids, I don't want the power to make them go away mindlessly whining this killing is wrong, this killing is wrong. I want them to go away and think is it wrong? I want them to work it out . . . (Jake Burns)

On another front, the continuing efforts of enthusiasts have ensured that more fifties rock'n'roll, and especially rockabilly, is now available on record than even twenty years ago. The seventies have also seen a growing number of young people wearing neo-Teddy-Boy clothes, finding the power of the old music undiminished, and supporting British rockabilly and rock'n'roll bands. Some, like Crazy Cavan's band and the excellent Matchbox, have been playing for some years, but there are new much younger bands like Whirlwind too. Perhaps it's no accident that in the same month of '76 that the Pistols and Stones were playing in London, the Vintage Rock'n'Roll Appreciation Society organised a well-attended march to Broadcasting House to present a petition demanding more airspace for rock'n'roll.

In a wider pop sense, though, there has been the steady rise of 'disco'. As the Discography makes clear, disco covers a variety of different musical styles. Whereas r'n'b was the black music of the fifties, and soul that of the sixties, disco increasingly held the ring in the seventies. Like country, disco too has become a crossover style for commercial pop to plunder. At its most middle-of-the-road it is easily assimilable into Top Forty radio programme-planning, which is reflected by the charts. The music has also been greatly helped by the success of the film *Saturday Night Fever* and the media star of '78, John Travolta.

6

Of course the music has to be in the grooves if it's to be successful, but today's marketplace also demands a strong organisation, sophisticated marketing techniques and a hard-headed, very business-like approach to the logistical marketing, promotional and sales functions. (Walter Yetnikoff, President of CBS Records)

Perhaps we'd rather they spent their money buying guitars and amplifiers than records. (The Mekons on BBC TV, October 1978)

And the recording industry itself? Nothing better illustrates the emphasis on marketing instead of creativity than the tie-up between records, films and such spin-offs as books-of-the-film, books-on-the-making-of-the-film, poster magazines and general ephemera from the media blitz surrounding the films *Saturday Night Fever* and *Grease*. Bart Mills in the *Guardian* has called such films 'dramatised soundtracks', pointing out that by August '78 the *Saturday Night Fever* album had already outgrossed the film.

Marketing of records through TV advertisements has also become commonplace and profitable — so much so that EMI has designated a special catalogue prefix (EMTV-) for such ventures. Pop is now a bigger business than ever before and it was partly this marketing stranglehold over the means to play and produce music which fuelled the reaction of the new wave.

For that explosion was not just musical and social. It couldn't have taken place in the way it did without alternative means of producing records. Just as fifties rock'n'roll in the States grew from small, independent local labels, so did the new wave in Britain. The first small labels were Stiff and Chiswick, the latter significantly growing out of the specialist record shop *Rock On*. Both labels were close to their audience and signed artists and bands whom the major companies were unwilling to invest in. Sometimes they saw no world-wide marketing potential; alternatively, they were too far removed from, and hence ignorant of, what was actually going on outside the Top 50 single and album charts. As the new wave gathered momentum, there came a host of smaller labels, some extremely specialist, some one-offs, many to eventually find licensing links with the major companies who belatedly came to realise that money could be made from this new music. At present Fast and Rough Trade are the most radically experimental of the remaining independents. The small labels' importance lies in easy and relatively cheap and fast access for bands to their audiences and for audiences to the music they want; it is possible, too, to employ unusual approaches to marketing and publicity. The new labels also offered the opportunity for the musicians themselves to be involved in the production and marketing of their music. Though it is proving difficult, many bands who later signed to the major companies have tried to keep this freedom as a basic principle.

7

And the radio is in the hands
Of such a lot of fools who try
To anaesthetise the way that you feel. (Elvis Costello, 1978)

The record charts (once Top 50, now Top 75) remain unrepresentative of everything that is being bought. They are made up from the returns of a (supposedly) secret list of selected shops throughout the country. In turn many of the bigger shops — often chain stores such as Boots and W.H. Smith — stock just those singles which appear in the charts. Therefore customers eeeking other types of record tend to find them only in specialist shops (like those who stock reggae) or smaller stores (*Rock On* or *Rough Trade* for example). But these shops are not asked for chart returns. It follows that the actual sales of many new-wave, reggae, rock'n'roll and disco records are not accurately reflected in their chart positions. For this reason, *Top Of The Pops* (which, according to its producer, considers itself a news programme reflecting what the public is buying) remains for the most part the comfortable, unstimulating show it has always been.

So, despite the new wave, much pop is still the rock music of before re-channelled for the late seventies. Of the established major artists prior to the new wave, it is mainly the Who and David Bowie who retain the respect of the newer bands. The Who have always remained close to their audience, and Pete Townshend (together with the presently-retired John Lennon) is the most articulate and deeply-thoughtful musician of his generation. The Who's music has always been powerful and even their sixties recordings fit well with the new bands of the late seventies. Despite the tragic death of drummer Keith Moon in the summer of 1978 they are continuing as a band and are at present involved in two film projects, one a record of their career and the other a version of *Quadrophenia*.

Bowie has always seemed in total control of his various changes of style and the different personas he has adopted — although hindsight leaves some of his work in a less favourable light than its impact at the time suggested. Nevertheless, almost alone among contemporary rock stars, he has never been afraid to experiment with new forms and ideas, usually successfully. Yet he has not been sucked into the industry's sterile image-making process in the way that, arguably, Bryan Ferry and Roxy Music were in the mid-seventies. Bowie's *Station To Station* and *Low* albums have proved satisfying departures, the latter recorded in Germany in collaboration with Brian Eno, once a member of Roxy Music. Together, they have looked away from America towards Europe, and to West Germany and Berlin in particular — with what ultimate result it is too soon to judge.

From Germany has come the electronic music of Tangerine Dream, and the colder machine-like music of Kraftwerk and Neu. Echoes can be found in the work of a range of bands, such as the later work of both Bowie and Eno, and Sheffield's Human League. This influence is also found in the highly-produced disco music of both Boney M and Donna Summer in their respective productions by Frank Farian and Giorgio Moroder. It is perhaps Bowie and Eno, but also bands like the Human League, who may well make most use of the wider potentialities of this resource. In the United States there are vague echoes too in the music of Devo and Père Ubu. Although they might argue against such a description Devo's approach is de-humanising and de-individualising. However, their music is not as impressive as the genuinely original work of Père Ubu. The future of all the above is difficult to predict. What can be said is that such developments will continue into the eighties.

And beyond? When I wrote the main chapter for the first edition of this book the time was the mid-seventies, and the concerns and music of the sixties were time-torn and dusty, but standing — though very still in most cases. It was easier then to draw to a close, and to attempt to summarise and evaluate, even if sometimes mistakenly, in the light of subsequent events. At the moment — encouragingly — it is hard to come to any firm conclusion. Rock music stemming from the late sixties has become one part in the array of differing styles of music and stances, which together make up the pop music world at the turn of the seventies.

When the seventies began, much rock music was tending to look in at itself, as the industry surrounding it grew into the giant world-wide entertainment business of the present. Today some dents, however temporary, have been made in that corporate structure. Though it is in the nature of the pop industry to assimilate what shakes it and recycle it into undisturbing product, the breadth and depth of music-making and access to it have grown beyond anything that could have been conceived in 1975. The early punk bands suffered from those comfortably British public traits such as mistrust of those who are loudly definite in their opinions and their advocacy of change, and a belief that popular music is solely entertainment and no place for what that public thinks of as politics. Bands like Clash and Sham 69 were watched closely from the start for any tiny sign of compromised principles. Clash have survived this enormous pressure, while Sham 69's Jimmy Pursey has doggedly put into practice some of punk's original ideals by using the band's earnings in helping other bands and forming an alternative and accessible record company. Through all this he has insisted on staying as far as possible part of his own audience, although at times much too close for comfort, as he publicly grapples with the essential paradox of such a position. He is perhaps the most defiantly genuine of all the new performers of the late seventies and the one who perhaps most mirrors what punk was originally all about.

The trend then is for musicians and their audiences both to reflect and to be involved in the society of which they are a part. This is the healthiest sign of change in years. In a Velvet Underground song of the sixties Lou Reed sang 'Between thought and expression lies a lifetime'. For a time at least in the last years of the seventies, thanks to the upsurge of accessible new-wave music, the small labels, clubs and halls which conveyed it, and the will and determination for involvement — musical and social — the gap between thought and expression has narrowed dramatically.

'The seventies are going to have to learn to cope with the eighties the same way that the sixties learned to cope with the seventies . . . and the fifties had to cope with the sixties and everybody had to learn to cope with rock'n'roll when it started in the first place.
We've still got a long way to go.'
                                  Charles Shaar Murray, *New Musical Express*, 31 March 1979.

April 1979

Recorded illustrations

A stereo cassette recording is available of the following pieces of music referred to in the text.

	Track	Page	Chapter/ example	
Side 1	1	101–3	5.1–4	Classroom blues
	2	103–5	5.5	'Baby I may not be much now'
	3	105–7	5.7	Psalm 107 – choral extract
	4	105–7	5.8	Psalm 107 – organ solo
	5	107–8	5.9	'Jazz Fantasia'
	6	109–10	5.10	Recorder and xylophone
	7	109–10	5.11	Recorder and cymbals
	8	110–12	5.12	Piano and percussion
	9	112–13	5.13	'Moonlight Mist'
	10	113–14	5.14	'Seen her at the club'
	11	114	5	Explorations of 5.14
	12	114–17	5.15	'I was so alone'
	13	114–17	5.16	'I was so alone' – second version
	14	117–20	5.17	Suspension song
	15	117–20	5.20	Suspension song – final version
	16	120–1	5	'Now summer's gone away'
Side 2	1	130, 132	6	End of term song
	2	136	6	Electronic music
	3	136	6	'Lady on the moor'
	4	136	6	Multi-instrumental solo
	5	139	6	Jam
	6	153, 168	7	'Brighten Your Night'
	7	153–4	7	'You are the Sunshine of my Life'
	8	153, 156	7	'Kind of Homesick Blues'
	9	153, 156	7	'Easter Song'
	10	153, 156	7	'Fools'

The recordings are of varying quality technically. Some tracks were made in the classroom with very limited equipment or in spontaneous sessions and some were made in near-professional or professional conditions, notably tracks 6–10 on side 2 which were recorded by Radio Humberside, to whom thanks are due. However they all give some indication of what can be achieved by pupils and teachers in the differing approaches and situations described by Piers Spencer, Malcolm Nicholls and Tony Robins, and advocated throughout the book.

The pieces on side 1 are fully analysed by Piers Spencer; Ed Lee provides some notes on side 2, picking our some additional points of musical content and practical interest.

Side 2

Track 1. A folk-influenced piece, which explores the hemiola (3 against 6) rhythm very effectively. Also of interest are the quality of the lyric, the use of mandolin and of the classical oboe player (improvised backing, written solo). Note the quality of the recording and the importance of a lively audience in creating the atmosphere of a pop concert.

Track 2. This was created with a Philicorda organ, radio tuner, home-made oscillator and Revox tape recorder. Note the use of silences, and of extremes of volume. The composer makes much use of stereo effects (which can be heard on the stereo cassette).

Track 3. A piece in 'contemporary folk' style, created entirely by the composer using superimposition. Note the clear but potentially very flat studio sound, and the interesting, intuitively derived vocal harmonies characteristic of this style, which ignore the rules of conventional 'classical' part writing.

Track 4. This track is an extract from a piece created for CSE examination, and like track 3 uses superimposition, in this case of guitar, glockenspiel, synthesiser and organ. It is conceived in the style of Mike Oldfield's *Tubular Bells*, and unfortunately tends to illustrate the danger of monotony in the use of ostinati as the main device for the creation of texture and structure. However, the composer creates some rather crude sforzando effects, which grow in interest and appeal on subsequent hearings.

Track 5. This performance arose spontaneously after a 'Sounds' concert; consequently the recording is unbalanced. Nevertheless guitars, harmonica and singer can be heard faintly. Note the emphasis on excitement, but also the degree of discipline (the percussionists follow and 'answer' each other), which reflects the insights gained in Adrian's drum ensemble.

Track 6. This is an example of the work of Tony Robins' choral and instrumental group. The rhythm section can be clearly heard in the introduction, and this is followed by voices both in harmony and used antiphonally with a soloist. The scope which this idiom offers to the arranger is well demonstrated (note especially the effective final section).

Track 7. The arrangement demonstrates the tasteful use of vocalists (long backing notes on 'ah'), as well as the possibility of extending instrumentalists' capabilities by the introduction of a modulation (last chorus).

Track 8. This piece, like tracks 9 and 10, was written and sung by a pupil, Chris Lazenby. It is typical of blues-based music and uses two of the most characteristic basic beats of the idiom. Note the use of reverberation and the blend of acoustic and electric instruments. This was achieved by mixing and, though easy enough to record, such a blend is often more difficult to achieve effectively in live performance. One aspect of this mixing process is that it is possible to bring into the foreground detail which would otherwise be lost. In this case Lazenby's fierce attack means that he hits both strings and guitar body with such force that at times one has the illusion of the presence of drums.

Track 9. This song, which uses 'Afro' or 'Latin' techniques in a blues-derived idiom, illustrates some potential strengths and weaknesses of the style. The undiscriminating use of reverberation finally disintegrates into an unwanted echo (for instance, at one point the claves strokes are doubled). Yet the piece clearly demonstrates the possibility of developing a high level of musical competence and sensitivity in improvised solos, in the choice and use of guitar tones — compare the tones of the two solos and of the solo in track 8 — and in the subtly varied combinations of percussion rhythms and tones.

   The track illustrates another important point — namely that *repetition* is as central to this idiom as *variation* is to classical music. Appreciating the role of repetition in pop is perhaps the most important realignment which the classically trained musician must make if he wishes to become involved with pop. Repetition is often described as 'monotonous' only because the listener finds the idiom as a whole unappealing. On the other hand, we should not advocate the uncritical acceptance of all repetition for, as Graham Vulliamy argues in Chapter 2, there are criteria of 'good' repetition in Afro-American music. Thus final judgement as to the effectiveness of, for example, the repetitive bass lines on this track must lie with the listener.

Track 10. This song manifests both the composer's self-awareness and his grasp of lyric writing. It is also a fitting reminder of two points frequently made by contributors, that pop listeners are acutely aware of distinctions within the idiom, and that songs should be regarded as a form distinct from either music or poetry. Just as a simple lyric may be transformed by the music with which it is combined, conversely (as in this case), a not very distinguished piece of music is often the best setting for a lyric with a great deal to say, if our attention is not to be distracted.

Bibliography

Using the Bibliography (notes by Ed Lee)

It has been pointed out at various times in this book that the teacher who uses pop will have to create his own curriculum. My aim here is therefore to make some suggestions on how the Bibliography may be used in formulating classroom projects or courses. The structure of the Bibliography follows that of the main body of the book: Part 1, Historical and theoretical studies of pop music; Part 2, Information and resources for the teacher.

In view of the rapid growth in the number of relevant publications, we have for the most part confined our recommendations to books currently in print. However, in a few instances we have felt that a book is of such significance that we have made an exception; in such cases the teacher should consult his local library, which will often have the book in stock, or be able to obtain it through the inter-library lending scheme. Given our limitations of space here, we have also slanted our references in this second edition towards those not already included in the first edition. Teachers requiring a fuller or more specialised range of materials are therefore advised to consult the first edition as well.

For courses of a historical nature the titles given under 'Popular music before 1956' are very suitable as reference books. The books on the various aspects of pop after 1956 will be of interest to both teachers and pupils. Books about individual performers are likely to be of special interest to the pupils in a secondary school. However, the teacher who is initiating project work on such performers will need to give considerable thought on how best to guide the pupil away from the adulating regurgitation of unimportant biographical details.

The texts on the major styles are more demanding, as are those in subsequent sections of Part 1, though good sixth-form pupils will be able to use them profitably. However, the teacher is strongly advised not to recommend books from these sections which he has not read himself (this is particularly true of the books on jazz, sociology and aesthetics); they are not children's books or school texts. Before the teacher can make effective use of them, he needs to have made his own assessment of the large amount of information and ideas which they contain. He is therefore advised to see this group of books as a part of his own preparation for a proposed classroom course. This is also true of the titles under 'Pop and the music teacher: general'.

In order to meet the teacher's need for material of more immediate and practical use, we have devoted much of the Bibliography to 'Information and resources'. A large number of titles have been given, and many others could be added (even though in our view some are preferable to others), because it was felt that it would be more useful to give a wide range of choice, to enable the teacher to cope with problems of cost and availability.

Any teacher who is contemplating a divergence from orthodox musical education, whether by using pop or not, is likely to find another work in the *Resources of Music* series most helpful. This is *Folk Music in School* (Leach, R., and Palmer, R., eds., Cambridge University Press, 1978). Though aimed at the teacher who wishes to use traditional folk music, the book is of great value, both because of the many links which exist between folk and popular music, and because of the very large number of practical ideas for classroom work which are offered. Above all, though the contributors often differ sharply in taste from those in our book, their advocacy of a revaluation of popular culture, and of traditional methods of teaching music, closely parallels some of the suggestions made in the present work.

The teacher can begin to use pop straightaway, without much adaptation of traditional class-singing procedures, if he buys albums of songs. These usually contain a simple piano part, as well as chord symbols which can be used by guitarists and bassists.

The least troublesome way of incorporating instrumentalists is by the use of band orchestrations; these are uninspiring but technically competent, and will enable the teacher to bridge the gap until he is able to give time to writing special orchestrations of the type advocated by Tony Robins. The theoretical knowledge needed for this and other purposes can be obtained by both teacher and pupils from the recommended texts. Since Graham Collier is a professional jazz musician, his book is excellent in this respect, but Coker (1964) and Philips (1965) are not to be undervalued. The latter is particularly useful for pupils, because of its low cost. Baker (1978) is another helpful publication in that it gives all the basic information clearly, cheaply and under the name of an author well known to guitar students.

An introduction to jazz and jazz-rock improvisation as yet little known is the series by Abersold (1976). This consists of a series of rhythm section records illustrating different facets of the subject, over which the listener is to improvise. The records can be bought singly, and are accompanied by a handbook containing an excellent and detailed account of the relevant theory. The series, which is likely to be valuable to teacher and pupil alike, is not yet available in all music shops, but can certainly be obtained from Chappells, 50 New Bond Street, London, W1.

Many teachers find it convenient to begin the study of the guitar with folk music; it solves problems of amplification and gives basic skills from which many other fields of music, including the classical, can be approached. For this reason several titles of folk guitar tutors are given. All works by Stefan Grossman and Jerry Silverman are excellent, as is Terry Gould's cheap but little-known tutor. In my own teaching, I have found it useful to begin a course with Lomax (1957); this is simple and clear, and does not rely on notation. After the pupils have gained confidence, Silverman (1964) makes an excellent revision and extension of what has been learned. I have not yet used Taussig (1971), but it looks sound, and is based on a 'programmed learning' approach; there are revision questions at the end of each lesson.

Silverman's *Beginning the Folk Guitar* is valuable in that it has an accompanying record, which is included in the purchase price of the book. This type of tutor has several important advantages. First, it gives a clear indication of tempo and phrasing, as well as elements such as tone which cannot be notated. At the same time teaching based on a record encourages aural development. Secondly, and perhaps most important to the teacher, a record offers a means of approach to those pupils who do not read music, and leads easily into self-directed work. If the pupils use headphones, they can be set to work independently at once, without the need for the collection and organisation of material by the teacher.

For this reason the tutors by B.B. King (1973) and Green Note Music (1973) are invaluable introductions to the electric guitar. The Green Note tutor *Improvising Blues Guitar* (1975) is also useful in that, like most of the titles listed, it uses both a form of tablature and diagrammatic notation. Teachers should not be too quick to judge the use of this kind of aid unfavourably. The development of musicality is unaffected, and I have known many pupils who, after learning by such methods, have made an easy transition to notation. However, before buying a guitar tutor, it is important to be clear exactly what is meant by such labels as 'delta blues' or 'folk blues'. The differences are not only stylistic but, as far as the beginner is concerned, involve significant differences of technique. In this connection it is worth noting that 'slide guitar' is a technique which has formed an important part of the musical vocabulary of many leading electric guitar players. A new, comparatively unknown, but well-presented book in this field is Dickler (1976).

Tutors for the very earliest stages of the bass guitar tend to be very unsuitable. However, after a little assistance at that point from the teacher, the pupil can graduate to Douglas and Macdevitt. Better still would be a move to Volume I of Hammick (1975). Though this goes very quickly over the groundwork, it is a more thorough and, more important, *idiomatic* tutor. The series by Carol Kaye are also excellent sources of materials, not least because they include parts which can be heard on record (for example she played the bass part on the Beach Boys' 'Good Vibrations'). However, these books are not clearly graded, and little guidance is given about problems of technique and fingering.

I do not know of any piano tutor which is really suited to the absolute beginner. I am inclined to advise the teacher to devise his own course for the first few weeks, based on the needs of the particular situation. I find that the finger movements used in *Musicianship for Students* (a classical text) are excellent for this purpose, if they are combined with the appropriate pop rhythms. The titles we have given are largely self-explanatory, and can all be recommended. Lee Sims' book, though valuable for older styles and theory, is not suitable for beginners. One book which the teacher should undoubtedly obtain without delay is Gutcheon (1978). Pupils will not be able to master this text without assistance from the teacher, as there is enough material in any one lesson to keep the learner busy for several weeks. But as a source of typical rock rhythm patterns and fill-ins, it is as yet far ahead of any other work.

Another valuable work for piano is Kerper (1977). It gives a selection of typical jazz and jazz-rock phrases, since it works from the assumption (discussed on pp. 165–6 above) that an essential part of an Afro-American training is the mastery of standard melodic patterns. Such a process develops technique, and gives the players a way of constructing adequate improvised solos, as well as acting as a starting point for a more creative exploration of an idiom.

For the drummer, the book by Buddy Rich (1942) is a standard work, but the tutors by Appice (1972) and Grossman (1972) have the advantage of covering a wider range of techniques. However, the recent book by John Savage is the best single introduction to drumming, and is accompanied by a C60 cassette, which is a valuable aid. This is a field in which the absolute beginner is often best helped by a little guidance from a more experienced fellow pupil and seems to be the main way in which Malcolm Nicholls' drummers take their first steps.

We have not included a section on music for wind instruments, since we believe that, as with bowed instruments, the initial stages of study can only be successfully carried out under the close supervision of a teacher. Though ideally this would apply to all instruments, it seems to us that bad habits of embouchure etc. are of another order of gravity from the problems which confront guitarists and others. Once pupils can play a little, they may be introduced to popular orchestrations, or to transcriptions of jazz solos, of which there are an increasing number. There is also a valuable companion volume entitled *Improvising Rock Saxophone* in the same series as Gutcheon (1978).

Song writing can be approached in many ways. One can start with a study of lyrics from the anthologies given, or from transcriptions of words made by the pupils. But the music specialist may wish to begin at once with musical techniques. In this case Harris (1973) gives a simple but clear and satisfactory introduction to the subject. Martin's book (1955) is more advanced; the Cooke title is included for the guidance of the teacher, though it might be valuable for pupils studying Advanced Level music. Another valuable approach is to make new melodies over known chord sequences. Piers Spencer (chapters 4 and 5 above) discusses various of these approaches.

Many music teachers have, as students, taken a subsidiary subject, which can be put to good use in the classroom. In such cases the articles for teachers of other subjects may prove valuable; those on rock lyrics clearly relate to song-writing projects. I have found that both John (1971) and Paynter and Aston (1970) are very useful to teachers who are attempting musical drama for the first time, and they are worth reconsideration even by the experienced teacher.

Musical instrument construction is clearly for the dedicated minority, but Brune (1974) and Romney (1975) are both useful for younger children, especially when resources are limited. It is worth mentioning that the article on 'Making an Electric Guitar' was drawn to my attention when I read a letter from a thirteen year old who, by following it, had constructed a guitar in his spare time. Teachers are warned against underestimating the intensity of interest of many young players in the technicalities of guitar construction about which they can often debate with considerable knowledge and insight.

It becomes daily less possible for the music teacher to ignore electronics; it is neither cultured nor prudent to do so. Fortunately there is now a range of excellent texts in this field. As far as the music itself is concerned the teacher would be advised to start with Schwartz, and to follow up with the broader based work by Jenkins and Smith (1975). As confidence comes, materials for pupils can be drawn from EAV (1972) and above all from Dwyer (1975). As the latter author points out, one does not need to learn electronics. It is obvious, however, that a few practical insights would be useful, and to this end he recommends the work by Strange (1975).

Our list of magazines can be useful in providing information both about the music itself and, perhaps more important, about the musical and reading tastes of the pupils. We have also felt that it would be helpful to mention some organisations and shops. The National Youth Jazz Association can be invaluable, not only as a source of material, but of guidance on all aspects of the music, such as which school music festivals will accept entries from school jazz and pop groups. Though the Association is naturally interested primarily in the promotion of jazz activities, its organiser, Bill Ashton, has an exceptional knowledge of commercial music at a professional level. As far as shops are concerned, the specialist shops, such as Bill Lewington's, are used by professionals. For both personal and educational purposes I tend to find that the smaller shops, such as Scarth's, may have a less impressive range actually in stock (though they can order most things for you), but are far more helpful, possibly because they are often run by ex-professionals, rather than by off-hand young assistants who are more concerned with 'being on the scene' than serving the customer.

It should now be clear that a wealth of material exists, which the teacher can use with confidence until time and experience permit him to plan his own courses in their entirety. I found that the Lomax guitar tutor, for instance, was more than adequate for beginners, until I could work out a course more exactly suited to my needs, and based on insights I had gained from examining a range of material.

A final word of caution is needed. We felt it was necessary to give some indications of the above sort, because, though not all books which have gone unmentioned are bad, there are, unfortunately, a range of books which have been pushed out quickly by firms desirous of exploiting a rapidly growing but uninformed market. Such books do not take account of the idiosyncracies of the instruments they set out to teach, nor are they (if only for copyright reasons) based on real examples of the idiom. Gutcheon's book on the piano is a rare example of the use of specially composed material which is nevertheless totally convincing. Above all, many books do not meet the teacher's need for carefully graded and clearly explained material, which is then thoughtfully reinforced. Though the books we have listed are by no means perfect in this respect, the teacher can rely on them, and particularly on the ones we have recommended. They will certainly act as a basis for study until the pupil is ready to enter upon the individualised process of self-education, which has always been an essential element in the acquisition of a mastery of pop music styles.

Part 1: Historical and theoretical studies of pop music

Popular music before 1956: General surveys

Ewen, D., *All the Years of American Popular Music*, Prentice Hall, 1977.
Mackerness, E.D., *A Social History of English Music*, Routledge and Kegan Paul, 1964.
Spaeth, S., *A History of Popular Music in America*, Phoenix House, 1948.

Folk music

Karpeles, M., *An Introduction to English Folk Song*, Oxford University Press, 1973.
Lloyd, A.L., *Folk Song in England*, Lawrence and Wishart, 1967.

Victorian song and music hall

Hudd, R., *Music Hall*, Eyre Methuen, 1976. (Illustrated; very useful for the classroom.)
Leslie, P., *A Hard Act to Follow: A Music Hall Review*, Paddington Press, 1978.
Pearsall, R., *Victorian Popular Music*, David and Charles, 1973.
Pearsall, R., *Edwardian Popular Music*, David and Charles, 1975.
Turner, M., *The Parlour Song Book: A Casquet of Vocal Gems*, Michael Joseph, 1975.

1900—56 ('Tin Pan Alley')

Barnes, K., *Sinatra and the Great Song Stylists*, Ian Allan, 1972.
McCarthy, A., *The Dance Band Era*, Hamlyn, 1974.
Pearsall, R., *Popular Music of the Twenties*, David and Charles, 1976.
Whitcomb, I., *Tin Pan Alley: A Pictorial History (1919—39)*, Paddington, 1975.
Wilder, A., *American Popular Song: The Great Innovators 1900—50*, Oxford University Press, 1972. (Musical analysis of many great 'standards'.)

Pop music after 1956: General

Belz, C., *The Story of Rock*, Harper and Row, 2nd edition, 1973.
Gillett, C., *The Sound of the City*, Sphere Books, 1971.
Gillett, C., *Making Tracks: Atlantic Records and the Growth of a Multi-Billion Dollar Industry*, Panther, 1975.
Marcus, G., *Mystery Train: Images of America in Rock 'n' Roll Music*, Dutton, 1975.

Miller, J. (ed.), *The Rolling Stone Illustrated History of Rock 'n' Roll*, Rolling Stone Press, Random House, 1976.
Orloff, K., *Rock'n'Roll Woman*, Nash, 1974.
Peelaert, G. and Cohn, N., *Rock Dreams*, Pan Books, 1976.
Pollock, B. and Wagman, J., *The Face of Rock and Roll: Images of a Generation*, New English Library, 1978.

Pop music in the 1950s

Escott, C. and Hawkins, M., *Catalyst: The Sun Records Story*, Aquarius Books, 1975.
Groia, P., *They All Sang on the Corner*, Edmund Publishing Co., 1973.
May, C., *Rock'n'Roll*, Sociopack Publications Ltd., 1974.
Nite, N., *Rock On*, Popular Library, 1977.
Shaw, A., *The Rockin' Fifties*, Hawthorne, 1974.

Performers of the 1950s

Farren, M., *Elvis in His Own Words*, Omnibus Press, 1977.
Goldrosen, J., *Buddy Holly, His Life and Music*, Charisma Books, 1975.
Hopkins, J., *Elvis*, Sphere Books, 1974.
Millar, B., *The Drifters: The Rise and Fall of the Black Vocal Group*, November Books, 1971.
Millar, B., *The Coasters*, Star Books, 1975.
Richard, C. and Latham, B., *Which One's Cliff?*, Hodder and Stoughton, 1977.

Pop music in the 1960s and 1970s

Eisen, J. (ed.), *The Age of Rock: Sounds of the American Cultural Revolution*, Random House, 1969.
Eisen, J. (ed.), *The Age of Rock, Volume 2*, Random House, 1970.
Fong-Torres, B. (ed.), *Rolling Stone Rock'n'Roll Reader*, Bantam, 1974.
Gold, M. (ed.), *Rock on the Road*, Futura, 1976.
Lydon, M., *Rock Folk*, Dial, 1971.
May, C. and Phillips, T., *British Beat*, Sociopack Publications Ltd., 1974.
Reid, J., *The Improbable Rise of Redneck Rock*, Da Capo, 1977.

Punk and the new wave

Burchill, J. and Parsons, T., *The Boy Looked at Johnny: The Obituary of Rock and Roll*, Pluto Press, 1978.
Coon, C., *1988: The New Wave Punk Rock Explosion*, Orbach and Chambers, 1977.
Davis, J. (ed.), *Punk*, Davison Publishing, 1977.
Dempsey, M., *100 Nights at the Roxy*, Big O Publishing Ltd., 1978. (Photographs taken at the Roxy Club, Covent Garden, December 1976–April 1977.)
Perry, M. (ed.), *The Bible*, Omnibus, 1978. (All the issues of Mark Perry's 'Sniffin' Glue', packaged in one book.)

Performers of the 1960s and 1970s

Carr, R., *The Rolling Stones: An Illustrated Record*, Harmony, 1976.

Carr, R. and Clarke, S., *Fleetwood Mac: Rumours 'n' Fax*, Harmony, 1979.
Cohen, M.S., *Carole King: A Biography in Words and Pictures*, B & N, 1976.
Dalton, D., *Janis*, Calder, 1972.
Edgington, H., *Abba*, Magnum Books, 1978.
Elsner, C., *Stevie Wonder*, Everest, 1977.
Gallo, A., *Genesis*, Sidgwick and Jackson, 1978.
Gambaccini, P., *Paul McCartney in His Own Words*, Omnibus Press, 1976.
Gelly, D., *The Facts About a Pop Group (Featuring Wings)*, G. Whizzard Publications, 1976.
Golden, B., *The Beach Boys: A Southern California Pastoral*, Burgo Press, 1976.
Gross, M., *Bob Dylan: An Illustrated History*, Elm Tree Books, 1978.
Harrison, H., *Grateful Dead*, Star Books, 1975.
Marchbank, P. and Miles, *Beatles in Their Own Words*, Omnibus Press, 1978.
Pidgeon, J., *Rod Stewart and the Changing Faces*, Panther, 1976.
Sanders, R., *Pink Floyd*, Futura, 1976.
Schaffner, N., *The Beatles Forever*, McGraw Hill, 1978.
Tatham, D., *Elton John*, Octopus Books, 1976.
Turner, S., *Conversations with Eric Clapton*, Sphere, 1976.
Wenner, J. (ed.), *Lennon Remembers: The Rolling Stone Interviews*, Penguin, 1972.
Williams, R., *Out of His Head: The Sound of Phil Spector*, Sphere Books, 1975.
Wooding, D., *Rick Wakeman*, Robert Hale, 1978.

Punk and the New Wave performers

Stevenson, R. (ed.), *The Sex Pistols File*, Omnibus Press, 1978.
Vermorel, F. and J., *The Sex Pistols*, Universal Books, 1978.

Pop music after 1956: Reference works

Encyclopedias
Hardy, P. and Laing, D., *The Encyclopedia of Rock*, Volumes 1, 2 and 3, Panther, 1976; also all packaged in one cheap hardback edition by Aquarius Books, 1977.
Logan, N. and Woffinden, B., *The Illustrated New Musical Express Encyclopedia of Rock*, Salamander Books, 1977.
Stambler, I., *Encyclopedia of Pop, Rock and Soul*, St James Press, 1975; also published in paperback in 1977 since its listing in the Postscript of the first edition of *Pop Music in School*.
Marchbank, P. and Miles, *The Illustrated Rock Almanac*, Paddington Press, 1977. (A listing of significant dates set out for each day of the year.)

Chart entries and record information
Charlie Gillett and Simon Frith edit the *Rock File* series, published by Panther. Each book (five to date) contains a mixture of articles and record chart analysis. The most comprehensive is *Rock File 4*, which has chart information on all British and American top 20 hits 1955–74.
Jasper, T., *20 Years of British Record Charts 1955–1975*, Queen Anne Press, 1976. (Covers the charts chronologically week by week, thus giving an overall picture at any chosen date.)
Leadbitter, M. and Slaven, N., *Blues Records, 1943–1966*, Hanover, 1968. (The major source on blues of this period.)
Rees, D., *Star File*, Star Books, 1977. *Star File Annual 2*, Hamlyn Paperbacks, 1978. (Covers both America and Britain for the years 1976 and 1977.)

Propes, S., *Those Oldies but Goodies: A Guide to 50s Record Collecting*, Collier Macmillan, 1973.
Propes, S., *Golden Oldies: A Guide to 60s Record Collecting*, Chilton, 1974.
Propes, S., *Golden Goodies: A Guide to 50s and 60s Rock 'n' Roll Record Collecting*, Chilton, 1975.
(These last three books give hints on rarity and value, but also include discographies of a large number of singers and groups generally unavailable elsewhere, except in specialist magazines.)
Record Information Services produce a still-growing number of record company label listings, including London, Capitol, and Tamla Motown.
Finally, J. Whitburn edits a very comprehensive (but also expensive) series on American chart entries, all of which have updating annual supplements.

The influence of various styles: Black music traditions

Background to Afro-American music
Mellers, W., *Music in a New Found Land*, Part 2, Barrie and Rockliff, 1964.
Pleasants, H., *Serious Music and all that Jazz*, Gollancz, 1969.
Roberts, J.S., *Black Music of Two Worlds*, Allen Lane, 1973.
Southern, E., *The Music of Black Americans: A History*, Norton, 1971.

Jazz
Berendt, J., *The Jazz Book*, Paladin, 1976.
Case, B. and Britt, S., *The Illustrated Encyclopedia of Jazz*, Salamander Books, 1978.
Coryell, J. and Friedman, L., *Jazz-Rock Fusion*, Marion Boyars, 1978.
Schuller, G., *Early Jazz*, Oxford University Press, 1968.
Shapiro, N. and Hentoff, N., *Hear Me Talkin' to Ya*, Penguin, 1962.
Wilmer, V., *As Serious As Your Life*, Quartet, 1977.

Blues and Rhythm'n'Blues
Broven, J., *Walking to New Orleans*, Blues Unlimited, 1974.
Cook, B., *Listen to the Blues*, Robson Books, 1975.
Guralnick, P., *Feel Like Going Home: Portraits in Blues and Rock'n'Roll*, Omnibus Press, 1978.
Haralambos, M., *Right On: From Blues to Soul in Black America*, Eddison Press, 1974.
Oakley, G., *The Devil's Music*, BBC, 1976.
Oliver, P., *The Story of the Blues*, Barrie and Jenkins, 1978.
Rowe, M., *Chicago Breakdown*, Eddison Press, 1973.
Mention should also be made of the excellent *Blues Paperbacks* series, edited by Paul Oliver and published by Studio Vista Ltd.

Gospel, Soul and Tamla Motown
Cummings, T., *The Sound of Philadelphia*, Eyre Methuen, 1975.
Heilbut, T., *The Gospel Sound: Good News and Bad Times*, Anchor, 1975.
Hoare, I., Anderson, C., Cummings, T. and Frith, S., *The Soul Book*, Methuen, 1975.

Reggae/Caribbean
Barrette, L.E., *The Rastafarians: The Dreadlocks of Jamaica*, Heinemann, 1977.
Boot, A. and Thomas, M., *Jamaica: Babylon on a Thin Wire*, Thames and Hudson, 1976.
Dalrymple, H. and Kallyndyr, R., *Reggae: A People's Music*, Carib-Arawak, 1974.

Davis, S. and Simon, P., *Reggae Bloodlines: In Search of the Music and Culture of Jamaica*, Anchor Books, 1977.
Elder, J.D., *From Conga Drum to Steel Band*, University of West Indies, 1972.
McKnight, C. and Tobler, J., *Bob Marley. The Roots of Reggae*, Star Books, 1977.
Nettleford, R.M., *Identity, Race and Protest in Jamaica*, Morrow, 1972.
Plummer, J., *Movement of Jah People*, Press Gang, 1979.

The influence of various styles: White music traditions

Country music
Arks, B., *Bluegrass*, Hawthorn, 1975.
Dellar, F. and Thompson, R., *The Illustrated Encyclopedia of Country Music*, Salamander Books, 1977.
Green, J.B., *Country Roots: The Origins of Country Music*, Hawthorn, 1976.
Hemphill, P., *The Nashville Sound: Bright Lights and Country Music*, Ballantine, 1975.
Malone, B., *Country Music USA: A Fifty Year History*, University of Texas, 1967.

Urban folk/Folk-rock
Baggelaar, K. and Milton, D., *The Folk Music Encyclopedia*, Omnibus Press, 1977.
Guthrie, W., *Bound for Glory*, Picador, 1977.
Laing, D., Dallas, K., Denselow, R. and Shelton, R., *The Electric Muse: The Story of Folk into Rock*, Methuen, 1975.
Rodnitzky, J.L., *Minstrels of the Dawn: The Folk Protest Singer as a Cultural Hero*, Nelson Hall, 1976.

The social and economic background of pop music

Bogdanor, V. and Skidelsky, R. (ed.), *The Age of Affluence 1951–1964*, Macmillan, 1970.
Chapple, S. and Garofolo, R., *Rock'n'roll is Here to Pay: The History and Politics of the Music Industry*, Chicago University Press, 1977.
Cohen, S., *Folk Devils and Moral Panics: The Creation of the Mods and Rockers*, Paladin, 1973.
Davis, C., *Clive: Inside the Record Business*, Munrow, 1975.
Grossman, L., *A Social History of Rock Music*, David McKay, 1976.
Hall, S. and Jefferson, T. (ed.), *Resistance through Rituals: Youth Subcultures in Post-war Britain*, Hutchinson, 1976.
Jenkinson, P. and Warner, A., *Celluloid Rock*, Lorrimer, 1975.
Krivine, J., *Jukebox Saturday Night*, New English Library, 1977.
Lewis, R., *Outlaws of America*, Penguin, 1972.
MacInnes, C., *Absolute Beginners*, Panther, 1973.
Mungham, G. and Pearson, G. (eds.), *Working Class Youth Culture*, Routledge and Kegan Paul, 1976.

Sociological studies of pop and rock music

Frith, S., *The Sociology of Rock*, Constable, 1978.
Murdock, G. and Phelps, G., *Mass Media and the Secondary School*, Macmillan, 1973.
Shepherd, J., Virden, P., Vulliamy, G. and Wishart, T., *Whose Music? A Sociology of Musical Languages*, Latimer, 1977.

Willis, P., *Profane Culture*, Routledge and Kegan Paul, 1978.
The American journal *Popular Music and Society* specialises in academic articles on the social background of popular music of all types. A British journal, *Popular Music Journal*, is also planned.

Musicological and aesthetic discussions of pop music

Chester, A., 'Second Thoughts on a Rock Aesthetic: The Band', *New Left Review*, No. 62 (1970).
Keil, C., 'Motion and Feeling through Music', *Journal of Aesthetics and Art Criticism*, Vol. 24 (1966).
Mellers, W., *Twilight of the Gods: The Beatles in Retrospect*, Faber, 1973.
Meltzer, R., *The Aesthetics of Rock*, Something Else Press, 1970.
Middleton, R., *Pop Music and the Blues*, Gollancz, 1972.
Pleasants, H., *The Great American Popular Singers*, Gollancz, 1974.
Titon, J., *Early Downhome Blues: A Musical and Cultural Analysis*, University of Illinois Press, 1977.
The following are a few of the highly critical appraisals of pop music, to which the reader was referred in the introduction:
Gipps, R., 'The Use of Trendy, Amplified Pop in School Music Classes', *Incorporated Society of Musicians Music Journal* (October 1976).
Holbrook, D., 'Pop and Truth', chapter 10 of *English in Australia Now*, Cambridge University Press, 1973.
Holbrook, D., 'Folksong and the Culture of Hate', *Use of English* (Autumn 1966).
Parker, C., 'Pop Song, the Manipulated Ritual', in Abbs, P. (ed.), *The Black Rainbow*, Heinemann Educational, 1975.

Part 2: Information and resources for the teacher

Pop and the music teacher: general

The first book in this field was:
Swanwick, K., *Popular Music and the Teacher*, Pergamon Press, 1968. (This is now out of print, but is still worth reading, if a copy can be obtained from a library.)
Music teachers will also find the following series of articles helpful:
Burnett, M., 'Coming to Terms with Pop', *Music Teacher* (1972).
A second book on the use of pop and rock in music teaching, edited by Graham Vulliamy and Ed Lee, is to be published by Cambridge University Press in 1981.

Albums of songs

A range of useful material of this type has been issued since the publication of the first edition of this book. The following are both of reasonable price and contain a large amount of classic material under one cover:
60 Old Time Variety Songs, EMI, 1977.
1001 Show Tunes and Themes, Hansen.
The Best of Broadway: 80 Great Songs, Chappell, 1973.
The Best of Jerome Kern, Chappell. (Contains a useful essay on Kern.)
Several series of albums now exist:
The Great Ones, Wise. (Notably *Great Groups*, containing 41 rock numbers, 1973.)
The Music Masters, EMI. (Notably *Al Jolson*, 1977, and *Marie Lloyd*, 1977.)

EMI have published a historical series, illustrated with a short essay in each. They are entitled *The Twenties, The Thirties, The Forties*, and *The Fifties*. The series would make a good first approach to popular music between 1919 and 1956.
Also recommended are the following works by named editors:
Arnett, H., *I Hear America Singing*, Praeger, 1975. (An account with musical examples of 250 years of American folksong.)
Gammond, P., *The Music Hall Songbook, 1890–1920*, David and Charles, 1975.
Garrett, J.M., *Sixty Years of British Music Hall*, Chappell, 1976. (Contains essay, illustrations, music.)
Hart, M., *The Cole Porter Song Book*, Simon and Schuster, 1959.
More recent pop songs tend to be issued in albums of the work of particular groups or artists. The work of most well-known performers, including some punk and new wave, is readily available. There is also a collection of *100 Super Hits of the ·Seventies*, published by Wise Publications.

Band orchestrations

In the first instance the needs of bands are best covered by Chappells' *Club* series (Chappells also do albums of the work of individual artists). Also invaluable are Campbell Connolly's *Book for Buskers* series and Francis and Day's *Pocket Book for Buskers* series (these are arranged for C, B flat and E flat instruments). Many bands these days are using *Pop Plan* arrangements, though these are not highly spoken of. For swinging big band arrangements teachers should use the series produced by Stanza Music.
A constant source of stimulus to more advanced instrumental pupils could be:
Feather, L., *200 Omnibus of Jazz*, Crown, 1975. (This contains two hundred original jazz themes.)

Pop and Jazz: harmony, arrangement and improvisation

Harmony
Bobitt, R., *Harmony in the Rock Idiom*, Wadsworth.
Philips, A., *Jazz Improvisation and Harmony*, Robbins, 1965.
Ricigliano, D., *Popular and Jazz Harmony*, Donato Music Publishing Co., 1969.

Arrangement
Baker, M., *Complete Handbook for the Musical Arranger*, Clifford Essex, 1978.
Garcia, R., *The Professional Arranger Composer*, Criterion Music, 1960.

Improvisation
Abersold, J., *Jazz*, Studio P.R. Publications, 1976. (A series of LPs each with an accompanying handbook.)
Coker, J., *Improvising Jazz*, Prentice Hall, 1964.
Collier, G., *Jazz: A Student's and Teacher's Guide*, Cambridge University Press, 1975. (An accompanying LP disc, Graham Collier, *Jazz Illustrations*, and a tape or cassette of backing tracks, Graham Collier, *Jazz Rhythm Section*, are also available from Cambridge University Press.)
Gray, J., *Bluesblues*, Mitchell Madison, 1973. (A useful first step into blues and other improvisation.)
Tanner, P. and Geeson, M., *A Study of Jazz*, revised edition W.C. Brown, 1977. (Contains examples in score and illustrative record.)

Instrumental tutors

Where the phrase 'plus record' is used below this indicates that when you buy the book you also receive an accompanying record of musical examples, which is obviously invaluable for clarifying points of tone and expression, as well as for non-readers. In some cases tuning notes or accompaniments for improvisation are given.

Guitar: general
The following texts do not confine themselves to one style:
Easy-Play Speed Music series, Sight and Sound Systems Inc., 1976. (Includes rock'n' roll, Paul McCartney etc.; a halfway house in that it uses a simplified staff notation.)
Morgan, D., *Guitar*, Corgi Books, revised edition, 1974.
Musicianship and Sight Reading for Guitarists, Musical New Services, 1977. (Though starting from basics, really a book to give to those who are fairly advanced.)
White, H., *Guitar Method and Song Folio*, Leeds Music. (A strange book which will put off some pupils and greatly appeal to others. It contains music, words and chord symbols, for a range of folk songs, and for popular songs of the 1950s before rock'n'roll.)

Folk guitar
Though more limited in field, and not always directly relevant to the needs of pop music, folk books tend to be the best value and the best written texts for absolute beginners, especially when amplification is impossible or undesirable.

Elementary stages
Gould, T., *Folk Guitar*, Sing Productions, 1966.
Lomax, A., *American Folk Guitar*, Robbins, 1957.
Noad, F., *Playing the Guitar*, Omnibus, 1972. (Does not go far, but useful for self-directed work, as it contains very full explanations.)
Silverman, J., *Beginning the Folk Guitar* (plus record), Oak, 1964.
Silverman, J., *The Folk Guitar Method Book*, Grosset and Dunlap, 1974.
Taussig, H., *Teach Yourself Guitar*, Oak, 1971. (Useful educationally in that each lesson has a set of revision questions at the end, to test what has been learned.)

More advanced (finger picking styles)
Green Note Publishing, *The Art of Ragtime Guitar* (plus record), 1974.
Grossman, S., *Contemporary Ragtime Guitar*, Oak, 1972.
Taussig, H., *Advanced Guitar*, Oak, 1975.

Country styles
Auldridge, M., *Bluegrass Dobro*, Guitar Player Books, 1975.
Green Note Publications, *Country Rock Guitar*, 1978.
Roth, A., *Nashville Guitar* (plus record), Oak, 1977.
Traum, H., *Flat-picking Country Guitar*, Oak, 1973.

Blues
Dickler, P., *Bottleneck and Blues Guitar*, Tara Publishers, 1976. (With instructional photos plus record.)
Green Note Music, *Improvising Blues Guitar*, 1975. (Notation plus diagrams.)
Green Note Music, *Slide Guitar* (plus record), 1974.
King, B.B. (ed. Jerry Snyder), *Blues Guitar* (plus record), Hansen, 1973. (Illustrates the style of the 'father' of rock guitar.)

Electric guitar
Green Note Music, *Improvising Rock Guitar* (plus record), 1973.
Lee, R., *Jazz Guitar*, 2 vols., Mel Bay Publications, 1970.

Bass guitar
De Witt, J., *Rhythmic Figures for Bassists*, Hansen, 1976.
Douglas, S. and Macdevitt, C., *Easy Guide to Rhythm and Blues for Bass Guitar*, Wise Publications.
Hammick, V., *Electric Bass Technique*, 2 vols., Gwyn Publishing, 1975. (Contemporary and thorough.)
Kaye, C., *How to Play the Electric Bass*, 5 vols., Ashley Fields, 1969-71. (Starts with the needs of beginners, but also introduces 'legitimate' scale approaches etc.; Vol. 4 is a set of transcriptions from records.)

Piano
Boogie Woogie Beat, MCA, 1975. (Teaches 25 bass parts for the left hand.)
Dale, B., Jacob, G. and Anson, H., *Musicianship for Students*, Novello, 1940. (A classical music tutor in two volumes; Part 3 of each gives simple, but valuable material as an approach to *classical* improvisation.)
Gutcheon, J., *Improvising Rock Piano*, Consolidated Music Publishers, 1978.
Haerle, D., *Jazz-Rock Voicings for the Contemporary Keyboard Player*, Studio P.R. Publications, 1974.
Harvey, E., *Teach Yourself Jazz Piano*, English Universities Press, 1975.
Kerper, M., *Jazz Riffs for Piano*, Amsco, 1977.
Sims, L., *Piano Method (Jazz)*, Keith Prowse, 1928. (Excellent for traditional styles, with strong left hand; good introduction to theory.)

Drums
Appice, C., *Realistic Rock*, Robbins, 1972.
Grossman, N., *Complete Book of Modern Drumming*, Wise Publications, 1972.
Rich, B., *Snare Drum Rudiments*, Peter Maurice, 1942.
Savage, J., *The Art of the Drummer*, John Savage Music Centre, 1978. (Plus C60 cassette.)

Violin
Krassen, M., *Appalachian Fiddle*, Oak, 1973.
Mel Bay's Bluegrass Fiddle, Mel Bay, 1974.
Mel Bay's Old Time Fiddle Solos, Mel Bay, 1974.
Timpany, J., *And Out of His Knapsack He Drew a Fine Fiddle*, English Folk Dance and Song Society, 1973. (English folk style.)
None of the above are beginners' tutors: they are recommended for use by teachers as an extension of pupils' repertoire and technique after a sound grounding has been given.

Other instruments
Glover, T., *Blues Harp*, Oak, 1965. (Harmonica styles.)
Silverman, J., *A Folksingers' Guide to Chords and Tunings*, Oak, 1967. (Invaluable for guitar, banjo, mandolin and ukelele.)

Words and music

How to write songs
Few books on this topic seem to be very useful or successful. As in tipping winners,

if you can do it you don't write about it, and probably couldn't explain your success anyway! But the following may be of use:

Cooke, D., *The Language of Music*, Oxford University Press, 1955. (This is not an instruction manual, but shows, with popular as well as classical examples, the use and prevalence of various melodic formulae. These could be used as suggestions to pupils in the same way as Piers Spencer illustrates the introduction of harmonic progressions to Dene in Chapter 5.)

Harris, Rolf, *Write Your Own Pop Song*, Wolfe Publishing and Keith Prowse Music, 1973. (Lively, as one might expect, and sound. More important, it makes no assumptions about musical literacy.)

Martin, L., *Teach Yourself Songwriting*, English Universities Press, 1955. (Sound, but difficult for real beginners.)

Collections of lyrics

Atkinson, B., *Songs of the Open Road: The Poetry of Folk Rock*, Signet, 1974.

The Beatles Lyrics, Futura, 1978.

Charters, S., *The Poetry of the Blues*, Oak, 1963.

Dylan, B., *The Writings and Drawings of Bob Dylan*, Panther, 1974.

Gershwin, I., *Lyrics on Several Occasions*, Elm Tree Books, 1977.

Goldstein, R., *The Poetry of Rock*, Bantam Books, 1969.

Lomax, A., *The Penguin Book of American Folk Songs*, Penguin, 1964.

Nicholas, A.X., *The Poetry of Soul*, Bantam Books, 1971.

Oliver, P., *Screening the Blues*, Cassell, 1968.

Vaughan Williams, R. and Lloyd, A., *The Penguin Book of English Folk Songs* Penguin, 1968.

Musical drama

John, M. (ed.), *Music Drama in Schools*, Cambridge University Press, 1971. (Valuable chapters by teachers and actors from theatre and education groups describing projects involving various forms of music and drama.)

Paynter, J. and Aston, P., *Sound and Silence*, Cambridge University Press, 1970. (This has several projects involving drama and movement.)

Instrument construction and repair

Construction projects for young pupils

Brune, J., *Resonant Rubbish*, English Folk Dance and Song Society, 1974.

Burton, J.A., *Musical Instruments from Odds and Ends*, Carousel, 1976.

Dankworth, A., *Make Music Fun*, Dryad, 1977.

Romney, E., *The Musical Instrument Recipe Book*, Penguin, 1975.

Older pupils

Garnett, H., *Musical Instruments You Can Make*, Pitman, 1976.

Guitar making and repair

Achard, K., *The Fender Guitar*, Musical New Services, 1977.

Bishop, I.C., *The Bishop Guitar from 1950*, Musical New Services, 1977.

Brosnac, D., *The Electric Guitar: its history and construction*. Omnibus, 1975.

Guitar Player Books, *Fix Your Axe – Easy Guitar Repairs You Can Do at Home*, 1976.

Kaminoto, H., *Complete Guitar Repair Book*, Oak, 1975.

Longworth, M., *Making Guitars: A History*, Omnibus, 1976.

'Making an Electric Guitar', *Everyday Electronics* (October, 1974).

Sloane, I., *Guitar Repair*, Omnibus, 1976.

The use of electronics

Technical manuals
Douglas, A., *The Electronic Musical Instrument Manual: a Guide to Theory and Design*, Pitman, 1976.
Sear, W., *A Guide to Electronic Music and Synthesisers*, Omnibus, 1977.
Strange, A., *Electronic Music*, Brown Co., 1975.
Towers, T.D., *Master Electronics in Music*, Newnes Technical Books, 1976.

Electronic music
Anderton, C., *Electronic Projects for Musicians*, Guitar Player Books, 1975.
Dwyer, T., *Making Electronic Music*, Oxford University Press, 1975. (A graded approach for schools; two pupils' books, teacher's handbook, two source material records.)
EAV Ltd., *Electronic Music*, EAV, 1972. (Tape/slide sequence.)
Ernst, D., *The Evolution of Electronic Music*, Collier Macmillan, 1977.
Schwartz, *Electronic Music – a Listener's Guide*, Secker and Warburg, 1973.
The following book also deals with electronic 'serious' music, but has the advantage of being the only book also to consider the use of electronics in other areas of music:
Jenkins, J. and Smith, J., *Electric Music: a Practical Manual for Musicians*, David and Charles, 1975.

Books for use by pupils and teachers

G. Vulliamy and E. Lee have edited a series of books designed specifically for use by school pupils and to be published by Routledge and Kegan Paul. The following will appear in 1980:
Carroll, B., *Contemporary Folk Song*
Frith, S., *Soul and Motown*
Hebdidge, D., *Reggae*
Lee, E., *Folk Song and Music Hall*
Rogers, D., *Rock'n'roll*
Rogers, D., *Rock Music*
Shepherd, J., *Tin Pan Alley*
Vulliamy, G., *Jazz and Blues*
There will be a *Teachers Handbook* to accompany the series, containing both follow-up resource material and suggestions for practical classroom projects.
Another teachers' handbook which music teachers will find particularly valuable is an American publication:
Standifer, J.A. and Reeder, B., *Source Book of African and Afro-American Materials for Music Educators*, Contemporary Music Project, Music Educators National Conference, 1972. (This contains not only a comprehensive list of source materials but also practical projects involving little or no outlay, which are suitable for immediate implementation in the classroom.)
T. Attwood and P. Farmer have produced a number of publications designed as resource material for teachers and pupils in the classroom, for use in both music and social studies lessons:
The Pop Business, E.J. Arnold, 1978. (Filmstrips and worksheets.)
In Concert, Syston Publishing Co. Ltd., 1978. (A file of lessons on pop.)
Pop Workbook, E.J. Arnold, 1978. (This is basically a set of comprehension exercises the texts of which deal with pop music. It is therefore likely to be equally useful to teachers of English and Communications.)

Farmer, P., *Pop*, Longman, 1979.

Records designed as teaching aids

In addition to records accompanying books already mentioned, teachers may find the following useful:
Pop Music in the Twentieth Century. (A filmstrip with 3 LPs, Education Audio Visual Ltd.)
Rock. (A filmstrip with 2 tapes, Educational Audio Visual Ltd.)
Soul. (A filmstrip with tape, Educational Audio Visual Ltd.)
Graham Collier, *Jazz Lecture Concert* (LP disc and booklet published in Cambridge University Press *Resources of Music* series).

Magazines and papers

The major music weeklies are *New Musical Express, Melody Maker, Sounds, Record Mirror*, and *Black Echoes*. Once lagging behind, *Melody Maker* has now caught up in its coverage of new wave music, while still devoting its traditional space to jazz, blues, folk and (recently) rock'n'roll. With the exception of some of *Melody Maker*'s contributors, the most challenging weekly is *New Musical Express*, followed by *Sounds. Record Mirror* is mainly chart-oriented in its coverage, publishing each week all the British Market Research Bureau record-sales charts, and, importantly, a disco section.

Black Echoes is the only weekly devoted entirely to black music, which is also covered by the fortnightly *Blues and Soul* and the highly recommended monthly *Black Music & Jazz Review*. The latter and *Black Echoes* both include reggae as does *Pressure Drop*, an occasional magazine edited by Nick Kimberley of Compendium Books. Two excellent, more specialist blues magazines are *Blues Unlimited* and *Living Blues*.

Country music publications include *Country Music Review, Country Music People* and *Country Music Round Up*. Particularly recommended for its depth of historical analysis is the quarterly *Old Time Music*.

Also published quarterly are various magazines dealing with rock'n'roll. They include *SMG* and *Red Hot* (both extend coverage to 1960s music as well), the Vintage Rock'n'Roll Appreciation Society's magazine *Not Fade Away*, and, the best of them all, *New Kommotion*.

Privately produced magazines such as these have grown in number through the 1970s. They inevitably reflect the tastes and interests of their editors and contributors and are worth seeking out for the greater depth of research and analysis they contain. *Zigzag* began in much this way but has changed with the new wave to its present concentration on contemporary music. *BamBalam* and *Hot Wacks* deal with aspects of the 1960s and 1970s, as do *Nuggets* and *Omaha Rainbow*. At different times there are many more: they tend to complement each other in the areas they cover rather than overlap. Of the punk/new wave magazines which had a hand in the changes of 1976/7, Mark Perry's *Sniffin' Glue* is now defunct, but, at the time of writing, *Ripped And Torn*, once the best of the rest, is still being produced.

From the United States, *Rolling Stone* is but a shadow of its former self, having become, in one commentator's phrase, a sort of hip executive's *Time* magazine. However, *Trouser Press* and *New York Rocker* are both worth finding, as is the always excellent *Bomp* magazine.

Excepting the widely available weeklies and some of the monthly magazines all the above are easily obtained from Compendium Books, 234 Camden High Street, London NW1.

Organisations

The Basement Youth Club Music Workshop (part of the Central London Youth Project Ltd., 29 Shelton Street, London WC2, phone 01-240-3266) provides instruction in pop and rock music for pupils in London schools.

Dance-for-Everyone (David Hadda, 22 Mapesbury Road, London NW2, phone 01-452-2903) presents all forms of dance, including pop, to schoolchildren.

National Youth Jazz Association, 11 Victor Road, Harrow, Middlesex. (Orchestrations, advice, Easter course, pupil orchestras.)

Shops

Collets Record Shop, 180 Shaftesbury Avenue, London WC2. (Jazz, folk and African specialists.)

Dobells, 77 Charing Cross Road, London WC2. (Jazz record specialists; folk shop next door at 75.)

Drum City, 114 Shaftesbury Avenue, London W1.

EFDSS Folk Shop, Cecil Sharp House, 2 Regent's Park Road, London NW1. (Send large s.a.e. for catalogue.)

Francis, Day and Hunter, 138–40 Charing Cross Road, London WC2. (Music publishers.)

Hunt, Bill, 10 Archer Street, London W1. (Drum specialists.)

Lewington, Bill, 144 Shaftesbury Avenue, London WC2. (Wind instrument specialists.)

Scarth, G. Ltd, 55 Charing Cross Road, London WC2. (A small and reliable firm with a stock of 1500 band orchestrations.)

Selmer Musical Instruments, 114 Charing Cross Road, London WC2.

Sound City, 124 Shaftesbury Avenue, London WC2.

Sterns, 126 Tottenham Court Road, London W1. (Third World record specialists.)

Top Gear, 5 Denmark Street, London WC2. (Very good for second-hand amplifiers and instruments.)

Discography

The main body of the Discography follows fairly closely the structure of Dave
Rogers' history of pop in both Chapter 1 and the postscript 'Pop into the eighties'.
The field is clearly so vast that this can be no more than an introduction to some of
the more important records in particular fields.

Folk anthologies

The following could prove useful for historical and other projects:
Songs of the Open Road, Topic 12T 253.
The Valiant Sailor, Topic 12T 232.
Songs of Courtship, Topic 12T 157.
Sea Songs and Shanties, Topic TPS 205.
Sailormen and Servingmaids, Topic 12T 194.
Fair Game and Foul (poaching), Topic 12T 195.
The Child Ballads, Topic 12T 160 and 12T 161.
English and Scottish Folk Ballads, Topic 12T 103.
The Iron Muse: A Panorama of Industrial Folk Music, Topic 12T 86.
(The above is only an indication of the wide range of material which this company
produces.)

Popular music prior to rock'n'roll

After the Ball, Starline MRSSP 513. (An anthology to accompany the book of the
    same name by I. Whitcomb.)
The Parlour Song Book: An Evening of Victorian Gems, Charisma CAS 1078.
Music Hall and Variety, EMI SH 145.
On the Halls, EMI SHB 43.
Stars Who Made the Music Hall (less well-known artists), Ace of Clubs, ACL 1170.
Dance Bands on the Air (pre-war), Vol. 1, BBC REC 139; Vol. 2, BBC REC 140.
Glenn Miller: A Memorial, RCA GM 1.
Kings of Swing (double LP, Benny Goodman etc.), Verve 2683 055.
The Best of the Big Bands (Artie Shaw, etc.), Embassy EMB 31017.
Million Sellers of the Fifties (Frankie Laine etc.; pre-rock'n'roll), Embassy EMB
    31078.
(Though the particular albums listed above may have been deleted by the date of
publication, this list should nevertheless prove a useful starting point, since it appears
that the cheap label companies are following a policy of making a certain amount of
earlier popular music available at any one time.)

Blues and rhythm'n'blues

The two compilation albums accompanying Paul Oliver's book *The Story of the Blues* provide perhaps the best introduction to recorded blues:
The Story of the Blues, Vol. 1, CBS 66218.
The Story of the Blues, Vol. 2, CBS 66238.

A second excellent compilation is the following series of boxed sets (each containing four LPs) charting the important part played in recording blues music in the 1940s and 1950s by Chess Records of Chicago. They include much of Muddy Waters' early influential recordings.
Genesis 1, Chess 6641 047.
Genesis 2, Chess 6641 125.
Genesis 3, Chess 6641 174.

In addition the following are directly relevant to music after 1956:
Robert Johnson, *King of the Delta Blues Singers*, CBS 62456.
B.B. King, *The Best of B.B. King*, Anchor ABCL 5026.
Elmore James, *Elmore James*, DJM DJCMD 8008.

In Chicago:
Howlin' Wolf, *Howlin' Wolf*, Chess ZACMB 201.
Jimmy Reed, *Big Boss Man*, DJM DJD 28033.

In Detroit:
John Lee Hooker, *Dimples*, DJM DJD 28026.

In and around Memphis:
Arthur Crudup, *That's All Right Mama*, DJM DJM 22025.

Various:
The Blues Came Down from Memphis, Charly CR 30125.

The following illustrate the often fuller instrumentation, and the more outgoing and danceable rhythms of r'n'b.

In New Orleans:
The Sound of the City, United Artists UAS 29215.
This is Where it All Began Vol. I, Specialty SNTF 5002.
The Ace Story Vol. 1, Ace/Chiswick CH 11.
The Ace Story Vol. 2, Ace/Chiswick CH 12.
Huey 'Piano' Smith, *New Orleans Rock'n'Roll*, Ace/Chiswick CH 9.

In New York:
Joe Turner, *His Greatest Recordings*, Atlantic 1540525.
The Roots of Rock'n'Roll, Savoy SJL 2221.
Louis Jordan and his Tympany Five, *The Best of Louis Jordan*, MCA MCFM 2715.

Country music

The two major artists in this field prior to the rise of rock'n'roll were undoubtedly Jimmie Rodgers (in the 1920s and 1930s) and Hank Williams who died at the age of twenty-nine in 1953. Both strongly influenced those rock'n'roll singers who had country leanings.
Jimmie Rodgers, *Country Music Hall of Fame*, RCA RD 7505.
Hank Williams, *40 Greatest Hits*, Polydor MGM 2683 071.

Others:
Bob Wills and his Texas Playboys, *The Bob Wills Anthology*, CBS Embassy 31611.
Bill Monroe and his Bluegrass Boys, *Best of Bill Monroe*, MCF 2696.

Rockabilly — the fusion into rock'n'roll

The successful synthesis of country music and r'n'b into rockabilly — the first white
rock'n'roll — was made at Sam Phillips' Sun Records in Memphis:
Good Rockin' Tonight, Bopcat 100.
Elvis Presley, *The Sun Sessions*, RCA HY 1001.
(Both of the above clearly show the fusing of country and blues styles in Presley's
singing.)
Carl Perkins, *The Original Carl Perkins*, Charly CR 30110.
The Best of Sun Rockabilly Vol. 1, Charly CR 30123.
The Best of Sun Rockabilly Vol. 2, Charly CR 30124.

Inspired by the pre-1956 success of Sun Records and Elvis Presley, other artists and
companies recorded in the new rockabilly style:
Buddy Holly and Bob Montgomery, *Western and Bop*, MCA CDLM 8055.
Johnny Burnette and the Rock'n'Roll Trio, MCA Coral CDLM 8054.
Imperial Rockabillies, United Artists, UAS 30101.
Chess Rockabillies, Phonogram 9124 213.
Rare Rockabilly, MCA MCFM 2697.
CBS Rockabilly Classics Vol. 1, CBS 82401.

Thanks to the enthusiasm and work of Charly Records, together with Colin Escott,
Martin Hawkins and especially Bill Millar amongst several others, more recorded
rockabilly (and rock'n'roll) is now available than at any time in the 1950s. This
music has reached a new and young audience. British bands playing rockabilly/
rock'n'roll and related music have deservedly prospered. Among the best are:
Matchbox, *Setting the Woods on Fire*, Chiswick WIK 10, 1978.
Crazy Cavan'n'The Rhythm Rockers, *Our Own Way of Rockin'*, Chorley CRL 5004,
    1976.
Whirlwind, *Blowin' Up a Storm*, Chiswick WIK 7, 1978.
Darts, *The Amazing Darts*, K-Tel DLP 7981, 1978.
Best of British Rockabilly, Charly CBM 2002, 1979.

The above bands are not just an exercise in nostalgia. The continuing power and
excitement of their music has brought wide popularity to several of the surviving
original rockabilly singers, some of whom were perhaps less well known in the
fifties, notably:
Warren Smith, Buddy Knox, Charlie Feathers, Jack Scott, *Four Rock'n'Roll*
    Legends, EMI Heritage SHSM 2024. (Recorded live in London, April 1977.)
Ray Campi & His Rockabilly Rebels, *Wildcat Shakeout*, Radar RAD 9, 1979.
Mac Curtis, *Ruffabilly*, Rollin' Rock LP002.

Guitarist Link Wray joined the much younger New York singer Robert Gordon to
produce two albums of which the best is:
Robert Gordon with Link Wray, *Robert Gordon*, Private Stock PVLP 1027, 1977.
Like Gordon, George Thorogood was also born in the 1950s. His fine r'n'b/rock'n'
roll guitar playing and singing is well worth hearing on:
George Thorogood and the Destroyers, *Move It On Over*, Sonet STNF 781, 1978.

Rock'n'roll

Bill Haley and his Comets, *Golden Hits*, MCA MCF 2555.
Elvis Presley, *40 Greatest*, RCA PL 42691.
Jerry Lee Lewis, *The Original Jerry Lee Lewis*, Chorley CR 30111.
Gene Vincent, *Gene Vincent Greatest*, Capitol CAPS 1001.
Wanda Jackson, *Rockin' with Wanda*, Capitol CAPS 1007.
Chuck Berry, *Motorvatin'*, Chess 9286 690.
Little Richard, *20 Original Hits*, Sonet SNTF 5017.
Fats Domino, *20 Greatest Hits*, United Artists UAS 29967.
Bo Diddley, *Golden Decade*, Chess 6310 123.
Buddy Holly, *20 Golden Greats*, MCA EMTV 8.
Eddie Cochran, *15th Anniversary Album*, United Artists UAG 29760.
Everly Brothers, *Don and Phil's Fabulous Fifties Treasury*, Phonogram 6310 300.
Ricky Nelson, *Legendary Master Series*, United Artists UAD 60019/20.
Sam Cooke, *The Golden Age of Sam Cooke*, RCA RS 1054.

Black vocal groups flourished too, both in a more recognizably r'n'b style and with doo-wop:
Drifters, *24 Original Hits*, Atlantic K 60106.
Platters, *The Original Platters*, Phonogram 9100 049.
Coasters, *20 Great Originals*, Atlantic K 30057.
Frankie Lymon and the Teenagers, *Why do Fools Fall in Love?* Pye NSPL 28251.
Doo-Wop, Specialty SN TF 5016.
Doowop Doowop, DJM DJSLM 2026.

In Britain

Skiffle:
Lonnie Donegan, *The Donegan File*, Pye FILD 011.

Rock'n'roll in Britain, as well as the performers' hits of the early 1960s, can be found on:
Tommy Steele, *Focus on Tommy Steele*, Decca FOS 21/2.
Marty Wilde, *Good Rockin' Then And Now*, Philips 6382 102.
Cliff Richard, *40 Golden Greats*, EMI TVS 6.
Billy Fury, *The Billy Fury Story*, Decca DPA 3033/4.
Johnny Kidd and the Pirates, *Best of Johnny Kidd and the Pirates*, EMI NUTM 12.

The following illustrate the important part played by Jack Good's late 1950s TV shows:
Eddie Cochran, *On The Air*, United Artists, UAS 29380.
Jack Good's Oh Boy!, EMI NUTM 13.

Instrumental rock'n'roll
Link Wray, *Link Wray: Early Recordings*, Chiswick CH6.
Duane Eddy, *Legend of Rock*, London DLL 500314.
Champs, *The Hits of the Champs*, London ZGH 141.
Shadows, *20 Golden Greats*, EMI EMTV 3.

1959/1960 Payola and the industry on top

From Bobby-sox to Stockings, MGM 2315 280.

Early to mid 1960s

Britain:
Adam Faith, *The Best of Adam Faith*, Starline SRS 5067.
Golden Hour of Original Golden Goodies, Pye GH 563.
See also the Billy Fury, Cliff Richard and Shadows compilations mentioned earlier.

America
Bobby Vee, *Legendary Masters Series*, United Artists UAD 60055/6.
Del Shannon, *The Best of Del Shannon*, Contempo CRMD 1001.
Brenda Lee, *The Brenda Lee Story*, MCA MCDW 428.
The Four Seasons, *Greatest Hits*, K-Tel NE942.

Female groups and the productions of Phil Spector were an important part of this period:
Phil Spector: 20 Greatest Hits, Polydor PSI 2307 012.
Shirelles, *The Shirelles Greatest Hits*, Pye GH 824.
Shangri-las, *Golden Hits of the Shangri-las*, Philips 6336 215.

But much closer to the spirit of rock'n'roll was:
Dion, *Dion's Greatest Hits*, Philips SON 004.

American folk boom
Peter, Paul and Mary, *Best of Peter, Paul and Mary*, Warner K46012.

Britain — the early 1960s and the clubs
Very little live music in r'n'b clubs of this time was actually recorded. The following can only give an indication:
Graham Bond Organization, *The Sound of '65*, Columbia SX 1711.
Georgie Fame and the Blue Flames, *R'n'B at the Flamingo*, Columbia SX 1599, 1963.
The Animals, *The Animals*, Starline SRS 5006, 1964.
Yardbirds, *Five Live Yardbirds*, Columbia SX 1677, 1964. (Three of the finest lead guitarists of the 1960s played for this group: Eric Clapton, Jeff Beck and Jimmy Page.)
The Animals and Sonny Boy Williamson, *Newcastle-on-Tyne December 1963*, Charly CR 3000016.

Britain — the Beatles, Stones and other groups
Beatles, *Please Please Me*, Parlophone PCS 3042, 1963.
Beatles, *1962–1966* (double album), Parlophone PCSP 717.
Rolling Stones, *The Rolling Stones*, Decca LK 4605, 1964.
Rolling Stones, *Rolled Gold*, Decca ROST 1/2.
Animals, *Most of the Animals*, Columbia SX 6035, 1964–6.
Manfred Mann, *Best of Manfred Mann*, EMI NUT 7.
Kinks, *Kinks File*, Pye FILD 001.
Spencer Davis Group, *Best of Spencer Davis*, Island ILPS 9070. 1965–7.
The Who, *The Story of the Who*, Polydor 2683 069.
Searchers, *The Searchers File*, Pye FILD 002.
Hollies, *20 Golden Greats*, EMI EMTV 11.
Various, *Hits of the Mersey Era*, EMI NUT 1.
The Beat Merchants 1963–1964, United Artists UDM 101/2.

America — the mid 1960s

Beach Boys, *20 Golden Greats*, Capitol EMTV 1.
Byrds, *History of the Byrds*, CBS 68242.
Mamas and Papas, *20 Golden Hits*, Probe GTSP 200.
Lovin' Spoonful, *The Lovin' Spoonful File*, Pye FILD 009.

The following compilation clearly shows the direct effect on American groups of the Beatles and other mid-1960s British groups. Released in Britain in 1973 it also became one of the basic reference points for some of the British punk rock of the late 1970s.

Nuggets, Elektra K62012. (Now deleted, but available on import.)

American folk/folk-rock
Woody Guthrie, *A Legendary Performer*, RCA PL 12099.
Pete Seeger, *Best of Pete Seeger*, CBS 68201.
Bob Dylan, *Bob Dylan*, CBS 62022, 1962.
Bob Dylan, *The Times, They Are A-Changing*, CBS 62251, 1964.
Joan Baez, *The Joan Baez File*, Pye FILD 010.
Tom Paxton, *The Compleat Tom Paxton*, Elektra K62004.
Phil Ochs, *Chords of Fame*, A&M AMLM 64599.

Whereas in Britain folk-rock (see below) was generally more closely related to traditional folk music, in America the term covered the music of the Byrds and the British singer Donovan (*The Donovan File*, Pye, FILD 004) as well as the largely pop music of the Mamas and Papas, Lovin' Spoonful and Sonny and Cher (*Best of Sonny and Cher*, Atlantic K40012.)

Its roots lay in the folk boom of the late 1950s/early 1960s. But its biggest influences were the Beatles, the protest song boom of 1964/5 set off by Dylan, and Dylan's move into electric music with the Band from the 1965 Newport Folk Festival onwards.

Changes 1966/67

Bob Dylan, *Royal Albert Hall Concert 1966*. (An unofficial bootleg recording which is well worth seeking out.)
Bob Dylan, *Highway 61 Revisited*, CBS 62572, 1965. (Contains 'Desolation Row'.)
Bob Dylan, *Blonde on Blonde*, CBS 66012, 1966.
Beatles, *Sergeant Pepper's Lonely Hearts Club Band*, Parlophone PCS 7027, 1967.
Beatles, *1967—70*, Parlophone PCSP 718.
Cream, *Best of Cream*, Polydor 583 060, 1966—8.
Cream, *Wheels of Fire* (double album), Polydor 2612 001, 1968.
Mothers of Invention, *Mothermania*, Polydor 2683 004, 1965—7.
Captain Beefheart and his Magic Band, *The Captain Beefheart File*, Pye FILD 008.
Pink Floyd, *A Nice Pair*, Harvest SHDW 403, 1967. (Their first two albums packaged as one.)

The late 1960s

Britain
Pink Floyd, *Ummagumma*, Harvest SHDW 1/2, 1969.
The Who, *Live at Leeds*, Track 2406 001, 1970.

Rolling Stones, *Get Yer Ya Yas Out*, Decca SKL 5065, 1970. (Live from an American tour.)
Beatles, *Abbey Road*, Parlophone PCS 7088, 1969.
Traffic, *Best of Traffic*, Island ILPS 9112, 1968–70.
King Crimson, *In the Court of the Crimson King*, Island ILPS 9111, 1969.
Soft Machine, *Volumes One and Two*, Probe GTSP 204, 1968 and 1969. (Their first two albums packaged as one.)
The Who, *Tommy* (double album), Track 2657 001, 1969.
Family, *Family Entertainment*, Reprise K44069, 1969.
Led Zeppelin, *Led Zeppelin*, Atlantic K40031, 1968.
Jethro Tull, *Living in the Past* (double album), Chrysalis CJT 1, 1968–73.
Free, *The Free Story* (double album), Island ISLD4, 1968–73.
John Mayall's Bluesbreakers, *Bluesbreakers*, Decca SITL 4804, 1965.
Fleetwood Mac, *Vintage Years*, CBS 88227.
Jimi Hendrix, *The Essential Jimi Hendrix*, Phonogram 2612 034. Also *Woodstock* (side 6), *Star Spangled Banner* and *Purple Haze*, Atlantic K60001, 1969.
Eric Clapton, *History of Eric Clapton*, Polydor 2659, 012.
Bonzo Dog Band, *History of the Bonzos*, United Artists, UAD 60071/72.

America
Most usually associated with San Francisco in the late 1960s are Jefferson Airplane and the Grateful Dead:
Jefferson Airplane, *Flight Log* (1966–76), RCA Grunt CYL 2-1255.
Grateful Dead, *Workingman's Dead*, Warner Bros. K46049, 1970.
Grateful Dead, *Live Dead*, Warner Bros. K66002, 1970.

Other groups recording on the West Coast included:
Buffalo Springfield, *Retrospective*, Atlantic K40071, 1966–8.
Canned Heat, *Rollin' and Tumblin'*, Sunset SLS 50321.
Captain Beefheart, *Trout Mask Replica*, Straight STS 1053, 1969.
Country Joe and the Fish, *Best of Country Joe and the Fish*. Vanguard VSD 7900.
Crosby, Stills, Nash and Young, *Déjà Vu*, Atlantic K50001, 1970.
The Doors, *Weird Scenes Inside the Goldmine*, Elektra K62009, 1967–71.
Janis Joplin with Big Brother and the Holding Company, *Cheap Thrills*, CBS 63392, 1968.
Love, *Forever Changes*, Elektra K 42015, 1967.
Steve Miller, *Sailor*, Capitol ST 2984, 1968.
Quicksilver Messenger Service, *Happy Trails*, Capitol EST 120, 1969.
Santana, *Abraxas*, CBS 64087, 1970.
Spirit, *Twelve Dreams of Dr Sardonicus*, Epic 64191, 1970.

Some American groups fused two important musical approaches into jazz-rock.
Blood, Sweat and Tears, *Blood, Sweat and Tears*, CBS 63505, 1968.
Chicago, *Chicago Transit Authority*, CBS 66221, 1969.
Miles Davis, *In a Silent Way*, CBS 63630, 1969.

During the same period there was a move back to re-working some of the roots of rock'n'roll and towards country music:
Byrds, *Sweetheart of the Rodeo*, CBS 63353, 1968.
The Band, *Music from Big Pink*, Capitol ST 2955, 1968.
The Band, *The Band*, Capitol EST 132, 1969.
Bob Dylan and the Band, *The Basement Tapes*, CBS 88147, recorded 1968.
Bob Dylan, *John Wesley Harding*, CBS 63252, 1968.

Bob Dylan, *Self Portrait*, CBS 66250, 1970.

The following had great success in the pop charts, but with very different styles:
Monkees, *Monkees*, EMI Sounds Superb SPR 90032.
Rascals, *Time Peace, The Rascals Greatest Hits*, Atlantic SD8190.
Creedence Clearwater Revival, *Creedence Gold*, Fantasy FT 501.
Simon and Garfunkel, *Greatest Hits*, CBS 69003.

Away from the West Coast, some much tougher music was being played in Detroit
and New York:
MC5, *Kick Out the Jams*, Elektra K42027, 1968. (Committed to 'the Revolution'
   stated the album cover; their manager was the imprisoned John Sinclair, cham-
   pioned by John Lennon in 'Sometime in New York City'.)
Velvet Underground, *Andy Warhol's Velvet Underground* (double LP), Polydor
   2683/006.
Velvet Underground, *Velvet Underground '69*, Mercury 6641 900. (A live recording.)
(From New York, and associated initially with Andy Warhol, they produced some
of the most effective, frightening and intelligent music of the time, often dealing
with subjects usually shunned by song writers, e.g. drug addiction, transvestism and
homosexuality.)

Also recorded in New York was Van Morrison's 'Astral Weeks'. Morrison was singer
with the excellent mid-1960s Irish band Them. Since the group split up in 1967 he
has lived and recorded in the USA.
Van Morrison, *Astral Weeks*, Warner K46024, 1968.

Black music in the 1960s

Two useful compilation albums of the more commercial side of black music are:
Black Music, Ronco BPR 2008, 1967—74.
Black Music, Arcade ADE P15, 1969—74. (Both include the O'Jays 'Love Train'
   mentioned in Chapter 3.)

Motown
Marvin Gaye, *Anthology* (2 LPs), Tamla Motown TMSP 1128, 1963—74. (Includes
   'I Heard it Through the Grapevine' mentioned in Chapter 3.)
Diana Ross and the Supremes, *20 Golden Greats*, Motown EMTV 5.
The Temptations, *Anthology* (3 LPs), Tamla Motown M782, 1964—73.
The Miracles, *Anthology* (3 LPs), Tamla Motown M793, 1960—72.
Stevie Wonder, *Greatest Hits*, Tamla Motown STML 11075, 1963—8.
The Motown Story (5 record set), Motown MS 5-726.

Soul
Otis Redding, *History of Otis Redding*, Atlantic K40066, 1064—7.
Aretha Franklin, *Aretha's Gold*, Atlantic K40036, 1967—8.
Sam and Dave, *Best of Sam and Dave*, Atlantic K40027, 1965—8.
Wilson Pickett, *Best of Wilson Pickett*, Atlantic K40015, 1961—6.
James Brown, *Best of James Brown*, Polydor 583 765, early 1960s to 1969.
Impressions, *The Impressions Big Sixteen*, Anchor ABCL 5104.
Booker T and the MG's, *Best of Booker T and the MG's*, Atlantic K40072.

British folk/folk-rock

Bert Jansch, *Bert Jansch*, Transatlantic TRA 125, 1965.

The Electric Muse — The History of Folk Into Rock, Island/Transatlantic FOLK
    1001.
Fairport Convention, *History of Fairport Convention*, Island ICD 4.
Incredible String Band, *Best of Incredible String Band*, Island ISLD9.
Steeleye Span, *Original Masters*, Chrysalis CJT 3.
Shirley Collins, *Anthems in Eden*, Harvest SHSM 2008.
Albion Country Dance Band, *Battle of the Field*, Island HELP 25.
Richard and Linda Thompson, *I Want To See the Bright Lights Tonight*, Island
    ILPS 9266.
Chieftains, *Chieftains 5*, Island ILPS 9334.
Horslips, *The Tain*, RCA MOO 5.

The 1970s

Mass pop
This category, in which popularity rather than a musical style is the criterion, is such
an all-embracing one that we have listed here only a few significant records from a
potentially very large selection.

Britain
Bay City Rollers, *Once Upon a Star*, Bell BELLS/8001, 1975.
Gary Glitter, *Greatest Hits*, Bell BELLS 262
Slade, *Sladest*, Polydor 2442 119, 1969—73.
Mud, *Mud Rock*, RAK SRAK 508, 1974.
Cockney Rebel, *The Best Years of Our Lives*, EMI EMC 3068, 1975.
10.c.c., *The Original Soundtrack*, Mercury 9201 500, 1976.
Sweet, *Strung Up*, RCA SPC 0001.
Marc Bolan and T Rex, *The Words and Music of M. Bolan 1947—77*, Cube HIFLD
    1-1/2.
Wizzard, *See My Baby Jive*, Harvest SHSP 4034.
Hot Chocolate, *XIV Greatest Hits*, RAK SRAK 524.
Rod Stewart, *The Best of Rod Stewart*, Mercury 6843 030.
Leo Sayer, *The Very Best of Leo Sayer*, Chrysalis CDL 1222.

From the mid 1970s
Abba, *Greatest Hits*, Epic EPC 69218. (From Sweden, ex-Eurovision Song Contest
    winners, Abba are the most phenomenally selling pop group of the decade.)
Queen, *A Night at the Opera*, EMI EMTC 103, 1976.
Showaddywaddy, *Greatest Hits*, Arista ARTY 145.
Smokie, *Greatest Hits*, RAK SRAK 526.
ELO (Electric Light Orchestra), *A New World Record*, United Artists UAG 30017,
    1976.
The Osmonds, *Greatest Hits*, Polydor 2675 153.
David Cassidy, *Greatest Hits*, Bell BELLS 250.
Raspberries, *Best of the Raspberries*, Capitol CAPS 1026.
Dr Hook, *A Little Bit More*, Capitol EST 2379.
Four Seasons, *Who Loves You*, Warner K 56179.
Peter Frampton, *Frampton Comes Alive*, A&M AMLM 63703.

And the following rock bands who moved close to mass pop, some compromising
more than others in the variety of styles they synthesised:
Aerosmith, *Get Your Wings*, CBS 80015.
Alice Cooper, *Greatest Hits*, Warner Bros K56043.

Bachman Turner Overdrive, *Best of Bachman Turner Overdrive*, Mercury 9100 026.
Boston, *Boston*, Epic EPC 81611.
Eagles, *Their Greatest Hits*, Asylum K53017.
Fleetwood Mac, *Rumours*, Warner Bros K56344.
Jefferson Starship, *Red Octopus*, RCA BFLI 0999. (With the name and some per-
    sonnel changed this is Jefferson Airplane of the 1960s.)
Steve Miller, *Fly Like an Eagle*, Mercury 9286 177.

Individual performers and singer/songwriters
(The range of styles and music here is wide — the heading is for convenience only.)

Britain
Elton John, *Tumbleweed Connection*, DJM DJLPS 410.
Elton John, *Greatest Hits*, DJM DJLPH 442.
Cat Stevens, *Tea for the Tillerman*, Island ILPS 9135.
Al Stewart, *Year of the Cat*, RCA RS 1082.
Rod Stewart, *Gasoline Alley*, Vertigo 6360 500, 1970.
Joan Armatrading, *Show Some Emotion*, A&M AMLH 68433.
Kevin Coyne, *Marjorie Razorblade*, Virgin VD 2501.
Nick Drake, *Bryter Later*, Island ILPS 9134, 1970.
Roy Harper, *Roy Harper 1970–1975*, Harvest SHSM 2025.
Peter Gabriel, *Peter Gabriel*, Charisma CDS 4013, 1978.
Kate Bush, *The Kick Inside*, EMI EMC 3223, 1978.

America
Carole King, *Tapestry*, A&M AMLS 2025.
Joni Mitchell, *Blue*, Reprise K44128.
Van Morrison, *It's Too Late to Stop Now*, K86007.
Van Morrison, *Wavelength*, Warner Bros K 56526, 1978.
Paul Simon, *Still Crazy After All These Years*, CBS 86001.
Neil Young, *After the Goldrush*, Reprise K44088.
Jackson Browne, *Late for the Sky*, Asylum K43007.
Leonard Cohen, *Death of a Ladies Man*, CBS 86042, 1977.
Joni Mitchell, *The Hissing of Summer Lawns*, Asylum SYLA 8763, 1976.
Randy Newman, *Little Criminals*, Reprise K56404, 1977.
Tom Waits, *Small Change*, Elektra K53050.

Country rock
A seminal influence here was the Byrds' *Sweetheart of the Rodeo* (CBS 63353
1968), heavily influenced by Gram Parsons, a member of the group at the time and
who then formed the Flying Burrito Bros.
Flying Burrito Bros. *The Gilded Palace of Sin*, A&M SP 4175.
Gram Parsons, *Grievous Angel*, Reprise K54018.
Emmylou Harris, *Elite Hotel*, Reprise K54060.

Meanwhile, both the following groups have borrowed from the country side of
rock'n'roll and from Western Swing:
Commander Cody and the Lost Planet Airmen, *Hot Licks, Cold Steel and Truckers
    Favourites*, Anchor ABCL 5079, 1972.
Asleep at the Wheel, *Comin' Right At Ya*, Sunset SLS 50415.

Heavy metal
High volume, riffing rock music (the name is particularly apt), much influenced by
the work of Cream, Jimi Hendrix and early Led Zeppelin.

Britain
Black Sabbath, *Greatest Hits*, NEMS NEL 6009.
Judas Priest, *Killing Machine*, CBS 83135, 1978.
Motorhead, *Overkill*, Bronze BRON 515, 1978.

America
Blue Oyster Cult, *Agents of Fortune*, CBS 81385.
Meat Loaf, *Bat Out of Hell*, Epic EPC 82419.
Rush, *A Farewell to Kings*, Phonogram 9100 042.

Boogie-inspired rock from the South
Allman Brothers, *The Road Goes on Forever*, Capricorn 2637 101.
The South's Greatest Hits, Capricorn 2429 153.

Black music in the 1970s
Marvin Gaye, *What's Going On*, Tamla Motown STML 11190, 1971.
Al Green, *Greatest Hits*, London SHU 8481, 1975.
Isaac Hayes, *The Best of Isaac Hayes*, Stax STX 1041.
Eddie Kendricks, *Eddie Kendricks*, Tamla Motown STML 11245, 1973.
Stevie Wonder, *Innervisions*, Tamla Motown, STMA 8011, 1973.
Bobby Womack, *I Can Understand It*, United Artists UAS 24715.
Curtis Mayfield, *Superbly*, Buddah 2318 065, 1972.
Shirley Brown, *Woman to Woman*, Stax STX 1031.
Millie Jackson, *Best of Millie Jackson*, Polydor 2391 247.
Gladys Knight and the Pips, *The Best of Gladys Knight and the Pips*, Buddah 5013.
Labelle, *Nightbirds*, Epic EPC 80566, 1974.
Diana Ross, *Touch Me In the Morning*, Tamla Motown, STML 11239, 1973.

By the mid 1970s in America there had been a tremendous rise in growth and popularity of discotheques. But although 'disco music' is sometimes spoken of as a single, separate musical genre, in fact the term merely describes a very wide range of black musical styles — the link being their disco popularity.

In Britain from the late 1960s there has been a large audience for soul music which has mainly been outside whatever mainstream manifests itself in the weekly pop charts. This specialist audience had its own disco venues in the Northern Soul scene. The music popular at such all-nighter discos often harked back to the obscurer reaches of 1960s soul. A taste of it can be found on:
Disco Demands Solid Soul Sensations, Pye DDLP 5001.

In both countries disco's mid- and late-1970s success was heralded partly by the differing styles of the following:
Souled Out, K-Tel NE 508. (A seminal record included here was George Macrae's 'Rock Your Baby'.)
Manu Dibango, *Makossa Music*, Creole CRLP 503.
Hamilton Bohannon, *Bohannon's Best*, London HSU 8522.
All Platinum Gold, All Platinum 9299 767.
Philadelphia Gold, Philadelphia International PIR 86049.

In the mid 1970s both the following achieved great pop chart success. The apparent softness of Barry White's music still retained an edge, the Stylistics increasingly moved towards lightweight pop:
Barry White, *Greatest Hits*, 20th Century BTH 8000.
Stylistics, *Best of the Stylistics*, AVCO 9109 003.

Where production of a disco beat was the main criterion came the soul-less dance

rhythms of Disco Tex and Gloria Gaynor of 1974–5; in this category also was music with the growing use of the drum machine and synthesised sounds, most widely employed in European-produced disco music, as in:
Silver Convention, *Get Up and Boogie*, MFP 50404.
Boney M, *Nightflight To Venus*, Atlantic K50498.
Cerrone, *Supernature*, Atlantic K50431.
Giorgio, *From Here to Eternity*, Oasis OASLP 501.

By 1978, the success of the film *Saturday Night Fever* brought disco (though not always necessarily black music) to the attention of a huge international popular audience. The soundtrack album contains not only the Trammps' excellent 'Disco Inferno', but also the enjoyable disco/pop hits of the white (originally Australian) group, The Bee Gees.
Saturday Night Fever, RSO 2658 123.

But a much stronger backbone of tougher, funkier black music has continued and grown in stature during the 1970s. This is apparent in the best work of the individual performers listed, in the music and performances of James Brown ('Soul Brother Number One') and in the following selection:
Kool and the Gang, *Greatest Hits*, Polydor 2310 401.
O'Jays, *Collectors Items, Greatest Hits*, Philadelphia International PIR 86058.
War, *Greatest Hits*, Island ILPS 9413.
Commodores, *Greatest Hits*, Tamla Motown, STML 12100.
Brothers Johnson, *Blam!*, A & M, AMLH 64714.
Chic, *Très Chic*, Atlantic K 50565, 1978.
Trammps, *Best Of The Trammps*, Atlantic K 50511.
Sister Sledge, *We Are Family*, Cotillion K 50587, 1979.
Alicia Bridges, *Alicia Bridges*, Polydor 2391 364, 1979.
Gloria Gaynor, *Love Tracks*, Polydor PD 1 6184, 1979.
Real Thing, *Can You Feel The Force?* Pye NSPH 18601, 1979. (Real Thing are a British group.)
Earth, Wind And Fire, *The Best of Earth, Wind And Fire*, CBS 83284.
Ohio Players, *Fire*, Mercury 9100 009, 1974.
Isley Brothers, *3 + 3*, Epic EPC 65740, 1973.
Bootsy, *Aah, The Name is Bootsy Baby!* Warner Brothers K56302.
Parliament, *The Clones of Doctor Funkenstein*, Casablance CAL 2003.
Sly and the Family Stone, *Greatest Hits*, Epic 69002.
Sly and the Family Stone, *There's a Riot Goin' On*, Epic EPC 64613, 1972.
(Sly's rhythmic and stylistic innovations were a huge influence in the 1970s not least on Norman Whitfield's production work.)
The Temptations, *All Directions*, Tamla Motown STML 11218. (This contains their classic 'Papa Was a Rolling Stone'.)
Rose Royce, *Best of Car Wash*, MCA MCF 2799.
Stargard, *Stargard*, MCA MCF 2834, 1978.

At the same time from the fringes of blues and jazz has come music with a much funkier feel:
Fatback Band, *The Best of the Fatback Band*, Polydor 2391 246.
Crusaders, *The Best of the Crusaders*, Anchor ABCD 612.
Herbie Hancock, *Head Hunters*, CBS 65928, 1974.
Herbie Hancock, *Feets Don't Fail Me Now*, CBS 83491, 1979.
Johnny 'Guitar' Watson, *Ain't That a Bitch*, DJM DJF 20485.

Finally, in 1977 Muddy Waters produced his finest recorded work for several years:

Muddy Waters, *Hard Again*, Blue Sky 81853.

Reggae

Compilations:
The Harder They Come, Island ILPS 9202, 1972. (Film soundtrack album featuring
    Jimmy Clift and other artists.)
The Trojan Story, Trojan TRLD 402.
This is Reggae Music, Island ICD 7.
Desmond Dekker, *Double Dekker*, Trojan TRLD 401.
Jimmy Cliff, *Best of Jimmy Clift*, Island ICD 6.
Wailers, *Burnin'*, Island ILPS 9256, 1973.
Bob Marley and the Wailers, *Live!*, Island ILPS 9376, 1975.
Bob Marley and the Wailers, *Exodus*, Island ILPS 9498, 1977.
Peter Tosh, *Equal Rights*, Virgin V2081.
Bunny Wailer, *Blackheart Man*, Island ILPS 9415. (Tosh and Bunny Wailer were orig-
    inal members of the Wailers.)
Max Romeo, *War in a Babylon*, Island ILPS 9392, 1977.
Inner Circle, *Everything Is Great*, Island ILPS 9558, 1979.
Dennis Brown, *Wolf and Leopard*, DEB Music MOR LPO1.
Vivian Jackson, *Deliver Me From My Enemies*, Grove GMLP 001, 1977.
Burning Spear, *Marcus Garvey*, Island ILPS 9377, 1975.
Gladiators, *Trench Town Mix Up*, Virgin V2062.
Abyssinians, *Forward On To Zion*, Island KLP 9023.
Culture, *Two 7s Clash*, Lightning LIP 1, 1977.
Count Ossie and the Mystic Revelation of Rastafari, *Grounation*, Vulcan VULX 301.

Dub
Reggae discs often had instrumental B-sides which were 'versions' of the top side:
the same track minus the vocal. In the 1970s the practice was modified: producers,
engineers and 'sound-system' DJs altering, boosting, lowering, phasing (etc.) the
various instruments, frequencies and channels, but always leaving a bass-heavy and
powerful basic rhythm. It has become a style in its own right.
    'Dub is the ancient art of layer after layer of reggae feeling one on top of the
until the random complexities are strange enough to be freaky. You get random
gaps, sale or return percussion, phasing in, phasing out and a general atmosphere of
Rebel Stockhausen.' (Idris Walters, *Let it Rock*, May 1975)
African Dub, *Chapter 3*, Joe Gibbs Records.
Aggrovators/Revolutionaries, *Aggrovators Meet the Revolutionaries at Channel One*,
    Third World TWS 900.
King Tubby Meets the Upsetter At the Grass Roots of Dub, Studio 16 WE 101.
Keith Hudson, *Brand*, Brand BRD 001, 1977.
Augustus Pablo, *King Tubby Meets the Rockers Uptown*, Clocktower CT 085.

Toasting
Often over backing or dub tracks, 'sound-system' DJs began to provide their own
vocals, talking to their audience, exhorting them, haranguing them, recounting
relevant anecdotes etc. Like dub, this practice has grown into a separate, recorded,
highly individual style.
Dr Alimantado, *Best Dressed Chicken in Town*, Greensleeves GREL 1.
U Roy, *Dread in a Babylon*, Virgin V2048.
I Roy, *Heart of a Lion*, Virgin FL 1001.
Tapper Zukie, *MPLA*, Klik 9022.

Dillinger versus Trinity, *Clash*, Burning Sounds BS 1003.
Dillinger, *Talking Blues*, Valdene JSLP 007.

British reggae bands have emerged as an increasingly separate force since the early 1970s. Musically, there is sometimes a sharper edge; the lyrics, whilst still dealing with Rastafarian beliefs, also reflect the social background of black Britons in the late 1970s — see in particular here the poems and songs of Linton Johnson.
Matumbi, *The Best of Matumbi*, Trojan TRLS 145.
Merger, *Exiles in a Babylon*, Sun-Star SUN 1001, 1978.
Rico, *Man from Wareika*, Island ILPS 9485.
Steel Pulse, *Handsworth Revolution*, Island ILPS 9502, 1978.
Linton Kwesi Johnson, *Dread Beat An' Blood*, Virgin Front Line FL 1017.
Linton Kwesi Johnson, *Forces of Victory*, Island ILPS 9566, 1979.
Third World, *Journey to Addis*, Island ILPS 9554.

American rock music in the 1970s
However excellent some of the music, much American rock through the 1970s lost some of its vital edge in appealing to a wider, older and more middle-class (and often seated rather than dancing) audience. As society and the tenor of life changed in different ways on each side of the Atlantic, much American music (especially the poppier side) became increasingly redundant and irrelevant to mid- and late-1970s British youth. As at other times in the past (the early 1960s, for example) this gap was mirrored in the music and is even apparent in the differences between the American and British New Wave. In their different ways, the following is some of the least indulgent and best non-New-Wave American music of the 1970s.
Steely Dan, *Greatest Hits*, ABC ABCD 616.
Joe Walsh, *The Smoker You Drink the Player You Get*, ABC ABCL 5033, 1973.
Little Feat, *The Last Record Album*, WEA K56156.
Doobie Brothers, *The Captain and Me*, Warner K46217, 1974.
Nils Lofgren, *Cry Tough*, A & M AMLH 64573, 1976.
Bob Seger, *Seven*, Reprise K44262, 1974.
Boz Scaggs, *Silk Degrees*, CBS 81193.
Tom Petty and the Heartbreakers, Shelter ISA 5014, 1977.
Bruce Springsteen, *Born To Run*, CBS 69170, 1975.
Mink de Ville, *Mink De Ville*, Capitol EST 11631, 1977.

The following, though, went their own way:
Captain Beefheart, *Clear Spot*, Reprise K 54007.
Frank Zappa, *Hot Rats*, Reprise K 44078, 1970.
Frank Zappa and Captain Beefheart, *Bongo Fury*, Discreet DS 2234, 1975.
Mothers of Invention, *Roxy and Elsewhere*, Discreet K69021, 1974.
Country Joe McDonald, *The Paris Sessions*, Vanguard VSD 79328, 1973.
Ry Cooder, *Chicken Skin Music*, Reprise K 54083, 1976.
Todd Rundgren, *A Wizard, A True Star*, Bearsville, K 45513, 1973.
Dr John, *In The Right Place*, Atlantic K 50017.
Lou Reed, *Berlin*, RCA APL1 0207, 1973.
Lou Reed, *Rock'n'Roll Animal*, RCA APL1 0472, 1974.

The fortunes and quality of Bob Dylan's work varied considerably. His best work of the 1970s is contained in:
Bob Dylan and The Band, *Before the Flood*, Island IDBD1, 1974. (Live recordings from an American tour.)
Bob Dylan, *Blood on the Tracks*, CBS 69097, 1975.
Bob Dylan, *Street Legal*, CBS 86067, 1978.

British rock music in the 1970s

It can be argued that by the mid 1970s, many rock bands had become what some music journalists chose to label 'dinosaurs' — contributing little that was innovative, and in some cases losing touch with their audiences (much was heard in this period of rock star 'tax exiles'). Nevertheless, the more famous of these bands have retained a fairly large and faithful audience, whilst the more experimental, and less commercial, ones have attracted a sufficient 'minority-taste' market to keep going. Most of these bands continue to work within wider musical and lyrical terms of reference than more conventional rock groups.

We have included some bands who, despite having broken up, are particularly worthy of note, and with other bands we have sometimes noted albums which are not their most recent, if we have felt that such material is significantly better than their later work.

Caravan, *If I Could Do It All Over Again*, Decca SKL-R-5052, 1970.
Audience, *The House on The Hill*, Charisma CAS 1032, 1971.
Emerson, Lake and Palmer, *Pictures At An Exhibition*, Manticore K533501, 1971.
Kingdom Come with Arthur Brown, *Galactic Zoo Dossier*, Polydor 2310 130, 1971.
Van Der Graaf Generator, *Pawn Hearts*, Charisma CAS 1051, 1971.
Genesis, *Foxtrot*, Charisma CAS 1058, 1972.
Khan, *Space Shanty*, Deram SDLR-11, 1972.
Wishbone Ash, *Argus*, MCA MCG 3510, 1972.
Yes, *Close To The Edge*, Atlantic K50012, 1972.
Led Zeppelin, *Runes*, Atlantic K50008, 1972.
Henry Cow, *Legend*, Virgin V2005, 1973.
Pink Floyd, *Dark Side of the Moon*, Harvest SHVL 804, 1973.
Procul Harum, *Grand Hotel*, Chrysalis CHR1037, 1973.
Mike Oldfield, *Tubular Bells*, Virgin 2001, 1973.
Bad Company, *Bad Company*, Island ILPS 9279, 1974. (Bad Company, with singer
    Paul Rodgers, grew out of the excellent Free.)
King Crimson, *Red*, Island ILPS 9308, 1974.
Man, *Winos, Rhinos and Lunatics*, United Artists UAG 29631, 1974.
Eno, *Another Green World*, Island ILPS 9370, 1975.
Hatfield and the North, *Rotters' Club*, Virgin V2030, 1975.
Stackbridge, *Extravaganza*, Rocket PIGL 11, 1975.
Supertramp, *Crisis? What Crisis?* A & M AMLH 683471, 1975.
Robert Wyatt, *Ruth is Stranger than Richard*, Virgin V2034, 1975.
Kevin Ayers, *Yes, We Have No Mananas*, Harvest SHSP 4057, 1976.
Genesis, *Trick of the Tail*, Charisma CDS 4001, 1976.
Steve Hillage, *L*, Virgin V2055, 1976.
Van Der Graaf Generator, *Still Life*, Charisma CAS 1116, 1976.
Camel, *Rain Dances*, Decca TXS R124, 1977.
Gentle Giant, *The Missing Piece*, Chrysalis, CHR 1152, 1977.
UK, *UK*, Polydor 2302 080, 1977.
Dire Straits, *Dire Straits*, Phonogram 9102 021, 1978.
Brian Eno, *Before And After Science*, Polydor 2302, 071, 1978.
National Health, *National Health*, Affinity AFF6, 1978.

Three German bands might also be included here:
Can, *Future Days*, United Artists, UAS 29505, 1973.
Tangerine Dream, *Rubycon*, Virgin V2025, 1975.
Kraftwerk, *Trans Europe Express*, Capitol EST 11603, 1976.

The long-heralded break-up of the Beatles as a unit came in 1970. Since then, despite continual rumours of a reunion, they have trod their separate paths. Harrison has not yet bettered *All Things Must Pass* or his achievement in organizing *The Concert for Bangla Desh*. Starr's best work is probably contained in *Ringo*, while, as expected, Paul McCartney and Wings have been very successful in the pop field. However, it is Lennon, as always, whose music has been the toughest, most interesting and uncompromising:

John Lennon, *John Lennon/Plastic Ono Band*, Parlophone PCS 7124, 1970.
John Lennon, *Imagine*, Parlophone PAS 10004, 1971.
John Lennon, *Sometime in New York City*, Parlophone PCSP 716, 1972.
John Lennon, *Shaved Fish*, Parlophone PCS 7173, 1975.
Paul McCartney and Wings, *Band On The Run*, Parlophone PAS 10007, 1973.
Wings, *Wings Greatest*, EMI PCTC 256.
Ringo Starr, *Ringo*, Parlophone PCTC 252, 1973.
George Harrison, *All Things Must Pass*, Parlophone STCH639/3 1970.
The Concert for Bangla Desh, Apple STCX 3385, 1972.

The following, arguably the major British rock artists and bands throughout the 1970s, have had mixed fortunes while retaining tremendous popularity. Bowie and the Who remain perhaps the most widely respected — deservedly so — by both their old audience and the new wave. The ever-thoughtful and articulate Pete Townshend and the Who have stayed closest to their audience; while Bowie alone continued to forge ahead and consistently excite with new and sometimes surprising ideas and methods.

Eric Clapton, *Layla and Other Assorted Love Songs*, Polydor 2625 005, 1971.
Eric Clapton, *461 Ocean Boulevard*, RSO 2479 118, 1974.
Rolling Stones, *Sticky Fingers*, Rolling Stones Records COC 59100, 1971.
Rolling Stones, *Exile On Main Street*, Rolling Stones Records COC 69100, 1972.
Rolling Stones, *Gimme Shelter*, Decca SKL 5101, 1971.
Rolling Stones, *Some Girls*, Rolling Stones Records CUN 39108, 1978.
Roxy Music, *Greatest Hits*, Polydor 2302 073.
Roxy Music, *Manifesto*, Polydor POLH 001, 1979.
Who, *Who's Next*, Track 2408 102, 1971.
Who, *Quadrophenia*, Track 2657 013, 1973.
Who, *The Who By Numbers*, Polydor 2490 129, 1975.
David Bowie, *The Rise and Fall of Ziggy Stardust*, RCA SF 8287, 1972.
David Bowie, *Diamond Dogs*, RCA APLI 0576, 1974.
David Bowie, *Young Americans*, RCA RS 1006, 1975.
David Bowie, *Station To Station*, RCA APLI 1327, 1976.
David Bowie, *Heroes*, RCA PL 12522, 1977.

From the early 1970s many of the most popular rock bands were playing at venues impossibly large for close audience contact, and playing music which seemed increasingly unrelated to the daily lives of their audience. Partly as a result of this, a number of different bands began playing in London pubs. As has always happened in the past, such grass roots contact has proved the most invigorating influence in rock and provided some of the strongest and most unpretentious music.

Ducks De Luxe (*Before The Wave*, RCA PL 25132) spawned the successful late 1970s Motors (*Motors 1*, Virgin V2089, 1977).

Out of Brinsley Schwartz (*15 Thoughts of Brinsley Schwartz*, United Artists UAK 30177) came the highly respected Nick Lowe (*Jesus of Cool*, RADAR RAD 1, 1978), whose presence and production work has had a marked effect on some sections of the new wave. Other members of Brinsley Schwartz went on to join the excellent Graham Parker (Graham Parker and the Rumour, *Heat Treatment*, Vertigo 6360 137, 1976).

By the mid 1970s Doctor Feelgood and the younger Eddie and the Hot Rods, both from Southend, were gaining a huge following with their own tough style of r'n'b.

Dr Feelgood, *Stupidity*, United Artists UAS 29990, 1976.

Eddie and the Hot Rods, *Teenage Depression*, Island ILPS 9457, 1976.

Finally, Thin Lizzy, originally from Ireland, continued to produce high-powered and, above all, relevant rock music into the late 1970s.

Thin Lizzy, *Jailbreak*, Vertigo 9102 008, 1976.

With David Bowie, it was these musicians who, if anything, provided part of the bridge to British punk rock and new wave music of the late 1970s.

The New Wave
New Wave is increasingly a blanket term covering the wide variety of music produced by the upsurge of new artists and bands of 1976 onwards in both Britain and the USA. Part of what they have in common is energy, originality, enthusiasm, a sense of direction and an empathy and close contact with their audience. In short, all the things which most of the major rock bands preceding them seemed to have lost by the mid 1970s.

America
It is noticeable that the most arresting bands of the late 1970s, in contrast to the West Coast sound of the 1960s, have come from urban environments, particularly New York.

Ramones, *Ramones*, Sire 9103 253, 1976.

Ramones, *The Ramones Leave Home*, Sire 9103 254, 1977.

Blondie, *Plastic Letters*, Chrysalis CHR 1166, 1977.

Talking Heads, *Talking Heads 77*, Sire 9103 328, 1977.

Television, *Marquee Moon*, Elektra K52046, 1977.

Richard Hell and the Voidoids, *Blank Generation*, Sire 9103 327, 1977.

Patti Smith, *Horses*, Arista ARTY 122, 1976.

Jonathan Richman, *Jonathan Richman and the Modern Lovers*, Beserkley B SERK 2.

Flamin' Groovies, *Shake Some Action*, Sire 9103 251, 1977. (Produced in Wales by Dave Edmunds.)

Devo, *Are We Not Men? We Are Devo*, Virgin V2106, 1978.

Père Ubu, *The Modern Dance*, Phonogram 9100 052, 1978.

Père Ubu, *Dub Housing*, Chrysalis CHR 1207, 1978.

The Akron Compilation, Stiff GET 3, 1978.

Nils Lofgren, *Cry Tough*, A & M AMLH 64573, 1976.

Britain
Some American antecedents and influences:

Stooges, *The Stooges*, Elektra K 42032, 1969.

Iggy and the Stooges, *Raw Power*, CBS 31464, 1973.

MC5, *Back in the USA*, Atlantic K50346, 1970.

New York Dolls, *New York Dolls*, Mercury 6641 631, 1973.

Flamin' Groovies, *Teenage Head*, Kama Sutra KSMD 101, 1971.

'The likes of Led Zeppelin, Queen and Pink Floyd need to be chucked in the "classical music" section' (Mark Perry).

'Punk rock is the generic term for the latest musical garbage bred by our troubled culture' (Derek Jewell in the *Sunday Times*).

'Its power, contrary to later allegations, lay in the fact that it was not created by the media but by teenage musicians and the kids themselves' (Caroline Coon).

'Every other group was riffing their way through the Black Sabbath catalogue. But hearing the Pistols I knew. I just knew. It was something you just knew without bothering to think about' (Joe Strummer of the Clash).

Adverts, *Crossing the Red Sea*, Bright BRL 201, 1978.
Buzzcocks, *Another Music in a Different Kitchen*, United Artists UAG 31059, 1978.
Buzzcocks, *Love Bites*, United Artists UAG 31097, 1978.
Clash, *The Clash*, CBS 82000, 1977.
Clash, *Give 'Em Enough Rope*, CBS 62431, 1978.
Jam, *In The City*, Polydor 2383 447, 1977.
Jam, *All Mod Cons*, Polydor POLD 5008, 1978.
Members, *At the Chelsea Nightclub*, Virgin V2120, 1979.
Penetration, *Moving Targets*, Virgin V2109, 1978.
Rezillos, *Can't Stand the Rezillos*, Sire K 56530, 1978.
Sex Pistols, *Never Mind the Bollocks, Here's the Sex Pistols*, Virgin V2086, 1977.
Sham 69, *Tell Us the Truth*, Polydor 2683 491, 1978.
Sham 69, *That's Life*, Polydor POLD 5010, 1978.
Siouxsie and the Banshees, *The Scream*, Polydor POLD 5009, 1978.
Skids, *Scared to Dance*, Virgin V2116, 1979.
Stiff Little Fingers, *Inflammable Material*, Rough Trade ROUGH I, 1979.
Stranglers, *No More Heroes*, United Artists UAG 30200, 1977.
Tom Robinson Band, *Power in the Darkness*, EMI EMC 3226, 1978.
X-Ray Spex, *Germ Free Adolescents*, EMI INS 3023, 1978.

And also:
Boomtown Rats, *A Tonic for the Troops*, Engisn ENVY 3, 1978.
Damned, *Damned, Damned, Damned*, Stiff SEEZ 1, 1977.
Generation X, *Generation X*, Chrysalis CHR 1169, 1978.
Heartbreakers, *L.A.M.F.*, Track 2409 218, 1977.
Johnny Moped, *Cycledelic*, Chiswick WIK 8, 1978.
Johnny Thunders, *So Alone*, Real RAL 1, 1978.
Lurkers, *Fulham Fallout*, Beggars Banquet BEGA 2, 1978.
999, *999*, United Artists UAG 30199, 1978.
Following the break-up of the original Sex Pistols, Steve Jones, Paul Cook and Sid Vicious continued to record under the group's name. Vicious died tragically in New York in February 1979. Johnny Rotten, under his real name John Lydon, formed Public Image Ltd.
Public Image Ltd., *Public Image*, Virgin V2114, 1978.
Radiators from Space, *TV Tube Heart*, Chiswick WIK 4, 1977.
Rich Kids, *Ghosts of Princes in Towers*, EMI EMC 3263, 1978. (The Rich Kids were
    formed by Glen Matlock, the Sex Pistols' first bassist.)
Vibrators, *V2*, Epic EPC 82495, 1978.

Although only partly representative, the following is an interesting compilation:
20 of Another Kind, Polydor POLS 1006, 1978.

Live recordings
The Roxy, London EC2, Jan.–Apr. 1977, Harvest SHSP 4069, 1977.
Hope and Anchor Festival, Warner K 66077, 1978.
Stiffs Live Stiffs, Stiff GET 1, 1978.

The following bands are currently breaking newer ground still in individual and highly distinctive ways:

Alternative TV, *The Image Has Cracked*, Deptford Fun City DLP 01, 1978.

The Fall, *Live at the Witch Trials*, Step Forward SFLP 1, 1979.

Magazine, *Real Life*, Virgin V2100, 1978. (Howard Devoto of Magazine was, with Pete Shelley, originally co-founder of the Buzzcocks.)

The Pop Group, *Y*, Radar RAD 20, 1979.

Wire, *Pink Flag*, Harvest SHSP 4076, 1977.

XTC, *Go 2*, Virgin V2108, 1978.

The following should also be noted. Their single releases and live performances promise well for their forthcoming albums:

The Cure

Gang of Four

The Human League

The Mekons

Scritti Politti

Subway Sect

The Teardrop Explodes

The Undertones

Finally, but by no means least:

Elvis Costello, *My Aim is True*, Stiff, SEEZ 3, 1977.

Elvis Costello, *This Year's Model*, Radar RAD 3, 1978.

Elvis Costello, *Armed Forces*, Radar RAD 14, 1979.

John Cooper Clarke, *Disguise in Love*, CBS 83132, 1978.

Ian Dury, *New Boots and Panties*, Stiff SEEZ 4, 1977.

Joe Jackson, *Look Sharp!*, A & M AMLH 64743, 1979.

Graham Parker and The Rumour, *Squeezing out Sparks*, Vertigo 910 2030, 1979.

The Rumour, *Frogs, Sprouts, Clogs and Krauts*, Stiff SEEZ 13, 1979.

Index

This is not an exhaustive index. The headings chosen are those that are particularly important or that have received more than passing reference in the text.